Environmental Law in Taiwan

Environmental Law in Taiwan

Anton Ming-Zhi Gao

This book was originally published as a monograph in the International Encyclopaedia of Laws/Environmental Law.

Founding Editor: Roger Blanpain
General Editor: Frank Hendrickx
Volume Editor: Kurt Deketelaere

Wolters Kluwer

Published by:
Kluwer Law International B.V.
PO Box 316
2400 AH Alphen aan den Rijn
The Netherlands
E-mail: lrs-sales@wolterskluwer.com
Website: www.wolterskluwer.com/en/solutions/kluwerlawinternational

Sold and distributed by:
Wolters Kluwer Legal & Regulatory U.S.
920 Links Avenue
Landisville, PA 17538
United States of America
E-mail: customer.service@wolterskluwer.com

ISBN 978-94-035-2826-7

e-Book: ISBN 978-94-035-2926-4
web-PDF: ISBN 978-94-035-2936-3

This title is available on www.kluwerlawonline.com

The Author

Prof. Gao received a Master's (MA) from the National Taiwan University and a second Master's in energy and environmental law (LLM) from the Institute of Environmental and Energy Law of KU Leuven, Belgium. He also received a PhD in Law from KU Leuven. Since then, he has devoted himself to energy and climate legal research and projects in Taiwan. He has published books and articles, hosted local and international energy law conferences and participated in international events. Prof. Gao envisions making the National Tsing Hua University one of the leading research institutes for energy law in East Asia. His main research interests lie in energy and environmental law and their interactions. Over the past few years, he has been very active in international publications centred on investigations of global legal issues, as well as European, Asian, and Taiwanese energy laws. He remains one of the most productive scholars in the field of energy law in Taiwan, publishing articles in international energy and environmental law journals (e.g., *European Environmental Law Review*, *International Energy Law Review*, *Renewable Energy Law and Policy*, *Carbon and Climate Law Review*), as well as in science-oriented energy journals (*Energy Policy, Renewable Energy and Sustainable Energy Review*).

In addition to international journals, Prof. Gao has also been devoted to studying and investigating energy law and policy development in Taiwan. He has participated in the formation of several legislations, such as the draft of the Nuclear-Free Homeland Act, the Nuclear Phase-out Act, the Basic Law for Sustainable Energy, as well as amendments to the Electricity Act and to the Renewable Energy Development Act, among others. His recent publications also include '100 questions regarding amendments to the Electricity Act' and '100 questions regarding amendments to the Renewable Energy Development Act'. He has also written opinion pieces on issues concerning energy transition, such as the Nuclear-Free Homeland Policy and offshore wind farms.

The Author

Table of Contents

The Author 3

List of Abbreviations 17

Acknowledgement 19

General Introduction 21

§1. General Background 21
I. Geography and Population 21
II. Legal and Political Structure 22
III. Economic Characteristics 26
IV. Social and Cultural Characteristics 27

§2. Basic Principles of Environmental Law 28
I. Definitions and Notions 28
A. Sustainable Development 29
B. Integration Principle 31
C. Intergenerational and/or Intragenerational Equity 32
D. State Responsibility and Liability 33
E. Polluter Pays Principle 34
F. Common but Differentiated Responsibilities 42
G. Prevention Principle 43
H. Environmental Impact Assessment 44
I. Precautionary Principle 45
J. The Obligation Not to Cause Damage (No-Harm Rule) 47
K. Human Rights 47
L. Equitable Utilisation 48
M. Common Heritage and the Common Concerns of Humankind 49
N. Good Governance 49
O. Duty to Adopt Effective National Law: The Duty to Enforce 50
P. Conservation 51
Q. Sovereignty over Natural Resources 51
R. Cooperation 52
S. Procedural Principles 52
1. Access to Information 53
2. Public Participation 55
3. Access to Justice 56

§3. Constitutional Provisions 59

§4. Historical Background of the Evolution of Environmental Law 60

§5. Role of Government Institutions in the Shaping and Administration of Environmental Law and Policy 62
I. The Governmental Institutions and Their Competencies 62
A. The Evolution of the Environmental Competent Authority EPA 62
B. Unfinished Works of Reorganisation of EPA 62
C. Other Ministries and Institutions 63
D. Moving Beyond Environment: Authority for Climate Change? 64
E. Office of Energy and Carbon Reduction Since 2016 65
F. NDC and Net Zero 65
G. Other Authorities Relating to Climate Change Mitigation/ Adaptation Works 66
H. Local Governments Relating to Environmental Affairs 67

§6. Sources of Environmental Law 67

Part I. Pollution Control 71

Chapter 1. General Law 71

§1. Environment Basic Act of 2002 71
I. General Provisions 73
A. Legal Purposes 73
B. Legal Definition 73
C. Basic Principles of Policy and Law 73
D. Responsibility of Actors 73
E. The Creation of Special Institutions 75
F. Development of Special Comprehensive Strategies and/or Plans 76
G. Important Mechanism under EBA 77
H. Financial and Incentive Instrument 77
I. International Cooperation 77
J. Educational and Information Campaign 78
K. The Relationship among These Eight Issues 78

§2. Environmental Education Act 79

§3. Environmental Impact Assessment Act 82
I. Project EIA 82
II. Policy EIA 85

Chapter 2. Air Pollution 87

§1. Air Pollution Control 87
I. Air Quality Control Regions 87
II. Air Pollution Control Plan 88
III. Cap-and-Trade Scheme 88
IV. Air Quality Monitoring Stations 90
V. Emergency Measures to Tackle Air Pollution 90
VI. Air Pollution Control Fees and Funds 91
VII. Control Measures Applying to Public and Private Premises with Stationary Pollution Sources 92
VIII. [Mobile Pollution Sources] Control Measures That Apply to Mobile Pollution Sources 94
IX. Volatile Organic Compounds 95
X. Other Measures to Improve Enforcement 95

§2. Indoor Air Quality 96
I. Premised at Stake 97
II. Measures 97

Chapter 3. Water Pollution 99

§1. Basic Measures 99
I. Principle 99
II. Public Authorities 99
III. Those Enterprises, Sewage Systems or Building Sewage Treatment Facilities 100

§2. Control Measures 100
I. Enterprises 100
A. Plan and Permit 100
B. Regulations 102
II. Sewage Systems That Discharge Wastewater or Sewage 102
III. Enterprises and Sewage Systems 103
A. Permit 103
B. Professional Personals 104
C. Reporting 104
D. Water Quality Analysis 104
E. Improvement Assistance 104
F. Emergency Measures 104
G. Automatic Monitoring System 105
IV. Enterprises and Sewage Systems 105
V. Administrative Inspection and Enforcement 105
VI. Water Pollution Control Zones 106
VII. Underground Water and Soil 106

§3. Public Interest Litigation Clause 107

Chapter 4. Soil and Underground Water Pollution Remediation 108

§1. INTRODUCTION 108
I. Purpose 108
II. The Relationship Between This Act and the Water Pollution Act 108
III. Regulated Media or Materials 109
IV. Responsibility Party 109
V. Seven Regulatory Tools 109

§2. MULTIPLE AUTHORITIES 110

§3. KEY MEASURES UNDER THE FOUR REGULATORY STAGES 112
I. Phase I Preventive Measures 112
A. The Duty of Authorities under Articles 6 and 7 113
1. Three Main Regulatory Regimes 113
2. Underground Water and Soil 113
3. Sediment 118
4. Administrative Inspection Power 119
II. The Behaviour Regulation of the 'Specified Industry' under Articles 8 and 9 119
III. Professionalism and Expertise Requirement 122
IV. Monitoring Wells and the Coordination of Information 122

§4. INVESTIGATION AND ASSESSMENT MEASURES: REGULATIONS ON DESIGNATED 'CONTROL' AND 'REMEDIATION' SITES 123
I. Control Sites 123
II. Remediation Sites 124

§5. REGULATORY MEASURES FOR CONTROL SITES AND REMEDIATION SITES 125
I. Competent Authorities 125
II. Control Zone 126
III. Compensation Scheme 127

§6. REMEDIATION AND RESTORATION MEASURES FOR REMEDIATION SITES 127
I. Remediation Plan 127
II. Ensuring the Plan Success 128

§7. OTHER REGULATORY MEASURES 129
I. Financial Mechanisms 129
II. Liability of the Soil and Groundwater Polluters 131
A. The Responsibility for Clean-up Costs 131
B. The Liability for Damage 131
III. Public Benefit Litigation Clause 132

Chapter 5. Marine Pollution Control 133

§1. Competent Authorities 133

§2. Basic Measures 134
I. General Measures 134
II. Major Marine Pollution Accident 134
III. Harbour Pollution 135
IV. Ocean as the Final Disposal Site 135
V. Emergency Plan, Financial Guarantee or Insurance 135
IV. Exemption from Sanction 136

§3. The Prevention of Pollution from Pollution Sources on Land 136

§4. The Prevention of Pollution from Marine Projects 136

§5. The Prevention of Pollution from the Disposal of Waste at Sea 137

§6. The Prevention of Sea Pollution by Ships 138

§7. Liability for Damage Compensation 139

§8. Public Interest Litigation Clause 140

Chapter 6. Waste Disposal 141

§1. Definition of Waste 141

§2. Competent and Enforcement Authority 142

§3. The Disposal of General Waste 143
I. Distribution of Cleaning Responsibility 143
II. Regulations 144
III. Recycle 144
A. Regulated Objects 144
B. Regulation 145
C. Fee and Fund 145
IV. Implementation of the Clearance and Disposal of General Waste by Special Municipality, County, or City Competent Authority 146
V. Designated Clearance Areas 147

§4. Disposal of Industrial Waste 147
I. Waste Disposal Hierarchy 147
II. Regulated Enterprise and Public Entities 148
III. Regulation 149

IV. Distribution of Responsibility 149
V. Unable to Perform the Disposal of Industrial Waste 150
VI. Import and Export Requirement and Import Ban 150
VII. Hazardous Industrial Waste 151
VIII. Reuse 151
IX. Emergency Measures 152

§5. The Management of Public and Private Waste Clearance and Disposal Organisations and Waste Analysis Laboratories 152

§6. Incentives to Improve the Waste Management 152
I. Reward to Report (An Offence) to the Authority by the Citizens 152
II. Tax Credit 152
III. Rewards 153

§7. Public Interests Litigation 153

Chapter 7. Noise Pollution Control 154

§1. Competent Authorities: EPA and Beyond 154

§2. Noise Control Zone 155

§3. Motor Vehicles and Civil Aircraft 156

§4. Airport 157

§5. Administrative Inspection Clause 158

§6. Soft Approach 158

Chapter 8. Ionising Radiation Protection 159

§1. Competent Authority: Atomic Energy Council 159

§2. AEC's Role 160

§3. The Duty of the Facility Operators 161

§4. The Regulation on Personnel and Employers 163
I. Age Limits, Pregnancy and Accident Training 163

§5. Regulation on Hospitals 164

§6. Product Regulation 165

§7. Construction and Building Regulations 165

§8. Regulation on Radiation Protection Service 166

§9. Management of Radioactive Material, Equipment Capable of Producing Ionising Radiation 166
I. Licence and/or Notification 166
II. Qualified Personnel and Training 167
III. Change of Nature in Registration 167
IV. Permanent Suspension 167

Chapter 9. Toxic Chemical Substances Control 169

§1. Competent Authority 169

§2. Assessment, Prevention and Management of Toxic Chemical Substances 171
I. Four Classes 171
II. Records and Disclosure 172
III. Operation 172
IV. Permission and Registration 173
V. Pollution Improvement 174
VI. The Handling of Toxic Chemical Substances by Government Agencies and Academic Organisations 175

§3. Assessment, Prevention and Management of Concerned Chemical Substances 175

§4. Registration and Reporting of Chemical Substances 176

§5. Accident Prevention and Emergency Response 177
I. General Measures 177
II. Prevention 178
III. Transportation 178
IV. Emergency Measures 179
V. Cost Bearing 180

§6. Audit, Inspection 180

§7. Fund 181

§8. Information Disclosure and Confidentiality 182

§9. Rewards 183

§10. Public Interest Litigation 183

Table of Contents

Part II. Nature Conservation and Management 185

Chapter 1. Heritage Preservation 185

§1. INTRODUCTION 185

§2. CULTURAL HERITAGE PRESERVATION ACT 185
I. Competent Authority 186
II. Monuments, Historic Buildings, Commemorative Buildings, and Groups of Buildings 187
A. Identifying Heritage 187
1. Identifying Heritage 187
2. Designation and Announcement 188
B. Maintenance Duty 189
1. Maintenance Duty 189
2. Reparation 190
3. Planning and Zoning 191
C. Historic Sites and Cultural Landscapes 192
1. Identification, Registration and Announcement 192
2. Planning and Zoning 192
3. Exemption 193
D. Natural Landscapes and Natural Monuments 193
1. Classification 193
2. Identification 194
3. Maintenance 194
4. Interim Natural Landscapes or Natural Monuments 194
5. Prohibition 195

§3. UNDERWATER CULTURAL HERITAGE PRESERVATION ACT 195
I. Competent Authority 195
II. General Principle 196
III. Identification and Research 196
IV. Duty of the Private Person, Government, and Public Companies 196
V. Education 197
VI. Regulation for Activities Directed at Underwater Cultural Heritage 197
A. Enforcement 198
VII. Preservation of Underwater Cultural Heritage in Situ 198
A. Zone Regulations 198
B. Enforcement 199
C. Education and Public Visit 199
VIII. Excavating Out of the Water 199
IX. Reward or Subsidies 200

Chapter 2. National Park 201

§1. Competent Authority 201

§2. Designation and Planning 201
I. Designation 201
II. Plan 202
III. Measures to Assist the Management 202

§3. Zoning and Zonal Regulations 203
I. General Rules 204
II. General Regulations 204
III. Permit 205

Chapter 3. Wild Life Conservation and Protection 207

§1. Competent Authority 207

§2. Conservation of Wildlife 208
I. Development Activities 208
II. Protection Zone 208
III. Enforcement 209
IV. Measures Relating to Protecting Wildlife 210
A. Protected Wildlife 210
B. General Wildlife 210
V. Hunting 211
VI. Personnel 212
VII. Rewards 212
VIII. Donation 212

§3. Import and Export of Wildlife 212
I. Import and Export 212
II. Export 213
III. Import 214

§4. Wildlife Management 214
I. Notification/Consent 214
II. Management Measures 215
A. Set Free 215
B. Raising or Breeding 215
C. Business Operation 215
D. Escape and Lost 216
E. Death 216

Table of Contents

Chapter 4. Forest 217

§1. COMPETENT AUTHORITY 217

§2. FORESTRY ADMINISTRATION 218
I. Principles 218
II. Classification of Forestland 218
III. Nationalization 218
IV. Regulations 219

§3. FORESTRY MANAGEMENT AND UTILISATION 220
I. Main Responsible Entity 220
II. Management of National Forests 220
III. Related Areas 221
IV. Personnel 221
V. Other Regulations 221

§4. CONSERVATION FORESTRY 222
I. Designation 222
II. Operation and Management 223
III. Application for Designation and Declassification 223

§5. FOREST PROTECTION 224
I. General 224
II. Fire Protection 224
III. Biological Hazards or Disturbances 225
IV. Forest in Aboriginal People's Area 225

§6. FORESTRY PROTECTION OUTSIDE THE FORESTS 225

§7. SUPERVISION 227

§8. INCENTIVE 228
I. Reforestation 228

Chapter 5. Fishery Resources 230

§1. FISHERIES ACT 230
I. Competent Authority 230
II. Licensing 230
A. Persons 230
B. Boat 231
C. Revoking of Licences 231
1. Legal Implications of Licence Revoking 232
III. Crews 232
IV. Conservation and Management 233
A. Restrains or Prohibitions 233

B. Zone and Planning 233
C. Survey 234
D. Enforcement 234
V. Fishery Development 234
A. Loan and Insurance 234
B. Government Measures 235
C. Rewards and Funds 235
D. Price Stabilisation Scheme 236
E. Tax Incentives 236

§2. DISTANT WATER FISHERIES ACT 236
I. Competent Authority 237
II. Planning 237
III. Licence 238
IV. Regulations 239
V. Prohibition 239
VI. Facilitation of Law Enforcement 241
VII. Port Regulations: Ban on Leaving or Entering the Port 242
VIII. Other Regulations 243
A. High-Risk Fishing Vessels 243
B. Export and Issuance of Catch Certificate Documents 243
C. Hire Foreign Crew Member 243
D. Dispatch Staff Stationed Abroad 244
E. Comprehensive Information System 244
F. Commission Professional Institution(s) 244
IX. Industry Development of Distant Water Fisheries 244
A. Planning 244
B. Assistance and Subsidy 245
C. Research and Development 245

Part III. Spatial Planning 247

Chapter 1. National Spatial Planning 248

§1. COMPETENT AUTHORITY 248
I. Main Authorities 249

§2. GENERAL PRINCIPLES AND WHITE PAPER 249

§3. NATIONAL AND LOCAL SPATIAL PLAN 250
I. Types of Spatial Plan 250
II. Preparation 251
III. Reviewing 251
IV. After Approval 252
V. After Publication 252
VI. Power to Ensure Enforcement 253

§4. Demarcation of Functional Zone and Land Use Control 254
I. Principles 254
II. Use Permit 255
III. The Effect of Functional Zone Map 257
IV. Public Interest Litigation Clause 258

§5. Environmental Restoration of National Land 258

§6. SD Fund for National Land 259

Part IV. Liability 261

Chapter 1. Private Law Liability 262

§1. General Introduction 262

§2. The RCA Case 263

Chapter 2. Administrative Law Liability 264

Chapter 3. Criminal Law Liability 266

§1. Criminal Code 266

§2. Environmental Law 267
I. Non-compliance with Adopting Emergency Measures 267
II. Other Criminal Offences in Environmental Law 269

Selected Bibliography 271

Index 273

List of Abbreviations

AC	Agriculture Council
AEC	Atomic Energy Council
ALARA	As Low As Reasonably Achievable
Amcham	American Chamber of Commerce Taiwan
CBDR	Common but Differentiated Responsibilities
CECER	Committee on Energy Conservation and Emission Reduction
COA	The Council of Agriculture of the Executive Yuan
COP	Conference of Parties
DPP	Democratic Progressive Party
EBA	Environmental Basic Act
EEA	Environmental Education Act
EECT	European Chamber of Commerce Taiwan
EHS	Environment, Health and Safety
EIA	Environmental Impact Assessment
EPA	Environmental Protection Administration
EU	European Union
ETS	Emission Trading Scheme
EU REACH	Registration, Evaluation, Authorisation and Restriction of Chemicals
GHG	Greenhouse Gas
IUU	Illegal, Unreported, and Unregulated
KMT	Kuomingtang
MOFA	Ministry of Foreign Affairs
MOI	Ministry of the Interior
NDC	National Development Council
NEPA	National Environmental Policy Act
NGOs	Non-governmental Organisations
PPP	Polluter Pays Principle
Radiation Act	The Ionizing Radiation Protection Act
ROC	Republic of China

List of Abbreviations

SD	Sustainable Development
SDG	Sustainable Development Goal
SEA	Strategic Environmental Assessment
Soil Act	Soil and Groundwater Pollution Remediation Act
SOP	Standard Operation Procedure
TCCSCA	Toxic and Concerned Chemical Substances Control Act
TCSCA	Toxic Chemical Substances Control Act
UNFCCC	United Nations Framework Convention on Climate Change
US	United States
VMS	Vessel Monitoring System
Waste Act	Waste Disposal Act

Acknowledgement

This manuscript owes its completion to the research funding of the Ministry of Science and technology (Project number: MOST 109-2410-H-007 -038 -MY2; 111-NU -E-007 -002 -NU) and the book publication incentive provided by the Research Center for Humanities and Social Sciences, National Tsing Hua University.

Acknowledgement

General Introduction

§1. General Background

I. Geography and Population

1. Taiwan, officially the Republic of China (ROC), is an island country located in East Asia. The main island of Taiwan, formerly known in Western literature as Formosa, measures 35,808 square kilometres (13,826 square miles) and makes up 99% of the country's land area. The main island lies some 180 kilometres (112 miles) across the Taiwan Strait from the southeastern coast of the People's ROC. The East China Sea is located to the north of the island, the Philippine Sea to its east, the Luzon Strait directly to its south and the South China Sea to its southwest. The ROC also controls a number of smaller islands, including the Penghu archipelago in the Taiwan Strait, the Kinmen and Matsu Islands near the Chinese mainland coast, and some of the South China Sea Islands.[1]

2. There are two types of terrain in Taiwan. The western third of the country is made up of flat to gently rolling plains; 90% of the 23 million people in Taiwan live in this area.[2] The eastern two-thirds of the country is mostly rugged, forest-covered mountains.[3] The island is highly urbanised, with nearly 9 million people living in the Taipei–Keelung–Taoyuan metropolitan area and over 2 million each in the urban areas of Kaohsiung and Taichung.[4] Taiwan is ranked as the fifty-seventh most populous nation in the world.[5]

3. This kind of geography and population distribution affected the environment and landscape of Taiwan in the post-industrialised era. The combination of limited

1. Taiwan – A Country Profile – Nations Online Project, available at: https://www.nationsonline.org/oneworld/taiwan.htm (visited on 15 May 2022).
   see also, Taiwan – New World Encyclopaedia, available at: https://www.newworldencyclopedia.org/entry/Taiwan (visited on 15 May 2022).
2. 1.1 Number of Villages, Neighbourhoods, Households and Resident Population. Monthly Bulletin of Interior Statistics. Ministry of the Interior, Republic of China (Taiwan). November 2012. Archived from the original (XLS) on 29 Mar. 2014.
3. Interesting facts about Taiwan, available at: http://justfunfacts.com/interesting-facts-about-taiwan/.
4. 'Taiwan: metropolitan areas'. World Gazetteer. Archived from the original on 9 Feb. 2013. Retrieved 19 Dec. 2012. https://archive.today/20130209115732/; http:/world-gazetteer.com/wg.php?x=&men=gcis&lng=en&des=wg&srt=dpnn&col=adhoq&msz=1500&pt=a&va=&geo=-218.
5. Worldometer, Taiwan Population (2022), available at: https://www.worldometers.info/world-population/taiwan-population/.

flatland/pains and very high population density in the cities (the capital city of Taipei city had 9,918 people/square kilometre in 2016)[6] led to a landscape that includes numerous housing complexes and serious traffic, air and noise pollution in the city.[7]

II. Legal and Political Structure

4. Taiwan adopted the civil law system of continental Europe instead of the common law system. Because of this, all legislations, including constitutional law and detailed implementation ordinances, are codified in the 'Six Codes'. This includes the constitution (憲法),[8] the civil code (民法),[9] the code of civil procedure (民事訴訟法)[10] and associated laws, the criminal code (刑法),[11] the code of criminal procedure (刑事訴訟法)[12] and associated laws, and the administrative and administrative procedure laws. Taiwan does have more than these six codes. As more complex social lives and technology development occur, many new laws and regulations are being developed, such as the Copyright Act,[13] Patent Act,[14] Air Pollution Act,[15] etc. Environmental law can be considered a similar type of 'new-generation' regulation. The existing six codes do address certain environmental issues; for example, Article 190-1 of the criminal code criminalises environmental pollution behaviours,[16] while the tort is also applied to environmental polluters.[17] Many new-generation environmental laws, such as the Greenhouse Gas Reduction

---

6. By the end of 2016, the population density in Taipei City was 9,918 people per square kilometre, available at: https://english.gov.taipei/cp.aspx?n=C619997124A6D293.
7. Yang, W.T. et al., Road Traffic Noise, Air Pollutants, and the Prevalence of Cardiovascular Disease in Taichung, Taiwan, *International Journal of Environmental Research and Public Health* 15(8), 1707 (2018).
8. MOJ, Constitution of the Republic of China (Taiwan), 1947-01-01, available at: https://law.moj.gov.tw/ENG/LawClass/LawAll.aspx?pcode=A0000001.
9. MOJ, Civil Code, Amended Date: 2019-06-19, available at: https://law.moj.gov.tw/ENG/LawClass/LawAll.aspx?pcode=B0000001.
10. MOJ, the Code of Civil Procedure, Amended Date: 2018-11-28, available at: https://law.moj.gov.tw/ENG/LawClass/LawAll.aspx?pcode=B0010001.
11. MOJ, Criminal Code of the Republic of China, Amended Date: 2020-01-15, available at: https://law.moj.gov.tw/ENG/LawClass/LawAll.aspx?pcode=C0000001.
12. MOJ, Code of Criminal Procedure, Amended Date: 2020-01-15, available at: https://law.moj.gov.tw/ENG/LawClass/LawAll.aspx?pcode=C0010001.
13. MOJ, Copyright Act, Amended Date: 2019-05-01, available at: https://law.moj.gov.tw/ENG/LawClass/LawAll.aspx?pcode=J0070017.
14. MOJ, Patent Act, Amended Date: 2019-05-01, available at: https://law.moj.gov.tw/ENG/LawClass/LawAll.aspx?pcode=J0070007.
15. MOJ, Air Pollution Control Act, Amended Date: 2018-08-01, available at: https://law.moj.gov.tw/ENG/LawClass/LawAll.aspx?pcode=O0020001.
16. Article 190-1 of the Criminal Code of Taiwan: 'A person who throws, abandons, drains, releases or uses other manner allowing a poisonous substance or any other substance that may harm health to pollute the air, soil, or rivers or other bodies of water and thereby causes harm shall be sentenced to imprisonment for no more than five years, detention, or a fine or combined with a fine no more than ten million dollars.'
17. Article 184 of the Civil code: 'A person who, intentionally or negligently, has wrongfully damaged the rights of another is bound to compensate him for any injury arising therefrom. The same rule shall be applied when the injury is done intentionally in a manner against the rules of morals.'

and Management Act[18] and Soil and Groundwater Pollution Remediation Act,[19] can also be classified as a kind of administrative regulation.

5. [公法/私法] There is another aspect to Taiwan's legal system, i.e., the public /private law system. Public law involves constitutional law, the criminal code, and administrative law, whereas private law includes mainly the civil code and other associated legislations. Key environmental legislations, including the Environmental Impact Assessment Act,[20] Air Pollution Control Act,[21] and Water Pollution Control Act,[22] can all be considered public law.

6. [法律影響] The development of related laws is greatly influenced by the Western world and Japan. For instance, Constitutional law was influenced by the German constitution (Grundgesetz für die Bundesrepublik Deutschland) and French constitutional law.[23] Civil code includes a mix of German, Japanese, and traditional Chinese civil code elements. Taiwanese intellectual property laws are heavily influenced by those in the United States (US). Law is often promulgated by legal scholars with different foreign education backgrounds. Many international components are involved in drafting environmental law, such as environmental and natural resources economics or environmental engineering think tanks, meaning that they include a unique mixture of different countries' legal regimes. How does this fact affect environmental law? For instance, Taiwan's air pollution legal regime is mainly based on US and California legislation. Thus, following the famous *Massachusetts v. Environmental Protection Agency*, 549 U.S. 497 (2007),[24] where US Supreme Court ruled that the Environmental Protection Administration (EPA) had the right to regulate carbon dioxide and other greenhouse gases (GHGs) as pollutants, Taiwan EPA designated six types of GHGs, such as carbon dioxide, methane, nitrous oxide, hydrofluorocarbons, sulphur hexafluoride, and perfluorocarbons, as

---

See also, Art. 191-1 of the Civil Code: 'The manufacturer is liable for the injury to another arising from the common use or consumption of his merchandise, unless there is no defectiveness in the production, manufacture, process, or design of the merchandise, or the injury is not caused by the defectiveness, or the manufacturer has exercised reasonable care to prevent the injury.'

18. Greenhouse Gas Reduction and Management Act, Date: 2015.07.01, Legislative: 1. Announced Date: 2015.07.01, Full text in thirty-four articles promulgated by Presidential Order Hua-Tsung-Yi-Yi-Tzu No. 10400077011 on 1 Jul. 2015, available at: https://oaout.epa.gov.tw/law/EngLawContent.aspx?lan=E&id=253.
19. Soil and Groundwater Pollution Remediation Act, Date: 2010.02.03, Legislative: Original 51 articles promulgated by Presidential Order, No. Yi-Yi 8900023580 on 2 Feb. 1990. Amendments to Arts 10, 34, and 42 promulgated by Presidential Order Yi-Yi 89100255710 on 8 Jan. 2003. All fifty-seven articles promulgated by Presidential Order Yi-Yi 09900024211 on 3 Feb. 2010, available at: https://oaout.epa.gov.tw/law/EngLawContent.aspx?lan=E&id=58.
20. Environmental Impact Assessment Act, 2003.01.08, available at: https://oaout.epa.gov.tw/law/EngLawContent.aspx?lan=E&id=28.
21. Air Pollution Control Act, 2018.08.01, available at: https://oaout.epa.gov.tw/law/EngLawContent.aspx?lan=E&id=205.
22. Water Pollution Control Act, 2016.12.07, available at: https://oaout.epa.gov.tw/law/EngLawContent.aspx?lan=E&id=282.
23. Shen, Y.C., Semi-presidentialism in Taiwan: A Shadow of the Constitution of the Weimar Republic, *Taiwan Journal of Democracy* 7(1), 135–152 (2011).
24. Sugar, M., Massachusetts v. Environmental Protection Agency, *Harvard Environmental Law Review* 31, 531 (2007).

air pollutants under the Air pollution Act in 2012.[25] However, when drafting climate change legislation, Taiwan EPA deviated from the US regulations and introduced and adopted a European-based emission trading scheme (EU ETS) in its 2015 GHG Greenhouse Gas Reduction and Management Act.[26] The recent Toxic and Concerned Chemical Substances Control Act (TCCSCA) has been influenced by EU REACH (Registration, Evaluation, Authorisation and Restriction of Chemicals).[27]

7. [建國] The ROC was established in 1911 after a successful revolution where Doctor Sun Yet-sen overthrew the corrupt Qing Empire and the dynasty. At that time, the ruling territory covered only mainland China and several islands; Taiwan was a Japanese colony, not a part of the ROC. After the Second World War, the ruling party – Kuomingtang (KMT) – won the battle with Japan and acquired Taiwan. It lost the battle with the Communist Party; however, it escaped to Taiwan and initiated a new ruling status in 1949.[28]

8. [五院、總統內閣] The constitutional law of Taiwan upholds the concept of 'separation of powers' and 'checks and balances' when designing governmental institutions. The Taiwanese government is mainly composed of five 'Yuan'. Borrowing from the concept of the three main branches of government, the Executive Yuan and the Examination Yuan exercise administrative power; the Judicial Yuan exercises judicial power; the Legislative Yuan (the Parliament) and the Control Yuan exercise legislative and auditing power. Even though the President was not a very important player in the original version of the constitutional law, the office has gained importance in the latest addition to constitutional law from 2005.[29] The entire constitutional system of Taiwan leans toward the presidential system, even though the original version preferred a cabinet. The presidential power to influence environmental policy and legislation cannot be ignored. For instance, facing the net zero by 2050 promise made by neighbouring countries such as South Korea and Japan,[30] Taiwan EPA remained originally reluctant to adopt a net-zero target in its draft amendment to the GHG Act in 2020. Later in 2021, however, President Tsai Ing-wen announced that the government was committed to working with academics and businesses to achieve net-zero carbon emissions by 2050.[31] This statement

---

25. Carbon dioxide, methane, nitrous oxide, hydrofluorocarbons, sulphur hexafluoride and perfluorocarbons are designated as air pollutants (二氧化碳、甲烷、氧化亞氮、氫氟碳化物、六氟化硫及全氟化碳等溫室氣體為空氣污染物), 9 May 2012, available at: https://oaout.epa.gov.tw/law/LawContent.aspx?id=GL007322.
26. Greenhouse Gas Reduction and Management Act, Announced Date: 2015-07-01, available at: https://law.moj.gov.tw/ENG/LawClass/LawAll.aspx?pcode=O0020098.
27. Taiwan Toxic Chemical Substance Control Act (TCSCA), available at: https://www.chemsafetypro.com/Topics/Taiwan/Taiwan_Toxic_Chemical_Substance_Control_Act_TCSCA.html.
28. Taiwan.gov.tw, History, available at: https://www.taiwan.gov.tw/content_3.php.
29. MOJ, Additional Articles of the Constitution of the Republic China, Amended Date: 2005-06-10, available at: https://law.moj.gov.tw/ENG/LawClass/LawAll.aspx?pcode=A0000002.
30. South Korea follows Japan and China in carbon neutral pledge, 27 Oct. 2020, available at: https://www.ft.com/content/185e5043-fd72-4fef-a05c-f2a5001c7f4b.
31. Taiwan ready to work with the world on net-zero target, 11/07/2021, available at: https://focustaiwan.tw/politics/202111070015.

caused a chain reaction, and Taiwan is now developing revisions to laws that will incorporate net-zero emissions targets by 2050.[32] It also announced an official policy document entitled 'Taiwan's Pathway to *Net-Zero* Emissions by 2050'.[33]

9. [環保署]Different ministries are created under the Executive Yuan. The EPA has environmental authority, meaning that it is in charge of proposing environmental policy and enforcing environmental and climate legislation, though its powers are neither absolute nor exclusive. For instance, the aforementioned net-zero roadmap was announced by The National Development Council (NDC).[34]

10. [政黨] After escaping to Taiwan, the KMT introduced martial law until the mid-1980s. The KMT remained the dominant ruling party during the terms of the five Yuan and the Presidency; there was no alternation of power during that time. The right to freedom of speech and to organise parties did not exist. Many political parties have begun since the abolition of marital law. After freedom of speech and of organisation was restored, civil society began to launch large-scale demonstrations over the development of electricity power plants, nuclear power, and other similar environmental issues. While Taiwan does have a multiparty system, there are only two main parties in the country, along with five small parties and numerous tiny parties in Taiwan. By 2000, most environmental legislation, along with many smaller parties and pollution control, were complete. In 2000, the chief opposition party, the Democratic Progressive Party (DPP), won the presidential election and became the ruling party. Because of its 'green' background, it began to launch the nuclear-phase-out scheme under the 'Nuclear-free Homeland' slogan but failed to complete this initiative after losing the election in 2008. During this period, Basic Environment Act was promoted and passed in the parliament.[35] The KMT returned to and remained in power until 2016; the key additional and new environmental legislation passed during this time were the GHG Reduction Act;[36] the Spatial Planning Act was also adopted in 2016.[37]

11. In 2016, the DPP government returned to the political stage again with renewed strength, having won both the presidential elections and a majority in the

---

32. Taiwan Net-Zero Emissions by 2050, 02/28/2022, available at:https://www.trade.gov/market-intelligence/taiwan-net-zero-emissions-2050.
33. NDC, Taiwan's Pathway to Net-Zero Emissions in 2050, 30 Mar. 2022, available at: https://ws.ndc.gov.tw/Download.ashx?u=LzAwMS9hZG1pbmlzdHJhdG9yLzEwL3JlbGZpbGUvMC8xNDc2Mi9jMGM3MTBlZC0yMTZhLTQwNGQtOThiMC00MTlkOWJmYWFiZGYucGRm&n=VGFpd2Fu4oCZcyBQYXRod2F5IHRvIE5ldC1aZXJvIEVtaXNzaW9ucyBpbiAyMDUwLnBkZg%3d%3d&icon=..pdf.
34. EUROVIEW, NDC publishes net zero roadmap, 30 Mar. 2022, available at: https://euroview.ecct.com.tw/category-inside.php?id=1007.
35. Basic Environment Act, Announced Date: 2002-12-11, available at: https://law.moj.gov.tw/ENG/LawClass/LawAll.aspx?pcode=O0100001.
36. Greenhouse Gas Reduction and Management Act, Announced Date: 2015-07-01, available at: https://law.moj.gov.tw/ENG/LawClass/LawAll.aspx?pcode=O0020098.
37. Spatial Planning Act, Announced Date: 2016-01-06, Amended Date: 2020-04-21, available at: https://law.moj.gov.tw/ENG/LawClass/LawHistory.aspx?pcode=D0070230.

Parliament for the first time in Taiwanese history. In addition to the goal of establishing a nuclear-free homeland by 2025, the DPP government invested a lot of effort in promoting energy transition and creating the very ambitious 20% renewable energy by 2025 agenda (from only around 5% in 2016).[38] The ruling party recently launched the aforementioned new agenda of net zero by 2050.

12. [兩岸關係] Finally, it is worth noting that Taiwan has had an acrimonious relationship with mainland China PRC since 1945. On 29 June 2010, both countries signed a free trade agreement called the Economic Cooperation Framework Agreement, but the cross-strait tension has not lessened. After the pro-independence party DPP won the election in 2016, the tension increased. This situation seemed to be merely a 'military' and 'diplomatic' issue and seemed less relevant to environmental affairs, but it did play a key role in influencing Taiwan's role in international environmental conventions. For instance, the Ministry of Foreign Affairs (MOFA) in Taiwan has worked to launch the 'Combating Climate Change: Taiwan Can Help' campaign[39] and wishes to join United Nations Framework Convention on Climate Change (UNFCCC) with observer status.[40] However, as tension increases, it seems less likely that China will support Taiwan's efforts to join these organisations.[41]

III. Economic Characteristics

13. In terms of economic development, Taiwan amazes the world. Taiwan evolved successfully from an agriculture-based society to a high-tech society in less than fifty years. In 1945, Taiwan's main export was agricultural products, such as bananas. Later, the government started to develop labour-intensive manufacturing industries, such as the clothes industry. After that, other energy-intensive industries, including petrochemical, steel, and cement, came into play. Currently, Taiwan is one of the world's most dynamic economies and an essential partner in a number of high-tech fields. Taiwan was the sixteenth largest exporter in 2021.[42]

14. Taiwan occupies an important position in the global economy. It is a top player in the world's information and communication technology industry and a major supplier of goods across the industrial spectrum, and its gross domestic product per capita reached USD 28,371 in 2020. In terms of nominal Gross Domestic

38. Energypedia, Energy Transition in Taiwan, last modified on 31 Oct. 2020, available at: https://energypedia.info/wiki/Energy_Transition_in_Taiwan.
39. MOFA outlines success of Taiwan's UNFCCC campaign, 17 Dec. 2019, available at: https://nspp.mofa.gov.tw/nsppe/news.php?unit=370&post=167968.
40. UNPO, Taiwan: Bid For Observer Status at UNFCCC, 13 Nov. 2013, available at: https://unpo.org/article/16583.
41. Kwei-Bo, H., *More International Space for Taiwan or Less?: Assessing the Presidency of Ma Ying-Jiu in Taiwan – Hopeful Beginning, Hopeless End?* 11 (2018).
42. Taiwan world's 16th largest trading economy in 2021: MOF, 04/15/2022, available at: https://focustaiwan.tw/business/202204150008.

Product (GDP), Taiwan ranks close to Switzerland and Poland, while its GDP per capita, expressed as purchasing power parity, is similar to that of Iceland and Sweden.[43]

15. However, there is an environmental cost to the rapid and expansive growth of Taiwan's economy. There are causal linkages between environmental pollution and healthcare expenditure,[44] as well as the pollution created by the manufacturing process of high technology and energy-intensive industries, e.g., the semiconductor factories,[45] the long unresolved issue of illegal factories manufacturing factories on farmland[46] would lead not just to environmental concerns but also concerns for food safety and human health.

IV. Social and Cultural Characteristics

16. [多民族社會、多元社會之形成] Taiwan is a multiethnic and multicultural society. About 4,000 years ago, Taiwan aborigines were settled in Taiwan. In the early 1600s, long before the Qing Empire of the Ming Dynasty, the Dutch and Spanish occupied parts of Taiwan. Many people fled Mainland China to escape the cruel control of the Ming Empire. Then, during the early Qing Empire, the Qing invaded Taiwan and set up an official government in Taiwan. They started to develop Taiwan but then lost the land to Japan during a battle. After fifty years of Japanese colonisation, Taiwan became part of China. The arrival of the KMT in Taiwan further heightened Taiwan's multicultural character. Taiwan was also under the influence of and receiving military support from the US, meaning that American culture had begun to take root in Taiwan. The integration and the fusion of these multiple cultures created a very special 'Taiwan culture'.[47]

17. [文化對環境之影響]These cultural elements may have had positive or negative effects on the environment. On the positive side, the effects of Buddhism led to a large population of vegetarians, which also made Taiwan Asia's top destination for vegans.[48] However, there are certain negative impacts from the existing

---

43. Taiwan.gov.tw, Economy, available at: https://www.taiwan.gov.tw/content_7.php.
44. Wu, C.F., et al., A Dynamic Relationship Between Environmental Degradation, Healthcare Expenditure and Economic Growth in Wavelet Analysis: Empirical Evidence from Taiwan, *International Journal of Environmental Research and Public Health* 17(4), 1386 (2020).
45. Yang, J.L. & Chen, L.H., Toxicity of Antimony, Gallium, and Indium Toward a Teleost Model and a Native Fish Species of Semiconductor Manufacturing Districts of Taiwan, *Journal of Elementology* 23(1) (2018).
46. Lee, B., Chang, H.H. & Wang, S.Y., Can Environmental Disamenities Increase Land Values? A Case Study of Manufacturing Factories on Farmland, *Journal of Cleaner Production* 279, 123–432 (2021).
47. LSE, Taiwan in comparative perspective, December 2008, vol. 2, available at: http://eprints.lse.ac.uk/50977/1/__libfile_REPOSITORY_Content_Taiwan%20Culture%20Research%20Programme_Taiwan%20in%20Comparative%20Perspective_Taiwan%20in%20Comparative%20Perspective_vol%202.pdf.
48. Why Taipei is Asia's top destination for vegans, Tue, 13 Feb. 2018 p. 13, available at: https://www.taipeitimes.com/News/feat/archives/2018/02/13/2003687547.

culture that led to a long unresolved environment problem. For instance, the practice of burning paper money in temples has long been criticised for creating air pollution.[49] In addition, a practice of overpackaging and overdecoration of gifts have been influenced by the Japan culture.

§2. Basic Principles of Environmental Law

I. Definitions and Notions

18. Basic principles of environmental law can be divided into two sub concepts: substantive and procedural principles. Taiwan environment law tries to adapt these concepts in related environmental legislation. This book will further discuss the principles in Table 1 as follows.[50]

Table 1 Basic Principles of Environmental Law in Taiwan

Substantive Principles	1. Sustainable Development 2. Integration Principle 3. Intergenerational and/or Intragenerational Equity 4. State Responsibility and Liability 5. Polluter Pays Principle 6. Common but Differentiated Responsibilities 7. Prevention Principle 8. Precautionary Principle 9. The Obligation Not to Cause Damage (No Harm) 10. Human Rights 11. Equitable Utilization 12. Common Heritage and the Common Concerns of Humankind 13. Good Governance 14. Duty to Adopt Effective National Law: The Duty to Enforce 15. Conservation 16. Sovereignty over Natural Resources 17. Cooperation
Procedural Principles	1. Access to Information 2. Public Participation 3. Access to Justice

(*Source*: compiled by this author).

49. Chen, W.L., Chang, C.C. & Chao, F.L., Redesign of a Traditional Ritual Furnace for Reducing Environmental Impact, *International Journal of Environmental Science and Development* 11(3) (2020).
50. This part has been adapted from my former book chapter: Anton Ming-Zhi Gao, *Transformation of the Principles of International Environmental Law in Taiwan*, in: Herausgegeben von Prof Dr Timo Hebeler eds, Protecting the Environment for International for Future Generations: Principles and Actors in International Environment Law, 231–278 (23 Jan. 2017) (ISBN: 978-3-503-17174-3).

A. Sustainable Development

19. As the concept of sustainable development (SD) is very broad, Taiwan's legislation often uses this term in the legislative purpose clause of Article 1 for the beginning and opening remarks of many environmental, natural resources, and energy acts[51] as well as other comprehensive acts;[52] there was even an attempt to draft a Sustainable Development Basic Act.[53] SD appears to be a prevailing theme in Taiwan's legislation; there are forty-eight provisions that reference SD.[54]

20. In most of the provisions, the term SD is mentioned without providing a *definition.* Article 2(2) of the Basic Environment Act, however, states: 'Sustainable development' means satisfying contemporary needs without sacrificing the ability of future generations to satisfy their needs.' Under this definition, the SD principle seems similar to the principle of intergenerational equity and may also be related to the principle of the equitable use of natural resources. However, this definition may not apply to all of the provisions that reference SD, even to the subsequent provisions in the same act (the Basic Environment Act). For instance, the SD indicators established by the central competent authority[55] may have a broader range of coverage than intergenerational equity.

21. Thus, the interpretation of SD in different provisions should depend on the legal context. For instance, the interpretation of the SD factor under Article 3-2 of

51. *See* e.g., Art. 1 of Sand and Gravel Excavation Act: 'To excavate sand and gravel resources rationally, protect natural environments, integrate administrative system, and prevent inappropriate sand and gravel excavation that may result in related hazards, this Act is then made accordingly for the purpose of achieving *sustained national development.* Provisions of other Acts shall apply when such are not included in this Act.'

    Article 1 of Renewable Energy Development Act: 'For purposes of encouraging renewable energy use, promoting energy diversification, improving environmental quality, assisting relevant industries and enhancing *sustainable development* of the country, this Act is specially formulated.'

    Article 1 of Coastal Zone Management Act: 'This Act is enacted to maintain natural systems, ensure zero loss of the natural coast, respond to climate change, prevent coastal disasters and damage to the environment, protect and restore coastal resources, implement integrated coastal zone management, and promote the *sustainable development* of coastal zones.'
52. *See* e.g., Art. 1 of the Fundamental Science and Technology Act: 'This Act is enacted for the purpose of establishing fundamental guidelines and principles for the government in promoting scientific and technological development so as to raise the standards of science and technology, maintain economic development, strengthen ecological preservation, improve public well-being, boost national competitiveness, and promote the *sustainable development* of human society.'
53. Environmental Protection Administration, The Sustainable Development Bill, available at: ivy5.epa.gov.tw/epalaw/prelaw/pre-b-00150.doc. Accessed on: 15 May 2022.
54. This is the updated information as of 18 Aug. 2015. Taiwan legislative database, http://law.moj.gov.tw/Eng/. Accessed on: 15 May 2022.
55. Article 7(1) of the Basic Environment Act: 'The central competent authority shall draft environmental protection laws and regulations, draw up national environmental protection plans, *establish sustainable development indicators* and promote and implement such laws and regulations, plans and indicators.'

the Land Expropriation Act[56] could have a very different meaning from the SD tourism concept under the Act for the Development of Tourism.[57] Thus, the interpretation of SD in different provisions should be decided on a case-by-case basis.

22. To emphasise the importance of SD in Taiwan, according to Article 29 of the Basic Environment Act,[58] the Cabinet (Executive Yuan) created the National Council for Sustainable Development Network.[59] This council is in charge of many important SD-related issues, such as the Taiwan Agenda 21,[60] the Sustainable Development Action Plan,[61] the Taiwan Sustainable Development Awards,[62] the Taiwan Sustainable Development Indicators,[63] and others.

---

56. Article 3(2) of the Land Expropriation Act: 'When considering expropriating land for establishing an undertaking, a land use applicant shall evaluate the public interest purpose and necessity of such undertaking and carry out overall evaluation and analysis of the following factors:

    1. Social factors: Including the size of population affected by the expropriation, the age structure of the affected population, and the extent of effects of the expropriation plan on the current status of the surrounding communities, the life style of and health risk to disadvantaged groups.
    2. Economic factors: Including the effects of the expropriation plan on tax revenue, food security, increase/decrease in jobs or population that might be forced to change jobs, the costs of expropriation, public facilities required of governments at all levels, the fiscal expenditure and burden of governments, the agriculture, forestry, fishery, or animal husbandry industry chain and the integrity of land use.
    3. Cultural and ecological factors: Including changes in natural urban/rural sceneries, cultural relics, living conditions or life style caused by the expropriation plan, and its impacts on the ecological environment of the area, surrounding residents or the society as a whole.
    4. *Sustainable development factors: Including national sustainable development policies, sustainability indicators, and national land use planning.*
    5. Others: Other relevant factors or factors that should be evaluated based on the individual expropriation plan.'

57. Article 19 of Act for the Development of Tourism: 'The competent authorities for the related matters shall employ professional guides in ecological and cultural environment reserves to preserve, maintain, and explain about the ecological resources unique to this country. Before entering such regions, tourists shall apply for accompanied visit with professional guides, who can give them detailed explanation, prevent acts of vandalism and *protect the sustainable development* of the natural resources.'
58. Article 29 of the Basic Environment Act: 'The Executive Yuan shall establish a *national sustainable development commission* to be responsible for relevant strategies and policies on national sustainable development matters. Said strategies and policies shall be conferred to relevant cabinet-level agencies for execution. Said commission shall be comprised of one-third each government representatives, academics and experts, and civic groups.'
59. *See* National Council for Sustainable Development Network, available at: http://nsdn.epa.gov.tw/en/index.htm.Accessed on: 15 May 2022.
60. Available at: http://nsdn.epa.gov.tw/en/agenda/index.htm. Accessed on: 15 May 2022.
61. Available at: http://nsdn.epa.gov.tw/en/project/index.htm. Accessed on: 15 May 2022.
62. Available at: http://nsdn.epa.gov.tw/en/TSDA/INDEX.htm. Accessed on: 15 May 2022.
63. *Ibid.*

B. Integration Principle

23. The integration principle in Taiwan is integrated into the fundamental law of the country, i.e., constitutional law. Even if there is no reference to the role of the environment in the original text of the Constitution,[64] the role of the environment is mentioned in the Seventh Amendment (2005),[65] which states that '[e]nvironmental and ecological protection shall be given equal consideration with economic and technological development'.[66] Considered from this point of view, the language itself can be seen as an 'advanced' version of the integration principle. On the one hand, the issue at stake has to consider the environment, which reflects the integration principle. On the other hand, when integrating environmental value, it should be considered to have the same value as economic development and technology development.

24. In addition, the Environment Basic Act advances the integration clause of the Constitution by providing an 'environmental priority' provision; the clause is even restated in the main clause of Article 3 of the Environment Basic Act.[67] It further advances the provision by stating: 'However, in the event that economic, technological or social development has a seriously negative impact on the environment or endangers the environment, the protection of the environment shall prevail.' Such an elaboration creates a conflict between the Constitution and the law. Fortunately, the court is of the opinion that the Environment Basic Act only has a 'policy declaration' function. Thus, the integration principle in the Constitution prevails.[68]

25. In fact, the day-to-day decision-making by the government always leads to conflict between environmental protection and economic growth. Thus, the integration consideration of environmental protection, along with other concerns of economic growth, social activities, and technology development, can be seen in individual acts. For instance, the development of the metro transportation system should consider the environment as well as other elements.[69] The use plan for wetlands should take multiple factors into account, including the environment.[70]

---

64. Constitution of the Republic of China (Taiwan) (1947), available at: http://law.moj.gov.tw/Eng/LawClass/LawContent.aspx?PCODE=A0000001. Accessed on: 15 May 2022.
65. The Additional Articles of the Constitution of the Republic of China (2005), available at: http://law.moj.gov.tw/Eng/LawClass/LawContent.aspx?PCODE=A0000002. Accessed on: 15 May 2022.
66. Article 10(2) of the Additional Articles of the Constitution of the Republic of China (2005).
67. 'Economic, technological and social development shall equally emphasize *environmental protection* based on long-term national interests.'
68. For further elaboration, please *see* Anton Ming-Zhi Gao & Katherine Yuhh-chinn, *The Effect of the Basic Environmental Act on Environmental Governance in Taiwan: From the Aspect of Judicial Review*, in: Konrad-Adenauer-Stiftung Foundation ed., Rule of Law for Good Environmental Governance (2015), 140–153.
69. Article 11 of the Mass Rapid Transit Act, 2014.06.04: 'The elements listed below shall be considered while planning the mass rapid transit system:

    1. Geographic conditions.
    2. Population distribution.
    3. Natural ecology and *environment.*

C. Intergenerational and/or Intragenerational Equity

26. The aforementioned definition of SD also embraces the concept of intergenerational and/or intragenerational equity. Article 2 of the Environment Basic Act states: 'Sustainable development means satisfying contemporary needs without sacrificing the ability of future generations to satisfy their needs.' The needs of the existing generation may be relevant to intragenerational equity, while those of future generations may be related to intergenerational equity.

27. [Intergenerational] The most controversial intergenerational issues regarding the application of the concept may be issues relating to the peaceful use of atomic energy and nuclear waste. Article 23 of the Environment Basic Act was affected by the German nuclear phase-out beginning in 1998, and the novel idea of a nuclear-free homeland was embedded.[71] Moreover, intragenerational issues are associated with the protection of aboriginal people's traditional knowledge and hunting practices.[72]

---

4. Land use planning and development.
5. Social and economic activities.
6. Trends in urban transportation development.
7. Integrated development of transportation systems.
8. Impact on the road traffic adjacent to the mass rapid transit system with non-exclusive right-of-way
9. Other relevant issues.'

70. Article 15 of the Wetland Conservation Act, 2013.07.03: 'The Wetland of Importance Conservation and Utilization Plan shall clearly states the following matters:

    I. The border and year period of the plan.
    II. The guidance of the superior and relevant programs.
    III. The investigation and analysis of local society and economy.
    IV. The rudimentary investigation and analysis of water resource system, ecological resources and *environment.*
    V. Land and building utilization status.
    VI. Primarily protected areas with critical scientific search, cultural heritage and ecological and environmental value.
    VII. Stipulations or measures governing the wetland system functional zoning, and its conservation, restoration, restricted or banned conducts, and maintenance.
    VIII. Permissible wise use items and management.
    IX. Water resource protection and utilization management.
    X. Emergency response and recovery.
    XI. Financial and implementation.
    XII. Other pertinent matters.'

71. Article 23 of the Environment Basic Act: 'The government shall establish plans to gradually achieve the goal of becoming a *nuclear-free homeland.* The government shall also strengthen nuclear safety management and control, protections against radiation, and the management of radioactive materials and monitoring of environmental radiation to safeguard the public from the dangers of radiation exposure.'
72. Ordinance of Hunting Wild Animals by Indigenous People for the Reason of Maintaining Traditional Cultural and Ritual Worship (原住民族基於傳統文化及祭儀需要獵捕宰殺利用野生動物管理辦法) (2015), available at: http://law.moj.gov.tw/LawClass/LawContentIf.aspx?PCODE=M012

28. [Intragenerational] Intragenerational equity is not mentioned specifically in the law, but its implicit reflection can be seen in *social welfare* legislation. The introduction of universal health care is a milestone for Taiwan in addressing the fundamental issue of equity.[73] The Senior Citizens Welfare Act[74] and Early Childhood Education and Care Act may also be relevant to facilitating intragenerational equity.

D. State Responsibility and Liability

29. Theoretically, the principle of state responsibility and liability could apply in both a domestic and an international context. However, from the above-referenced literature, this principle seems to be applied only in an international context.

30. [International] In Taiwan, a significant amount of legislation may be relevant to this principle. For instance, in the environmental impact assessment (EIA) ordinance, when determining the threshold for the likelihood of significant environmental effects for purposes of an EIA screening, the significant negative effects on 'another country's environment' should be taken into account.[75] Also, the state will intervene in violations related to fishing.[76]

31. [Domestic] However, in Taiwan, the law is more focused on the domestic aspect of state responsibility. Article 4 of the Environment Basic Act provides for the government's joint liability and ultimate responsibility for unknown polluters[77],

---

0007; The Ordinance on the Protection of Traditional Intelligent Creation by Indigenous People (2015), available at: http://law.moj.gov.tw/Hot/AddHotLawIf.ashx?PCode=D0130029&SelectType=A2&k1=%e4%b8%96%e4%bb%a3&k2=&k3=&k4=. Accessed on: 15 May 2022.

73. National Health Insurance Act, 1. Promulgated on 9 Aug. 1994 by the President's Order of Hua Chung (1) Yi Tze No. 4705, latest revision: 29 Jun. 2011, available at: http://law.moj.gov.tw/Eng//LawClass/LawContent.aspx?pcode=L0060001. Accessed on: 15 May 2022.

74. Senior Citizens Welfare Act, available at: http://law.moj.gov.tw/Eng//LawClass/LawContent.aspx?pcode=D0050037.

75. Article 19(7) of the EIA Ordinance (環境影響評估法施行細則) (2015), available at: http://ivy5.epa.gov.tw/epalaw/search/LordiDispFull.aspx?ltype=03&lname=0020. Accessed on: 15 May 2022.

76. Article 31 of Regulations on the Management of the Crew of Fishing Vessels: 'The fishermen shall not commit the following behaviors: … .6.to poach *other country's* economic waters during operation, or to fish in a water area specifically prohibited by the Regulations of the competent authority or to intentionally capture marine organisms that are protected by regulations of the competent authority.'

77. Article 4 of the Environment Basic Act: 'Citizens, enterprises and *government entities at all levels* shall jointly share the duties and responsibilities of protecting the environment.

Those who pollute or destroy the environment shall be responsible for the environmental harm or risk they create.

The government shall bear responsibility in the event that those who pollute or destroy the environment in the foregoing paragraph do not exist or cannot be confirmed.'

while other provisions in the Environment Basic Act also place the planning responsibility[78] and public procurement duty of environmentally friendly products[79] on the government.

32. Apart from state responsibility, interestingly, the Environment Basic Act also stipulates citizens' environmental responsibility.[80]

E. Polluter Pays Principle

33. There is both a direct and an indirect reference to the polluter pays principle (PPP) in Taiwan's Environment Basic Act.

34. [Direct] Article 28 of the Environment Basic Act provides the following:

> Environmental resources belong to all citizens and future generations. The central government shall establish a *system in which those who pollute or destroy the environment pay. Pollution control or environmental restoration fees that are collected from those who pollute or destroy* [emphasis by author] shall be used to preserve the sustainable use of the environment.

35. To internalise environmental costs, many environmental and energy-related acts have created associated funds, including the Air Pollution Control Fund,[81] the Water Pollution Fund,[82] the Waste Fund,[83] the Soil and Groundwater Pollution Remediation Fund,[84] and the GHG Reduction Fund,[85] as well as the Renewable Energy Fund,[86] the Energy R&D Fund,[87] and the Petroleum Fund.[88] The creation of

78. Article 7 of the Environment Basic Act: 'The central competent authority shall draft environmental protection laws and regulations, draw up *national environmental protection plans*, establish sustainable development indicators and promote and implement such laws and regulations, plans and indicators.'
79. Article 38 of the Environment Basic Act: '*Government entities at all levels* shall adopt necessary measures to promote the use of renewable resources and other materials, products or services that beneficially lessen environmental impact.'
80. Article 5 of the Environment Basic Act: '*Citizens* shall uphold environmental protection concepts and lessen the environmental impact of daily life. In terms of consumer behavior, citizens shall, as a principle, practice green consumption. In terms of daily life, citizens shall carry out waste disposal reduction, separation and recycling.

    Citizens shall actively carry out environmental protection and be responsible for assisting the government in implementing measures related to environmental protection.'
81. Articles 16 and 18 of the Air Pollution Control Act.
82. Article 11 of the Water Pollution Act.
83. Article 16 of the Waste Disposal Act.
84. Articles 28, 29, 30 of the Soil and Groundwater Pollution Remediation Act.
85. Article 19 of the GHG Reduction and Management Act states that the 'Central Competent Authority should set up a GHG Management Fund based on the funding sources of the following: 1. Revenue from the tendering of GHG emission rights … .'
86. Article 7 of the Renewable Energy Development Act.
87. Articles 5 & 5-1 of the Energy Management Act.
88. Articles 34, 35, 36, Ch. 6 Petroleum Fund, Petroleum Administration Act.

these funds is related to the German idea of 'Sonderabgaben', where funding is used for designated spending purposes rather than general ones.

36. [Indirect] On the other hand, according to Article 4(2) of the Environment Basic Act, those who pollute or destroy the environment shall be responsible for the environmental harm or risk they create. This could be seen as an indirect reference to PPP that can also be reflected in civil law through tort liability for environmental damage[89] and, even more broadly, *administrative or criminal penalties* for polluters under pollution laws.

37. [Beneficial's pay and user pay] The Environment Basic Act also sets forth the idea that the beneficiaries and users should pay, which may be partly associated with PPP as well. 'Government entities at all levels shall enhance environmental public construction projects, improve the quality of the environment, and collect appropriate fees from beneficiaries or users.'[90]

Table 2 illustrates the current special environmental levies in Taiwan.

Table 2 Summary of Special Environmental Levies in Taiwan

Legislations	*Who should pay?*	*Spending*
Air Pollution Control Fund under the Air Pollution Control Act	*Air pollution control fees* from stationary and mobile pollution sources that emit air pollutants.	1. Matters concerning the implementation of air pollution control work by competent authorities 2. Matters concerning the inspection of air pollution sources and the auditing of the implementation and efficacy of such inspections.

89. Article 184 of the Civil Code: 'A person who, intentionally or negligently, has wrongfully damaged the rights of another is bound to compensate him for any injury arising therefrom. The same rule shall be applied when the injury is done intentionally in a manner against the rules of morals.

A person, who violates a statutory provision enacted for the protection of others and therefore prejudice to others, is bound to compensate for the injury, except no negligence in his act can be proved.'

Article 213 of the Civil Code: 'Unless otherwise provided by the act or by the contract, a person who is bound to make compensation for an injury shall restore the injured party to the status quo before the injury.

If the restoration of the status quo ante shall be paid in money, interest shall be added from the time of the injury.

Under the circumstances of the first paragraph, the creditor may claim the necessary expenses for restoration instead of the restoration.'

Article 215 of the Civil Code: 'If it is impossible or obviously and greatly difficult for the restoration of the status quo ante, the injury sustained shall be compensated in money.'

90. Article 32(1) of the Environment Basic Act.

Legislations	*Who should pay?*	*Spending*
		3. Matters concerning subsidies and incentives for the performance of air pollution abatement work by each category of pollution source. 4. Matters concerning the commissioning and subsidising of analysis laboratories for the performance of motor vehicle emissions testing. 5. Matters concerning the commissioning or subsidising of professional organisations for the performance of the testing, guidance and evaluation of stationary pollution sources. 6. Matters concerning air pollution control technology research and development and strategy formulation. 7. Matters concerning international environmental protection work involving air pollution. 8. Matters concerning air quality monitoring and the auditing of the implementation and efficacy of such monitoring. 9. Matter concerning the expenses related to the collection of air pollution control fees. 10. The hiring of personnel required for work related to air pollution control. 11. Related matters concerning air pollution health risk assessments and management.

Legislations	*Who should pay?*	*Spending*
		12. Matters concerning incentives for promoting the use of clean energy and related research and development. 13. Other matters concerning air pollution control work.
Water Pollution Fund under the Water Pollution Act	Enterprises, sewage systems and households that discharge wastewater or sewage into surface water bodies based on their discharge water quality and water volume	1. Remediation of the pollution of surface water bodies and monitoring of water quality. 2. Improvement of water quality in drinking water source quality protection areas. 3. Improvement of water quality in water pollution total quantity control zones. 4. Construction of primary and secondary public sewage system main pipes. 5. Construction of wastewater treatment plants and wastewater and sewage interception facilities. 6. Construction of nightsoil dumping stations and nightsoil treatment plants. 7. Construction of centralised treatment facilities for sludge produced by wastewater and sewage treatment facilities. 8. Water pollution control technology research and development, acquisition and strategy research and development. 9. Necessary expenditures and the employment of required personnel related to the implementation of fee collection work. 10. Other relevant water pollution control work.

Legislations	*Who should pay?*	*Spending*
Waste Fund *(Resource Recycling Management Fund)* under the Waste Disposal Act	The enterprises responsible for recycling, clearance and disposal (a manufacturer; importer) *recycling, clearance and disposal fees*	1. The payment of recycling, clearance and disposal subsidies. 2. The provision of subsidies and incentives for recycling systems and reuse. 3. The covering of expenses when the enforcement authority performs disposal on behalf of others. 4. The covering of auditing and certification expenses of the impartial auditing and certification group selected and commissioned by the central competent authority. 5. Other uses related to general waste resource recycling approved by the central competent authority.
Soil and Groundwater Pollution Remediation Fund under the Soil and Groundwater Pollution Remediation Act	Manufacturers and importers, in accordance with the amounts of officially announced chemical substances, manufactured and imported by such enterprises	1. Expenditures made by competent authorities at all levels for verification, adoption of necessary response measures, supervision, and plan determination, review, investigation, assessment, implementation, and change pursuant to Article 7, paragraphs 1 and 5; Article 12, paragraph 1, paragraphs 5, 6, 8 through 10, and 13; Article 13, paragraphs 1 and 2; Article 14, paragraphs 1 and 3; Article 15; Article 22, paragraphs 1, 2, and 4; Article 24, paragraphs 3 through 5; and Article 27, paragraphs 1 and 2. 2. The funds claims for compensation and legal expenses.

Legislations	*Who should pay?*	*Spending*
		3. The funds personnel and administrative management expenses, personnel expenses incurred by soil and groundwater pollution prevention and remediation work. 4. Expense of soil and groundwater pollution control work performed by competent authorities at all levels. 5. Expense of audit of soil and groundwater pollution verification and implementation effectiveness. 6. Expense of international environmental protection work involving soil and groundwater pollution. 7. Expense of audits of soil and groundwater quality monitoring and implementation effectiveness. 8. Expense of levying soil and groundwater pollution remediation fees. 9. Expense of soil and groundwater pollution health risk assessment and management. 10. Expense of researching, promoting, developing, and creating incentives for soil and groundwater pollution remediation technology. 11. Matters concerning subsidies for soil and groundwater pollution prevention work. 12. To cover other costs in connection with soil pollution or groundwater pollution remediation approved by the central competent authority.

Legislations	*Who should pay?*	*Spending*
GHG Reduction Fund under the GHG Reduction Act	Primarily from the auction revenue of emission allowances	1. emission reduction measures; 2. emission audit measures; 3. assist, subsidise, and encourage the voluntary reduction of emission sources; 4. projects establishing informational platforms, auctions, allocations, and trade-related administration; 5. staff costs associated with GHG reduction and management; 6. adaptation-related collaboration and promotion events; 7. education, campaigns, and incentives regarding climate change and GHG reduction; 8. international activities on climate change and GHG reduction; and 9. other research issues on GHG reduction and climate adaptation.
Renewable Energy Fund	Electricity enterprises and anyone equipped with self-use power-generating facilities exceeding a certain installed capacity	1. to subsidise renewable energy facilities; 2. to conduct the resources inventories, subsidise demonstration cases, promote the use of renewable energy, and assist in setting up certification institutions; 3. to subsidise the development of power generation and storage of renewable energy; 4. to spend the fund on or subsidise the recognition and audit of renewable power generation facilities in relation to this Act; 5. for other purposes related to the development of renewable energy approved by the central competent authority.

Legislations	*Who should pay?*	*Spending*
Energy R&D Fund	The contribution of the vertically integrated electricity utilities (not exceeding half of 1% (0.5%) of the income of the vertically integrated utilities)	1. Research and development of technology relevant to exploitation of energy resources and alternative energies. 2. Research and development relevant to technology and methodology for the rational and efficient use of energy as well as energy conservation. 3. Economic analysis and collection of information on energy. 4. Training of experts in energy planning and technology. 5. Other expenses as approved.
Petroleum Fund	1. The exporter or importer of oil 2. Petroleum by-products produced by petrochemical feedstock manufacturers and sold to oil refinery operators	1. To maintain the government petroleum security stockpile. 2. To subsidise the setup of petroleum facilities in remote, aboriginal and offshore areas as well as transportation outlays and offer price subsidies. 3. To establish award of encouraging the exploration for and development of oil and natural gas reserves with feedback mechanism. 4. To implement research and development, application and promotion of energy policy, oil development technology, and alternative energies. 5. To make the security and reasonable, effective use of oil & gas (including LPG) as well as to develop and promote oil-saving technology and method. 6. Subsidy of rewarding the heat use of renewable energy to replace petroleum energy.

Legislations	*Who should pay?*	*Spending*
		7. Operation subsidy of a municipality, a county, or a city competent authority to implement the oil management and the ban, inspection or auditing that stated in the first paragraph of Article 54 in this Law. 8. To implement other necessary measures deemed necessary by the central competent authority to stabilise the oil supply and maintain the oil market order.

(*Source*: compiled by the author).

F. Common but Differentiated Responsibilities

38. [Implicit] Before the promulgation of the GHG Reduction Act of 2015, there was no explicit reference to common but differentiated responsibilities (CBDR) in Taiwan. However, the implicit reflection of the spirit of the CBDR principle was reflected in the attitude of parliament and the administrative sector in drafting and formulating environmental regulations. For instance, the relative lateness of Taiwan's parliament in passing the GHG Reduction Act could reflect how it was too harsh for Taiwan, which was a late developer in terms of the industrial revolution, to adopt legal schemes for GHG reductions at the same pace as Western countries. Also, the emission standards in Taiwan are usually less stringent than those in developing countries. For instance, the emissions standards for air pollutants in Germany are often stricter than in Taiwan (*see* Table 3).

Table 3 The Emissions Standards for Certain Air Pollutants in Taiwan and Germany

		Taiwan	*Germany*
PM_{10}	24 hours	125μg/m^3	50 μg/m^3
	Yearly	65μg/m^3	40 μg/m^3
(SO_2)	Hour	0.25 ppm	350 μg/m^3
	Day	0.1 ppm	125μg/m^3
	Yearly	0.03 ppm	50μg/m^3

	Taiwan	*Germany*
(Pb)	1.0μg/m^3 Monthly	0.5 (year) μg/m^3
Benzol	N/A	5 (year)

(*Source:* compiled by the author).

39. [Explicit] However, after the promulgation of the GHG Reduction Act on 1 July 2015, the CBDR principle finds formal and explicit legal grounds in Taiwan. According to Article 6 of the GHG Reduction Act, the formulation and adoption of the GHG reduction and management programme or plan should follow four principles. One of them is the CBDR: 'the setting and determination of a country's emission reduction target and schedule should follow the UNFCCC[United Nations Framework Convention on Climate Change]'s CBDR principle, and also take into account Taiwan's sustainable development of the environment, its economy, and society'. The national target for emissions reduction is a relatively lenient target where 2050 emissions should be cut by at least 50% of the 2005 emissions.[91] In addition, the target may be subject to change and may decrease depending on the circumstances.[92] Finally, the free allocation of emissions rights could also reflect the CBDR.[93]

G. Prevention Principle

40. This principle may be considered the fundamental basis for Taiwan's environmental pollution acts, and it has been widely implemented in Taiwan. This is reflected in the titles of certain legislation, such as the Air Pollution *Prevention* and Control Act, the Water *Prevention* and Control Act, the Marine Pollution *Prevention* and Control Act, etc. Several legal measures under these acts are related to the concepts of prevention principles, such as comprehensive pollution prevention planning,[94] permission systems,[95] the duty to adopt pollution prevention actions,[96] governmental actions,[97] etc.

91. Article 4(1) of the GHG Reduction Act.
92. Article 4(2) of the GHG Reduction Act.
93. Article 20 of the GHG Reduction Act.
94. *See* e.g., Art. 7 of the Air Pollution Act: 'Special municipality, county and city competent authorities shall determine and officially announce *air pollution control plans* [emphasis by author] pursuant to the foregoing article, and shall evaluate, revise and improve said plans and submit said plans to the central competent authority for approval every two years.'
95. *See* e.g., Art. 13(1) of the Water Pollution Act: 'Prior to establishment or modification, enterprises shall submit water pollution control measure plans and related documents for review and approval to the special municipality, county or city competent authority or an agency commissioned by the central competent authority.'

See also, Art. 26(1) of the Environment Basic Act: 'The central government shall establish pre-approval, random check and enterprise self-reporting mechanisms for environmental pollution activities to effectively control pollution sources.'

41. In addition, in the Environment Basic Act, there is also explicit reference to the preventive principle as follows:

> Government entities at all levels shall adopt *preventive measures* [emphasis by author] to protect non-renewable resources and shall regularly conduct surveys and assessments on rare resources that have surpassed limits or are nearing limits and undertake improvement or restrictive measures.[98]
>
> The central government shall establish an environmental impact assessment system to *prevent* [emphasis by author] and reduce the negative impact of government policies or development activities on the environment.[99]
>
> Government entities at all levels shall actively conduct research and establish environmental and health risk assessment systems, adopt preventive and medical healthcare measures, reduce health risks, and *prevent* [emphasis by author] or lessen diseases related to the environment.[100]

The establishment of the EIA scheme could be seen as also the specific action used to implement preventive principal issues. The EIA principle will be explained in greater detail later.

H. Environmental Impact Assessment

42. As noted above, one of the keys to preventing environmental harm is knowing the potential environmental impact beforehand. In some literature, the duty to perform an EIA is considered an independent legal principle of environmental law.[101] Originally, it was designed as an environmental 'procedural' right[102] *or* a requirement for the 'assessment and monitoring of environmental impacts'.[103] As the core of the EIA involves not only the EIA itself but also public participation and

---

96. *See* e.g., Art. 18 of the Water Pollution Act: 'Enterprises shall adopt water pollution control measures; the central competent authority in consultation with the relevant industry competent authorities shall determine management regulations for the applicable targets, scope, conditions, necessary facilities, specifications, installation, operation, monitoring, recordkeeping, time limit in years for the preservation of monitoring data, preventive management, emergency response, the collection, treatment and discharge of wastewater and sewage, and other binding matters for water pollution control measures.'
97. Article 20 of the Environment Basic Act: 'Government entities at all levels shall actively adopt measures to protect the marine environment, enhance coastal area management, and control groundwater overuse, ground subsidence, and coastal erosion.'
98. Article 19 of the Environment Basic Act.
99. Article 24 of the Environment Basic Act.
100. Article 22 of the Environment Basic Act.
101. Ved Nanda & George Rock Pring, *International Environmental Law and Policy for the 21st Century*, Martinus Nijhoff Publishers, 2012, 65-66.; Pierre-Marie Dupuy & Jorge E. Viñuales, International Environmental Law: A Modern Introduction (2015),68-70; Olufemi Elias, *Environmental Impact Assessment*, in: Fitzmaurice/Ong/Merkouris eds, *Research Handbook on International Environmental Law* (2010), 227–242.
102. Sumudu Atapattu, *Emerging Principles of International Environmental Law* (2007) 289–374.
103. Ben Boer, Ross Ramsay, Donald Rothwell, *International Environmental Law in the Asia Pacific* (1998) 11.

information disclosure during the EIA process, the EIA may also be relevant to participation rights.[104] Finally, the context of the EIA broadens to cover the EIA itself as well as the strategic environmental assessment (SEA).[105]

43. If the EIA is a procedural right, then why is the role of the EIA discussed in this section? This discussion is important because of the multiple characteristics of the substantive rights and procedural rights of EIAs in Taiwan. In Taiwan, the EIA statement prepared by the developers should receive permission from the competent authority as well.[106] Thus, an EIA statement alone does not fulfil the legal requirements of the EIA Act of Taiwan. Thus, in Taiwan, many scholars call this 'EIA veto power' for individual development projects. Even if the drafting of Taiwan's EIA Act was influenced by Western policies, EIA in Taiwan has moved beyond being simply a procedural right. The EIA reviewing results were given the legal meaning and nature of an 'administrative injunction', in parallel with development permits, planning permits, and other permits. This power makes the international community doubt if Taiwan is really an 'environmentally friendly nation'. In reality, to avoid allowing the rigid nature of the EIA to impede development or avoid conflict with other principles (such as SD noted above), most of the EIAs pass but with conditions added to the administrative injunction. This has created a SEA scheme in Taiwan.[107]

I. Precautionary Principle

44. [Early warning/pre-warning alert] Compared with the explicit role of the preventive principle in Taiwan's environmental law scheme, the role of the precautionary principle is less clear in Taiwan. In fact, the wording of the precautionary principle could be very confusing given the phrase 'early warning' (預警) in Taiwan, as this can mean either precautionary or early warning. Thus, the early warning or 'alert' in epidemic laws,[108] disaster laws,[109] bank laws,[110] national defence

---

104. Atapattu, above note, 353–374.
105. *Ibid*., at 344–352.
106. Article 14 of the Environmental Impact Assessment Act: 'The industry competent authority may not grant permission for a development activity prior to the completion of an environmental impact statement review or the authorization of an environmental impact assessment report; permission granted in violation of this regulation shall be invalid.'
107. The Ordinance on the Environmental Assessment of Policy and Programme, available at: http://law.moj.gov.tw/LawClass/LawContentIf.aspx?PCODE=O0090029. Accessed on: 15 May 2022.
108. Communicable Disease Control Act, available at: http://law.moj.gov.tw/Eng//LawClass/LawContent.aspx?pcode=L0050001; Regulations on Implementation of Communicable Disease Surveillance and Alert Systems, available at: http://law.moj.gov.tw/Eng//LawClass/LawContent.aspx?pcode=L0050006; Regulations on Implementation of Communicable Disease Surveillance and Alert Systems, available at: http://law.moj.gov.tw/Eng//LawClass/LawContent.aspx?pcode=L0050006. Accessed on: 15 May 2022.
109. *See* e.g., Art. 8 of the Ordinance on the Disclosure of Flood Data, available at: http://law.moj.gov.tw/LawClass/LawContentIf.aspx?PCODE=J0110078; Toxic Chemical Substances Hazard Prevention and Response Plan Regulations, available at: http://law.moj.gov.tw/Eng//LawClass/LawContent

laws,[111] and food laws[112] are all related to early warnings or early alerts. Even Article 27 of the Environment Basic Act could be related to an early warning: 'Government entities at all levels shall establish a strict environmental monitoring network, regularly publish monitoring results, establish *pre-warning* systems, and adopt necessary measures' [emphasis added by author].

45. [Precautionary] However, this does not mean that the precautionary principle is not reflected in Taiwan. The precautionary principle could be related to the use of nuclear power and GHG reduction issues in Taiwan. For instance, even though Taiwan has not experienced a major nuclear accident (similar to those at Chernobyl, Three Mile Island, or Fukushima), the Environment Basic Act adopted a schedule to gradually reach a nuclear-free homeland.[113] Also, the adoption of legal measures to tackle climate change 'mitigation' could be seen as the implementation and reflection of the precautionary principle.[114] The establishment of heavy regulations on the research, development, and demonstrations of Genetically Modified Organisms plants, animals, and aquaculture crops and livestock in Taiwan could also be relevant to precautionary principle issues.[115]

.aspx?pcode=O0060035; Enforcement Rules for the Implementation of the Nuclear Emergency Response Act, available at: http://law.moj.gov.tw/Eng//LawClass/LawContent.aspx?pcode=J0160060. Accessed on: 15 May 2022.

110. Regulations Governing the Deposit Accounts and Suspicious or Unusual Transactions, available at: http://law.moj.gov.tw/Eng//LawClass/LawContent.aspx?pcode=G0380199. Accessed on: 15 May 2022.

111. Article 10 of the Communication Security and Surveillance Act: 'Information gathered via communication surveillance pursuant to the provisions of Article 7 is to be used for national security *warning* intelligence purposes only. However, if circumstances as described in Article 5 are found, the information obtained should be forwarded to judicial police authorities, judicial authorities, or military courts to be processed in accordance with the law.'

    See also, The Implementing Regulation on Air-raid Practice, available at: http://law.moj.gov.tw/Eng//LawClass/LawContent.aspx?pcode=F0070021. Accessed on: 15 May 2022.

112. Article 5 of the Act Governing Food Safety and Sanitation: 'The competent authority at all levels shall establish a food sanitation and safety monitoring system based on scientific evidence. Upon discovery of incidents that may be harmful to food sanitation and safety during monitoring, an active inspection shall be conducted and *an alert* shall be issued or other necessary measures shall be implemented.

    The issuance of the active inspection and *alert* or implementation of necessary measures referred to in the preceding paragraph which will be done by the competent authority shall include conducting sampling and testing, investigating the source of raw material and the flow of the product, publishing testing results, disclosing other relevant information and ordering food businesses to perform testing on their own.' (Emphasis added).

113. Article 23 of the Environment Basic Act.

114. GHG Reduction Act of 2005, and Art. 21 of the Environment Basic Act: 'Government entities at all levels shall actively adopt measures to control carbon dioxide emissions and establish related plans to mitigate the greenhouse effect.'

115. *See* Juang Gao, *Genetic Technology and Food Safety in Taiwan*, in: Norer ed., Genetic Technology and Food Safety (2015), (ISBN: 978-621-8017-10-8).

J. The Obligation Not to Cause Damage (No-Harm Rule)

46. All of Taiwan's environmental laws can be related to the principle of an obligation not to cause damage or the no-harm rule as well. For instance, the adoption of the GHG Reduction Act of 2015 can be seen as a symbol of Taiwan's efforts to reduce carbon emissions and not harm the atmosphere. The regulations in the Marine Pollution Act can also be related to other countries' environmental pollution. In the EIA legal regime, the transboundary environmental effects could also be considered during the evaluation process.[116]

K. Human Rights

47. The right to a clean[117] and healthful[118] environment is confirmed as an important human right.[119] Some experts would expand its scope to cover not only substantive rights but procedural rights as well.[120]

48. Under Taiwan's original Constitution, this environmental right was not considered an independent human right. However, due to the effects of environmental damage and harm to existing human rights such as property rights or the right to live,[121] this environmental right could be considered an implicit right protected by the Constitution as well. As noted above, even if environmental rights are not considered to be independent rights under Article 10 of the Additional Articles of the Constitution of the ROC, the trend is to improve the importance of the environment in Taiwan's Constitution.[122]

49. Recently, Taiwan also wished to comply with two important human rights *conventions*,[123] where environmental rights were included in the concerns addressed

116. *See* Art. 19 of the EIA Ordinance (環境影響評估法施行細則).
117. M. Fitzmaurice, *Contemporary Issues in International Environmental Law* (2009) 170–206.
118. For the right to a clean, healthful environment, *see* e.g., Nanda & Pring, above note, 31–32.
119. *See also*, Elli Louka, *International Environmental Law Fairness, Effectiveness*, and World Order (2006), 54; Dinah Shelton, *Human Rights and the Environment: Substantive Rights*, in: Fitzmaurice, Malgosia, David M. Ong & Panos Merkouris eds, Research Handbook on International Environmental Law, 265–283 (2010).
120. Jona Razzaque, *Human Rights to a Clean Environment: Procedural Rights*, in: Fitzmaurice, Malgosia, David M. Ong & Panos Merkouris, eds, *Research handbook on international environmental law*. Edward Elgar Publishing, 284–302 (2010).
121. Article 15 of the Constitution of the Republic of China (Taiwan): 'The right of existence, the right of work, and the right of property shall be guaranteed to the people.'
122. 'Environmental and ecological protection shall be given equal consideration with economic and technological development.'
123. International Covenant on Economic, Social, and Cultural Rights, adopted and opened for signature, ratification, and accession by General Assembly Resolution 2200A (XXI) of 16 Dec. 1966 and entered into force 3 Jan. 1976 in accordance with Art. 27 of the International Covenant on Civil and Political Rights, G.A. Resolution 2200A (XXI), 21 U.N. GAOR Supp. (No. 16), 52, U.N. Doc. A/6316 (1966), 999 U.N.T.S. 171, entered into force 23 Mar. 1976.

by the two conventions.[124] In the Act to Implement the International Covenant on Civil and Political Rights and the International Covenant on Economic, Social, and Cultural Rights, Article 4 urges the government to facilitate the protection of human rights.[125]

50. Environmental quality[126] could also be considered an environmental human right in Taiwan.

L. *Equitable Utilisation*

51. Equity and non-discrimination have their foundation in the non-discrimination clause of Article 7 of the Taiwan constitution.[127] To further promote 'substantial equity', several additional provisions have been provided to raise equity in society.[128]

52. The Environment Basic Act provides further instruction on the issues of land development and the land of aboriginal peoples. The former provides the principle concerning land utilisation and environmental protection,[129] while the latter is related to limitations on land utilisation, paying special attention to protecting the land of aboriginal peoples.[130]

---

124. *See* e.g., International Covenant on Economic, Social, and Cultural Rights, adopted and opened for signature, ratification, and accession by General Assembly Resolution 2200A (XXI) of 16 Dec. 1966 and entered into force 3 Jan. 1976, in accordance with Art. 27.
Article 12: (1)The States Parties to the present Covenant recognize the right of everyone to the enjoyment of the highest attainable standard of physical and mental health. (2) The steps to be taken by the States Parties to the present Covenant to achieve the full realization of this right shall include those necessary for: (a) The provision for the reduction of the stillbirth-rate and of infant mortality and for the healthy development of the child; (b) The improvement of all aspects of *environmental* and industrial hygiene; (c) The prevention, treatment and control of epidemic, endemic, occupational and other diseases; (d) The creation of conditions which would assure to all medical service and medical attention in the event of sickness.
125. Article 4 of the Act to Implement the International Covenant on Civil and Political Rights and the International Covenant on Economic, Social and Cultural Rights: 'Whenever exercise their functions all levels of governmental institutions and agencies should confirm to human rights protection provisions in the two Covenants; avoid violating human rights; protect the people from infringement by others; positively promote realization of human rights.'
126. Alexandre Charles Kiss & Dinah Shelton, *A Guide to International Environmental Law* (2007)31.
127. Article 7 of the Constitution of the Republic of China (Taiwan): 'All citizens of the Republic of China, irrespective of sex, religion, race, class, or party affiliation, shall be equal before the law.'
128. For example, Arts 155 and 159 of the Constitution of the Republic of China (Taiwan).
Article 155: 'The State, in order to promote social welfare, shall establish a social insurance system. To the aged and the infirm who are unable to earn a living, and to victims of unusual calamities, the State shall give appropriate assistance and relief.'; Article 159: 'All citizens shall have equal opportunity to receive an education.'
129. Article 16 of the Basic Environment Act: 'With a high quality, comfortable and harmonious environment as the goal and on the basis of total environmental resource management concepts, government entities at all levels shall carry out reasonable plans for land development and use and promote such plans.'
130. Article 17 of the Basic Environment Act: 'Government entities at all levels may, with respect to natural conditions, actual needs, and preserving the rights of indigenous peoples, adopt necessary measures or limit human activity and use within designated areas to protect the natural, social and human environment.'

53. In other laws, certain provisions are also related to the allocation of resources. In general, fair rules are in place to award mining rights,[131] water rights,[132] or renewable energy utilisation rights.[133]

M. Common Heritage and the Common Concerns of Humankind

54. In terms of the legal regime relating to ‘environmental concerns’, the existing Environmental Basic Act (EBA) can be considered as a response to these common concerns. In addition, the existence of a wide range of environmental pollution acts will have the same meaning.

55. The Cultural Heritage Preservation Act is relevant when considering the protection of various types of cultural heritage, including (1) monuments, historical buildings, and settlements; (2) historical sites; (3) cultural landscapes; (4) traditional art; (5) folk customs and related cultural artefacts; (6) antiquities; and (7) natural landscapes. The act contains not just human-made but also natural heritage, and there is a partial overlap in the scope of protection between cultural heritage and the environment.

N. Good Governance

56. In Taiwan, there is no direct reference to the phrase good governance. However, all of the pollution prevention and control acts can be seen as legal instruments and efforts to improve the rule of law and environmental governance. The Environment Basic Act attempts to improve governance by providing the following key elements:

- professional experts and personnel for environmental matters;[134]
- professional authorities and institutions in charge of environmental matters at the central government level, including the establishment of a National Sustainable

---

131. Mining Act of 2016, available at: https://law.moj.gov.tw/ENG/LawClass/LawAll.aspx?pcode=J0020001.
132. Water Act, Amended 29 Jan. 2014, available at: http://law.moj.gov.tw/Eng/LawClass/LawContent.aspx?PCODE=J0110001. Accessed on: 15 May 2022.
133. Renewable energy Act of 2019, available at: https://law.moj.gov.tw/ENG/LawClass/LawAll.aspx?pcode=J0130032. Accessed on: 15 May 2022.
134. Article 13 of Basic Environment Act: ‘The central government shall carry out professional environmental protection training and establish a criteria system for environmental protection professionals to raise the quality of environmental protection work.

    Enterprises shall establish dedicated units or personnel in accordance with related environmental protection laws and regulations and draft and implement environmental protection plans.’

Development Council and the transformation of the existing EPA into a more powerful ministry for environmental resources[135] at the local government level;[136] and

- incentives and funds for facilitating environmental projects.[137]

O. Duty to Adopt Effective National Law: The Duty to Enforce

57. Environmental legislation in Taiwan is relevant to the principle of having a duty to adopt effective natural law and enforce it. With the view of highlighting this

---

135. Article 29 of Basic Environment Act: 'The Executive Yuan shall establish a national sustainable development commission to be responsible for relevant strategies and policies on national sustainable development matters. Said strategies and policies shall be conferred to relevant cabinet-level agencies for execution. Said commission shall be comprised of one-third each government representatives, academics and experts, and civic groups.'

    Article 30 of Basic Environment Act: 'The central government shall establish a cabinet-level agency dedicated to environmental resources to effectively integrate and promote government policies and related matters on environmental resource preservation.'

136. Article 10 of Basic Environment Act: 'Government entities at all levels shall have a dedicated agency or unit to plan, promote and provide guidance on environmental protection matters.

    Government entities at all levels shall liberally budget for environmental protection and reasonably allocate such budget according to actual needs.'

137. Article 31 of Basic Environment Act: 'The central government, in accordance with the law, shall establish environmental funds to bear responsibility for environmental cleaning, restoration and tracking and investigation of pollution sources and the promotion of matters beneficial to environmental development.'

    Article 35 of the Basic Environment Act: 'The central government shall provide incentives for academic and research organizations involved in environmental protection to upgrade facilities, recruit and train personnel, introduce advanced technologies, and integrate research resources, hastening the development of demonstration projects and research on environmental protection technology.'

    Article 36 of the Basic Environment Act: 'Government entities at all levels shall adopt incentives to promote the development of environmental protection enterprises and private environmental protection groups, as well as encourage private investment in the environmental protection industry.

    The central government shall promote and manage environmental protection enterprises to raise the quality of environmental protection engineering and services.'

    Article 37 of the Basic Environment Act: 'With the aim of rationally and effectively using resources and meeting environmental protection needs, government entities at all levels shall adopt appropriate incentive, promotion and compensation measures for the following activities.

    1. Protection of the natural, social and human environment
    2. Research and development of clean production technologies, equipment or products for production cleaning
    3. Research and development of resource recycling and reuse technologies
    4. Promotion and application of renewable energy
    5. Research and development of energy conservation technology and installation of products that conserve energy
    6. Manufacture or installation of pollution control equipment
    7. Moving for the purpose of protecting the environment
    8. Provision of land or other resources to be used to protect the environment
    9. Environmental reforestation and greenification
    10. Other activities related to environmental protection.'

principle, Article 39 of the EBA requires government entities at all levels to fully enforce environmental laws and regulations and to interdict and punish violations in accordance with the law.

P. Conservation

58. This principle,[138] known as the 'obligation to conserve the environment and natural resources',[139] is also related to the no-harm principle and the precautionary principle.[140]

59. In addition to the aforementioned no harm and precautionary principles, the EBA provides an additional clause for the conservation principle with particular focus on biodiversity and the natural environment: 'Government entities at all levels shall actively protect wildlife, ensure biodiversity, protect forests, estuaries and wetland environments, and maintain a diverse natural environment, while also enhancing water resource conservation, water and soil conservation, and revegetation and greenification work.'

Q. Sovereignty over Natural Resources

60. Sovereignty over natural resources[141] or State sovereignty[142] embodies the right of states and peoples to freely dispose of their natural resources.[143]

61. In Taiwan, sovereignty over natural resources can be seen in the Constitution's sovereignty clause[144] and its territory provision.[145] At the legislative level, there is a special law that provides for an Exclusive Economic Zone and the Continental Shelf of the ROC. For instance, Article 5 of the Law on the Exclusive Economic Zone and the Continental Shelf of the ROC[146] conveys the government of

138. Nanda & Pring, above note, 36–37.
139. Boer, Ramsay & Rothwell, above note, 10–11.
140. *Ibid.*, at 10.
141. Louka, above note, 49; Philippe Sands & Jacqueline Peel, *Principles of International Environmental Law* (2012)191–192.
142. Nanda, Pring, above note, 20.
143. Nicolaas Schrijver, Self-Determination of Peoples and Sovereignty over Natural Wealth and Resources, 96, available at: http://www.ohchr.org/Documents/Issues/Development/RTDBook/PartIIChapter5.pdf.
144. Article 2 of the Constitution of the Republic of China (Taiwan): 'The sovereignty of the Republic of China shall reside in the whole body of citizens.'
145. Article 4 of the Constitution of the Republic of China (Taiwan): 'The territory of the Republic of China according to its existing national boundaries shall not be altered except by resolution of the National Assembly.'
146. Law on the Exclusive Economic Zone and the Continental Shelf of the Republic of China, available at: http://law.moj.gov.tw/Eng/LawClass/LawContent.aspx?PCODE=A0000010 Accessed on: 15 May 2022.

Taiwan's sovereignty over the natural resources in the exclusive economic zone and the continental shelf of the ROC as follows:

> The Republic of China shall, in its exclusive economic zone or on its continental shelf, enjoy and exercise the following rights:
>
> 1. Sovereign rights for the purpose of exploring, exploiting, conserving, and managing the resources, living or non-living, of the waters superjacent to the seabed and of the seabed and its subsoil;
> 2. Jurisdiction over the construction, use, modification, or dismantlement of artificial islands, installations or structures;
> 3. Jurisdiction over marine scientific research;
> 4. Jurisdiction over preservation of marine environment; and
> 5. Other rights in accordance with international law.
>
> The Republic of China shall enjoy and exercise sovereign rights of utilising the energy stemming from the water, currents, and winds or other activities.
> The Republic of China shall enjoy and exercise jurisdiction over laying, maintaining, or modifying submarine cables or pipelines.

R. Cooperation

62. In environmental governance, the Taiwan legal regime also emphasises the importance of cooperation. For instance, Article 12 of the Environment Basic Act provides an international cooperation clause as follows:

> The central government shall promote international cooperation and technological assistance, engineering technology, and experimental research related to global sustainable development and publish related information to facilitate its use by citizens and enterprises. Local governments may also carry out such work as deemed necessary.

S. Procedural Principles

63. Apart from the substantive environmental principles, there are also procedural aspects of environmental principles that are sometimes called 'procedural environmental rights'.[147] There are several approaches that can be used in defining these procedural principles. Thus, this author attempts to follow three procedural rights as set forth under the Aarhus Convention[148] and will elaborate on the three aspects of these principles below.

---

147. Dupuy, Viñuales, above note, 316.
148. The UNECE Convention on Access to Information, Public Participation in Decision-making and Access to Justice in Environmental Matters, also known as the Aarhus Convention, available at: http://www.unece.org/env/pp/welcome.html.

1. Access to Information

64. Compared with the early development of substantive environmental principles via many of the environmental pollution control acts in Taiwan, the development of access to information rules is quite recent. This is also related to developments in democracy in Taiwan. Taiwan underwent a long age of martial law (July 1947–May 1991).[149] The transparency requirement was considered during the legislative process for the fundamental law of administrative behaviour, i.e., the Administrative Procedure Act.[150] Consequently, in 1999, a special section regarding information disclosure and four additional provisions were included to guide administrative transparency.[151] More detailed legislation was announced in 2005.[152]

---

149. Period of Mobilization for the Suppression of Communist Rebellion, available at: https://en.wikipedia.org/wiki/Period_of_mobilization_for_the_suppression_of_Communist_rebellion. Accessed on: 15 May 2022.
150. Administrative Procedure Act, available at: http://law.moj.gov.tw/Eng/LawClass/LawContent.aspx?PCODE=A0030055.Accessed on: 15 May 2022.
151. Section 7 Making Information Public of the Administrative Procedure Act.
   Article 46: 'The party or an affected person may apply to an administrative authority for examining, transcribing, copying or taking photographs of relevant materials or records; provided that the materials or records are necessary for claiming or protecting his legal interest.
   An application made under the preceding paragraph to an administrative authority may not be denied except for information specified as follows:

   1. Drafts and other preliminary operational documents prepared before an administrative decision is made;
   2. Information relating to national defense, military, diplomacy and any other general official secrets, which is legally required to be kept in confidence;
   3. Information relating to personal privacy, occupational secrets and trade secrets, which is legally required to be kept in confidence;
   4. Information [the disclosure of which] is likely to result in infringement of the right of any third party; and
   5. Information [the disclosure of which] is likely to result in serious impairment to the social security, public safety or the normal performance of any function in connection with the public interest.

   Examination shall be permitted of the part of the information specified under sub-paragraphs 2 and 3 of the preceding paragraph, if no confidentiality is necessary therefor.
   Where a party finds any error in the materials or records referred to in paragraph 1, concerning the party himself, he is entitled to request the administrative authority to make correction upon producing proofs of the facts.'
   Article 47: 'In the course of an administrative procedure, a government officer shall not enter into contact with a party thereto or any person representing the interest thereof for any purpose other than that of the administrative procedure, unless it is necessary for the performance of his duties.
   A government officer who has contacted a party or any person representing the interest thereof for any purpose other than that of the administrative procedure shall place in the file all written documents in connection with his communication with such party or person and shall make such documents open to all other parties, if any.
   Where the contact referred to the preceding paragraph was not made in writing, a written record thereof shall be kept, describing therein the person contacted, the time and place where the contact was made, and the contents thereof.'
152. The Freedom of Government Information Law, 28 Dec. 2005, available at: http://law.moj.gov.tw/Eng/LawClass/LawContent.aspx?PCODE=I0020026. Accessed on: 15 May 2022.

Provisions for active disclosure,[153] disclosure upon request,[154] and limitation on disclosures[155] are all included in this Act. This can be seen as the fundamental rule on information disclosure in all sectors, including the area of environmental administration. In the environmental law sphere, the Environment Basic Act of 2002 incorporated environmental information disclosure elements at approximately the same time, including:

- international cooperation and technology R&D information;[156]
- basic environmental information;[157] and
- monitoring information.[158]

65. Providing related information during the environmental education or learning process can also be indirectly linked to access to information.[159]

66. The right to information has also expanded from general administrative/environmental law to individual environmental laws. For instance, a disclosure clause is included in the revision of the Toxic Chemical Substances Control Act (TCSCA) in 2013.[160] Registration information must also be disclosed as part of the EU's Regulation on REACH.[161]

---

153. Chapter 2, Active Publication of Government Information: The Freedom of Government Information Law.
154. Chapter 3, Request for Providing Government Information: The Freedom of Government Information Law.
155. Chapter 4, Restrictions on Publication of Government Information: The Freedom of Government Information Law.
156. Article 12 of the Environment Basic Act: 'The central government shall promote international cooperation and technological assistance, engineering technology and experimental research related to global sustainable development and publish related information to facilitate its use by citizens and enterprises. Local governments may also carry out such work as deemed necessary.'
157. Article 15 of the Environment Basic Act: 'Government entities at all levels shall collect, survey and assess information on the condition of the natural, social and human environment within its jurisdiction, build an environmental information system and provide such system for checking.
    The environmental information system in the foregoing paragraph shall be open to the public on a regular basis.'
158. Article 27 of the Environment Basic Act: 'Government entities at all levels shall establish a strict environmental monitoring network, regularly publish monitoring results, establish pre-warning systems, and adopt necessary measures.'
159. Article 9 of the Environment Basic Act: 'Government entities at all levels shall make widely available environment first and sustainable development education and study and strengthen public education to improve the environmental knowledge of citizens, establish environmental protection concepts and realize such concepts in daily life.'
160. *See* e.g., Art. 41 of the Toxic Chemical Substances Control Act: 'Chemical substance registration information pursuant to this Act shall be disseminated to the public. However, the central competent authority possesses the authority to maintain confidentiality of information involving national defense, industrial or commercial confidentialities subject to the application submitted by the manufacturer or importer and received approval by the central competent authority.
    When one of the following circumstances occurs, information confidentiality in the foregoing paragraph shall not be subjected to this restriction pursuant to the authority of the central competent authority.

    I. It is necessary for benefitting the public.

2. Public Participation

67. The transformation of participation rules in Taiwan can be seen in general administrative procedural rules and the rules that form environmental laws. As to the former, there is one section in the Administrative Procedural Act specifying the hearing process.[162] Hearing procedures may be applicable to administrative behaviours such as administrative deposition,[163] administrative rules,[164] and administrative planning.[165] Additionally, the deponent undergoing an administrative deposition also has the right to state his/her opinion.[166]

II. It is necessary for protecting people's lives, bodies, health.
III. It is consented by the manufacturer or importer.

Confidentiality shall be maintained concerning reviews, checking, and the collection of samples and testing performed pursuant to this Act that involve national defense, industrial or commercial secrets. However, identities, physical, chemical, toxicity, classification, labeling and relevant safety information of chemical substances shall not be subjected to this restriction.

The Freedom of Government Information Law shall apply to application to the central, municipality, county and city competent authorities for provision of government information pursuant to the regulations in the foregoing three paragraphs.'

161. Article 7-2 of the Toxic Chemical Substances Control Act.
162. Articles 54–66, s. 10, Hearing procedure, Administrative Procedure Act.
163. Article 107 of the Administrative Procedure Act: 'In any of the following circumstances, the administrative authority shall *hold a hearing*:

1. Where the law requires explicitly the holding of a hearing; and
2. Where the administrative authority considers it necessary to hold a hearing.'

164. Chapter IV Legal Orders and Administrative Rules of the Administrative Procedure Act.

Article 155 of the Administrative Procedure Act: 'The administrative authority may hold *ex officio hearings* for the purpose of establishment of a legal order.'

Article 156 of the Administrative Procedure Act: 'In holding hearings for the purpose of establishment of a legal order, the administrative authority shall publish in a government gazette or newspaper a public notice thereof, giving the following details:

1. Name of the authority establishing the legal order, or the names of all authorities involved if it is required by law that the legal order be established jointly by several authorities;
2. The legal basis for establishing the legal order;
3. Full text or the essence of the draft;
4. The date and place of the hearing; and
5. The basic procedure of the hearing.'

165. Chapter V Administrative Planning of the Administrative Procedure Act.

Article 164 of the Administrative Procedure Act: 'The decision on an administrative planning that relates to specified utilization of land situated in specific districts or the construction of major infrastructures, which involves persons with diverse interest and the powers of a multiple number of administrative authorities, may be finalized only through open process and after the holding of a hearing proceeding, and such a planning may bring efficiency as a result of concentrated efforts and power.

The procedure for formulation and finalization of, revision to and cancellation of an administrative planning mentioned in the preceding paragraph shall be separately established by the Executive Yuan.'

166. Article 102 of the Administrative Procedure Act: 'An administrative authority shall, before rendering an administrative disposition to impose restraint on the freedom or right of a person or to

68. In the field of environmental law, Article 11 of the Environment Basic Act invites not only experts but also the public to participate in the environmental decision-making process:

> Government entities at all levels may employ *the services of an environmental protection organisation, group representative or academic expert* for consultation.
> Government entities at all levels may invite *relevant members of the public or groups* to jointly participate and strengthen the promotion of environmental protection work [emphasis by author].

69. Aside from the Basic Act, the individual environmental laws provide a participation scheme as well. For instance, a public hearing is required under the Environmental Impact Assessment Act.[167] Article 9 of the Coastal Zone Management Act requires the 'integrated coastal zone management plan' to involve citizens during the drafting process[168] and to make the draft available for further public comments.[169]

3. Access to Justice

70. In the Environment Basic Act, there are several provisions relating to access to justice or the role of justice. First, Article 14 seeks to improve the professionalism of the court regarding environmental matters by 'establishing a dedicated court

---

deprive him of the same, give the person subject to the disposition an opportunity to state his opinions, unless a notice has been given to the person subject to the disposition under article 39 hereof to enable him to state his opinions or it has been decided that a hearing will be held, except where it is otherwise prescribed by law.'

167. Article 12 of the EIA Act: 'The industry competent authority shall, in conjunction with the competent authority, members of the Committee and other relevant agencies, invite together experts, scholars, groups and local residents to conduct an on-site inspection and hold a public hearing within thirty days after receipt of the draft environmental impact assessment report; records of the on-site inspection and public hearing shall be maintained and submitted to the competent authority within thirty days after the on-site inspection and public hearing.'

168. Article 9(1) of the Coastal Zone Management Act: 'Forums or other suitable means shall be organized to widely gather opinions from scholars, experts, related departments, central democratic bodies, and *private organizations* for the formulation of the integrated coastal zone management plan. The opinions shall be documented and representatives of scholars, experts, related departments, and *private organizations* shall be appointed to jointly deliberate on the integrated coastal zone management plan. The number of scholar, expert, and *private organization representatives* shall be no less than one half of all representatives. The integrated coastal zone management plan shall be submitted to the Executive Yuan for ratification and take effect after it is announced. This shall also apply to any changes to the integrated coastal zone management.' (Emphasis added).

169. Article 9(2) of the Coastal Zone Management Act: 'The progress, results, response to opinions, and other related information of the deliberation shall be announced on the internet, government gazette or other suitable means. After the integrated coastal zone management plan is ratified, the Central Competent Authority shall announce the management plan within 40 days after receiving the ratification document, and shall notify municipal and county (city) governments and township (district) offices to publicly display the management plan for no less than 30 days. While on display, the integrated coastal zone management plan shall be maintained clean and complete for public access.'

or designating dedicated personnel for environmental protection disputes'. Furthermore, Article 33 seeks to improve the overall dispute resolution mechanisms for environmental matters.[170] Finally, Article 34 attempts to broaden the standing issue by awarding standing to citizens or public interest groups in the administrative litigation process.[171] This expansion of the standing rules can also be seen in the Administrative Litigation Act[172] and individual environmental laws such as:

- The EIA Act.[173]
- The Soil and Groundwater Pollution Remediation Act.[174]
- The Water Pollution Control Act.[175]

---

170. 'The central government shall establish a mechanism for resolving environmental disputes, strengthen technology to assess reasons for dispute and burden of proof education, training, research and development, and provide an appropriate dispute resolution mechanism.

 The central government shall establish emergency response, compensation, reparation and remediation mechanisms.'

171. Article 34: 'If a government entity at any level is negligent in enforcement, persons or public interest groups may, in accordance with laws and regulations, name said competent authority as a defendant and directly file a lawsuit with the Administrative Court.

 When issuing a verdict on such lawsuit, the Administrative Court pursuant to its authority may order the defendant competent authority to pay the appropriate lawyer fees, detection and appraisal fees and other litigation costs to plaintiffs that have made specific contributions to maintaining the quality of the environment.'

172. Article 9 of the Administrative Litigation Act: 'Citizens are allowed to bring administrative litigation against administrative authorities for the cases unrelated to his/her personal rights or legal interests. Yet, such standing should be further specified by individual laws.'

173. Article 23(7) of the Environmental Impact Assessment Act: 'For those competent authorities that have still failed to carry out implementation in accordance with the law within sixty days after receipt of the written notification, *the victims* or *public interest groups* may name the competent authority at issue as a defendant and directly file a lawsuit with an administrative court based on the negligent behavior of the competent authority in fulfilling its implementation duties in order to seek a ruling ordering the competent authority to carry out implementation.'

174. Article 54 Soil and Groundwater Pollution Remediation Act: 'When a public and private premises violates this Act or a legal order determined pursuant to the authorization of this Act and the competent authority is negligent in enforcement, victims or public interest groups may notify the competent authority in writing concerning the details of the negligent enforcement. When a competent authority has failed to carry out enforcement in accordance with the law within sixty days after receipt of the written notification, the victims or public interest groups may name the competent authority at issue as a defendant and file a lawsuit directly with an administrative court based on the negligent behavior of the competent authority in the execution of its duties in order to seek a ruling ordering the competent authority to implement its duties.

 When issuing a verdict on the lawsuit in the foregoing paragraph, the administrative court pursuant to its authority may order the defendant agency to pay the appropriate lawyer fees, detection and appraisal fees and other litigation costs to plaintiffs that have made specific contributions to soil or groundwater pollution remediation.

 The central competent authority shall determine the format of the written notification in Paragraph 1.'

175. Water Pollution Control Act Art. 72: 'When an enterprise or sewage system violates this Act or related orders determined pursuant to the authorization of this Act and the competent authority is negligent in enforcement, victims or public interest groups may notify the competent authority in writing of the details of the negligent enforcement. For those competent authorities that have still failed to carry out enforcement in accordance with the law within sixty days after receipt of the written notification, the victims or public interest groups may name the competent authority at issue

- The Air Pollution Control Act.[176]
- The Marine Pollution Control Act.[177]
- The Waste Disposal Act.[178]

---

as a defendant and directly file a lawsuit with a high administrative court based on the negligent behavior of the competent authority in the execution of its duties in order to seek a ruling ordering the competent authority to execute its duties.

When issuing a verdict on the lawsuit in the foregoing paragraph, the high administrative court pursuant to its authority may order the defendant agency to pay the appropriate lawyer fees, monitoring and appraisal fees and other litigation costs to plaintiffs that have made specific contributions to the maintenance of the quality of water bodies.

The central competent authority in consultation with the relevant agencies shall determine the format of the written notification in Paragraph 1.'

176. Air Pollution Control Act Art. 81: 'When a public and private premises violates this Act or related orders determined pursuant to the authorization of this Act and the competent authority is negligent in enforcement, victims or public interest groups may notify the competent authority in writing of the details of the negligent enforcement. For those competent authorities that have still failed to carry out enforcement in accordance with the law within sixty days after receipt of the written notification, the victims or public interest groups may name the competent authority at issue as a defendant and file a lawsuit directly with an administrative court based on the negligent behavior of the competent authority in the execution of its duties in order to seek a ruling ordering the competent authority to execute its duties.

When issuing a verdict on the lawsuit in the foregoing paragraph, the administrative court pursuant to its authority may order the defendant agency to pay the appropriate lawyer fees, detection and appraisal fees and other litigation costs to plaintiffs that have made specific contributions to the maintenance of air quality.

The central competent authority in consultation with the relevant agencies shall officially announce the format of the written notification in Paragraph 1.'

177. Article 59 of the Marine Pollution Control Act: 'When a public or private premises violates this Act or related orders determined pursuant to the authorization of this Act and the competent authority is negligent in enforcement, victims or public interest groups may notify the competent authority in writing of the details of the negligent enforcement. For those competent authorities that have still failed to carry out enforcement in accordance with the law within sixty days of the receipt of the written notification, the victims or public interest groups may name the competent authority at issue as a defendant and directly file a lawsuit with an administrative court based on the negligent behavior of the competent authority in fulfilling its enforcement duties in order to seek a ruling ordering the competent authority to carry out enforcement.

When issuing a verdict on the lawsuit in the foregoing paragraph, the administrative court pursuant to its authority may order the defendant competent authority to pay the appropriate lawyer fees, detection and appraisal fees and other litigation costs to plaintiffs that have made specific contributions to the prevention of marine pollution.

The central competent authority shall determine the format of the written notification in Paragraph 1.'

178. Article 72 of the Waste Disposal Act: 'When a public and private premises violates this Act or related orders determined pursuant to the authorization of this Act and the competent authority is negligent in enforcement, victims or public interest groups may notify the competent authority in writing of the details of the negligent enforcement. For those competent authorities that have still failed to carry out enforcement in accordance with the law within sixty days after receipt of the written notification, the victims or public interest groups may name the competent authority at issue as a defendant and directly file a lawsuit with a high administrative court based on the negligent behavior of the competent authority in the execution of its duties in order to seek a ruling ordering the competent authority to execute its duties.

When issuing a verdict on the lawsuit in the foregoing paragraph, the high administrative court pursuant to its authority may order the defendant agency to pay the appropriate lawyer fees, monitoring and appraisal fees and other litigation costs to plaintiffs that have made specific contributions to the effective clearance and disposal of waste.

71. From these laws, per se, Taiwan seems to have adopted broad standing requirements for environmental non-governmental organisations (NGOs) to be involved in the litigation process. However, in legal practice, broad standing is being awarded on a case-by-case basis by the court. In general, the rule to launch litigation in Taiwan follows the German-based principle of 'Schutznormlehre', where only the victims or the deponent undergoing an administrative deposition can initiate litigation. This rigid and narrow scope for standing is being challenged by environmental NGOs and local citizens. In recent cases, standing to initiate EIA litigation was expanded to local citizens instead of only the applicants directly concerned. Additionally, an NGO won a significant verdict in a pioneering EIA case regarding Miramar Resort.[179] Even so, the standing issue is typically quite controversial in other non-EIA cases. For instance, the court did not admit standing for local citizens against the demolition of a heritage hospital at the terminal station of Taipei METRO.[180]

§3. Constitutional Provisions

72. In the main provisions of Constitutional law, even though fundamental rights such as freedom of speech[181] and freedom of religious belief[182] are mentioned, there is no discussion of 'environment protection', even in the very lengthy chapter of 'Chapter XIII Fundamental National Policies' (from Articles 127–169), which relates to section 1 National Defence, section 2 Foreign Policy, section 3 National Economy, section 4 Social Security, section 5 Education and Culture, and section 6 Frontier Regions.

73. Until the 7th Additional Articles of the Constitution of the ROC promulgated in June 2005,[183] the term environmental protection is finally included in Article 10(2): 'Environmental and ecological protection shall be given equal consideration with economic and technological development.' As noted above, this can be seen as the realisation of the environmental principle of integration. Therefore, it is implemented on a case-by-case basis.

The central competent authority in consultation with the relevant agencies shall determine the format of the written notification in Paragraph 1.'

179. Miramar Resort EIA to be Revoked, Court Rules, Taipei Times, available at: http://www.taipeitimes.com/News/front/archives/2014/10/29/2003603163; Taitung Appeals Decision to Revoke Miramar EIA, Taipei Times, available at: http://www.taipeitimes.com/News/taiwan/archives/2014/12/03/2003605877.
180. For further discussion, *see* Juang, above note.
181. Article 11 of the Additional Articles of the Constitution of the Republic of China: 'The people shall have freedom of speech, teaching, writing and publication.'
182. Article 13 of the Additional Articles of the Constitution of the Republic of China: 'The people shall have freedom of religious belief.'
183. Additional Articles of the Constitution of the Republic of China, Amended Date: 2005-06-10 https://law.moj.gov.tw/ENG/LawClass/LawAll.aspx?pcode=A0000002.

§4. Historical Background of the Evolution of Environmental Law

74. High-speed growth accompanied by quick industrialisation began in the late 1950s. Taiwan became known for cheap manufactured exports that were produced by small enterprises bound together by flexible sub-contracting networks.[184] This led to serious pollution and conflict with the local people, and a large environmental movement began in the 1970s, especially after the famous Yu-cheng Rice Oil Poisoning Incident in 1979. In this incident, a Japanese-produced PCB mixture (Kanechlor 400, 500) was used as the heat-transfer medium to deodorise and decolourise rice oil by a company in central Taiwan. PCBs and their heat-degraded by-products, polychlorinated dibenzofurans, ter- and quaterphenyls (PCTs and PCQs), contaminated the rice oil and injured 2000 people who had consumed the oil, causing acne, pigmentation of the nails and skin, and hypersecretion of the meibomian glands.[185]

75. The emergence of the environmental movement in Taiwan was marked by protests against the Sunko Ink Co. chemical plant in Taichung County from 1982 to 1986. Local villagers began complaining about the poisonous gas emitted by Sunko in 1982, but their constant petitions to higher authorities were ignored.[186] After martial law was lifted on 15 July 1987, the number of environmental protests increased, with that number through the 1990s.[187]

76. These movements have played a key role in facilitating the development of environmental legislation. In the early 1970s, concerns about pollution led to the adoption of the Drinking Water Management Act of 1972, the Water Pollution Act of 1974, the Waste Disposal Act of 1974, and the Air Pollution Control Act of 1975.

77. It is important to note the quick upgrade in environmental authority that occurred in the 1980s, along with the promulgation of the Noise Control Act of 1983 and TCCSCA of 1986.

78. The Executive Yuan passed the Environmental Protection Act in Taiwan Area in April 1979 that comprehensively planned a sound system for EPA. The Environmental Health Division, the Department of Health, Executive Yuan, was changed to the Environmental Protection Bureau and took on the responsibilities of air pollution control and environmental health, the original tasks of the Department of Health, and also took control of matters related to water pollution and traffic noise that had originally belonged to the Ministry of Economic Affairs and the National

184. EH.net, The Economic History of Taiwan, available at: https://eh.net/encyclopedia/the-economic-history-of-taiwan/.

185. Hsu, C.C., et al., *The Yu-cheng Rice Oil Poisoning Incident*, in: Arnold Schecter, ed., *Dioxins and Health* (1994): https://doi.org/10.1007/978-1-4899-1462-0_20.

186. Ho, M.S., *Environmental Movement in Democratizing Taiwan (1980–2004): A Political Opportunity Structure Perspective*, in: Jeffrey Broadbent & Vicky Brockman eds, East Asian Social Movements, 283–314, 292 (2011).

187. Tong, Y., Environmental Movements in Transitional Societies: A Comparative Study of Taiwan and China, *Comparative Politics*, 167–188 (2005).

Police Agency. On 22 August 1987, the Environmental Protection Bureau, the Department of Health, Executive Yuan, then became the EPA, i.e., the current competent authority for environmental affairs, governing seven departments: comprehensive planning, air quality protection and noise control, water quality protection, waste management, environmental sanitation and toxic substance management, supervision evaluation and dispute resolution, environmental monitoring and information management.[188]

79. The establishment of EPA played a key role in legal reform in the 1990s. The Public Nuisance Dispute Mediation Act of 1992 and the Environmental Impact Assessment Act of 1994 were two important milestones during this period.

80. As noted above, in the 2000s, the new ruling party won the presidential election and led to the promulgation of the Environment Basic Act of 2002.[189] The key legislation subject to the EPA's authority is summarised in Table 4.

Table 4 The Key Environmental Legislations Governed by EPA

Organisational act	Organic Act of the EPA, Executive Yuan Organic Act of the National Institute of Environmental Analysis, EPA, Executive Yuan Organic Act of the Environmental Professionals Training Institute, EPA, Executive Yuan Organization Act of the Toxic and Chemical Substances Bureau, EPA, Executive Yuan
Cross-sectoral Acts	Basic Environment Act Environmental Impact Assessment Act Public Nuisance Dispute Mediation Act The Environmental Education Act
Pollution control	Air Pollution Control Act Greenhouse Gas Reduction and Management Act Indoor Air Quality Act Noise Control Act Water Pollution Control Act Drinking Water Management Act Waste Disposal Act Resource Recycling Act Environmental Agents Control Act Toxic and Concerned Chemical Substances Control Act Soil and Groundwater Pollution Remediation Act

(*Source*: compiled by this author using https://law.moj.gov.tw/ENG/Law/LawSearchLaw.aspx?TY=0126).

188. Taiwan EPA, EPA History, available at: https://www.epa.gov.tw/eng/DB6E2C29814EB83A.
189. Basic Environment Act, Announced Date: 2002-12-11, available at: https://law.moj.gov.tw/ENG/LawClass/LawAll.aspx?pcode=O0100001.

§5. Role of Government Institutions in the Shaping and Administration of Environmental Law and Policy

I. The Governmental Institutions and Their Competencies

A. The Evolution of the Environmental Competent Authority EPA

81. As noted above, it was many years before the EPA was created (in 1987). Originally, environmental matters were handled through a distributed approach. The Department of Health was established under the auspices of the Ministry of the Interior (MOI) before 17 March 1971; its responsibilities included infectious disease prevention, epidemic control and surveillance, international health inspection and quarantine, environmental sanitation, public health facilities, and medicine management. The Ministry of Economic Affairs created the Industrial Development Bureau in 1969. Section 7 of the Industrial Development Bureau, Ministry of Economic Affairs is responsible for managing industrial waste gas and water emissions as well as preventing or mitigating public hazards. In March 1971, the Environmental Health Division was created by the Department of Health, Executive Yuan. This division was responsible for monitoring and managing garbage and sewage disposal in public health facilities, public space, and food processing plants; the use of pesticides; studies, guidance, and supervision of air, water, and noise pollution control. In addition, the Ministry of Economic Affairs also set up the Water Pollution Control Section under the Water Resource Integrated Planning Commission to take care of water pollution control.[190]

82. According to Article 4 of the Organic Act of the EPA, Executive Yuan (30 January 2002), further subdivisions will be created under the EPA to manage detailed environmental regulations:

- Department of Comprehensive Planning.
- Department of Air Quality Protection and Noise Control.
- Department of Water Quality Protection.
- Department of Waste Management.
- Department of Environmental Sanitation and Toxic Substances Management.
- Department of Supervision Management and Dispute Resolution.
- Department of Environmental Monitoring and Information Management.

B. Unfinished Works of Reorganisation of EPA

83. Because of the increasing complexity of environmental matters, the government began to launch large-scale reform of the institutions and ministries through the *Organizational Act of the Executive Yuan* of 1980, which was revised and

190. EPA History, available at: https://www.epa.gov.tw/eng/DB6E2C29814EB83A.

updated in 2012.[191] According to Article 3 of the Act, the EPA would be merged with the function of other existing ministries and become) Ministry of Environment and Natural Resources.

84. However, this is a huge project that has led to incomplete tasks. Establishing the new Ministry of Environment and Natural Resources is one of the most difficult tasks for the government to accomplish. This integration includes the EPA (Environmental Professionals Training Institute, Environmental Analysis Laboratory), the Construction and Planning Office of the Ministry of the Interior (National Parks Division, Sewage Systems Office), the Ministry of Economic Affairs (Mines Department, Bureau of Mines, Central Geological Survey), the Ministry of Transportation and Communication (Central Weather Bureau), the Council of Agriculture (Forestry Bureau, Soil and Water Conservation Bureau, Taiwan Forestry Research Institute, Endemic Species Research Institute), and the Veterans Affairs Council (Forest Conservation and Management Administration). After the administrative adjustment, approximately 2,681 personnel will be integrated into the ministry; when personnel from the fourth-level agencies and the Taiwan Water Corporation are included, the total will be over 14,500 employees. Among them, approximately 5,700 will be working at the Taiwan Water Corporation. This represents a significant increase from the original 551 employees (including contracted personnel, nearly 1,000). The official budget was raised from TWD 6.5 billion to TWD 50 billion; including the underlying funding and the special budget, the total budget is TWD 150 billion.[192]

C. Other Ministries and Institutions

85. As noted above, the following ministries and institutions may deal with environmental-related matters as well:

- Construction and Planning Office of the Ministry of the Interior (National Parks Division, Sewage Systems Office).
- Ministry of Economic Affairs (Mines Department, Bureau of Mines, Central Geological Survey), the Ministry of Transportation and Communication (Central Weather Bureau).
- Council of Agriculture (Forestry Bureau, Soil and Water Conservation Bureau, Taiwan Forestry Research Institute, Endemic Species Research Institute).
- Veterans Affairs Council (Forest Conservation and Management Administration).

191. Amended and promulgated a total fifteen articles of the Act by the Presidential Order No. 09900024171 on 3 Feb. 2010, and enacted on 1 Jan. 2012, available at: https://law.moj.gov.tw/ENG/LawClass/LawAll.aspx?pcode=A0010032.
192. Legislative Gazette, Volume 101, Commission records No. 38, at 269–358.
See also, Country Report: Taiwan the Development of Organisational Reform and Environmental Law in Taiwan YingShih Hsieh at 399. https://www.iucnael.org/en/documents/1246-taiwan.

D. Moving Beyond Environment: Authority for Climate Change?

86. [節能減碳推動會] To comply with the Copenhagen Accord, particularly the implementation of Nationally Appropriate Mitigation Action, and to address cross -ministerial and comprehensive affairs regarding climate change and energy issues, Taiwan decided to create the *Committee on Energy Conservation and Emission Reduction (CECER)* and the *Committee on the Promotion of New Energy* in 2010. The CECER's function is to coordinate the climate and energy affairs that are distributed among numerous ministries and to provide advice and a comprehensive strategy. The Minister without Portfolio is the main organiser of the committee because of their professional competence in energy and climate-related issues. It should also be noted that, in spite of the CECER's cross-ministerial nature, its website is under the sub-net of the MOEABOE.[193] This situation also shows the weakness of the committee. Since it does not have its own staff, it remains under the direction of the existing authorities. The structure of this committee and related ministries is illustrated in Figure 1.

Figure 1 The Structure of the CECER

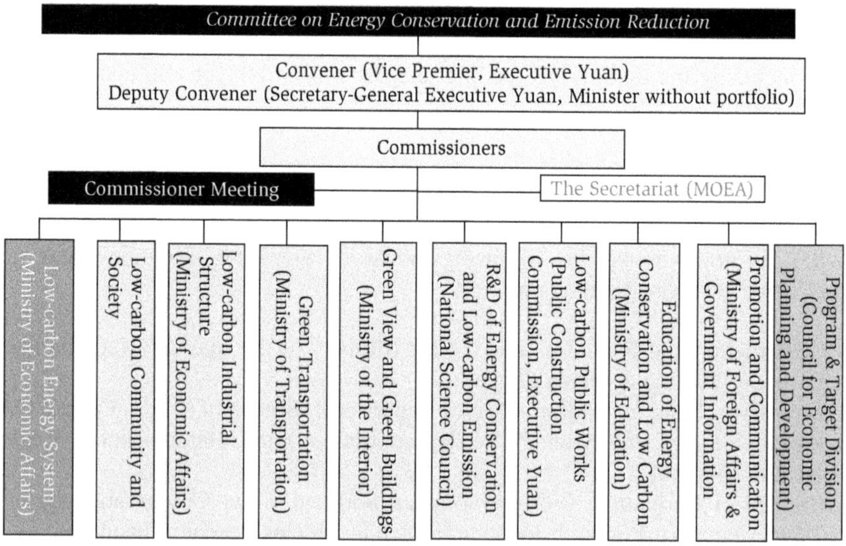

(*Source*: Compiled by the author).

193. MOEABOE, Website of Committee on Energy Conservation and Emission Reduction, The Executive Yuan., available at: https://www.moeaboe.gov.tw/ecw/reduceCO21_M/home/HomeMobile.aspx www.moeaboe.gov.tw/Policy/ReduceCO2Emission/default.html (visited on 15 May 2022).

87. An additional parliamentary decision was taken along with the changes to the EPA and Ministry of Economic Affairs that were included in the Governmental Reorganization Act of February 2010. This decision urged the Executive Yuan to realise the cross-ministerial nature of climate change affairs and encourage the creation of a *cross-ministerial climate change competent authority* to implement climate change policy and measures. This design was inspired by the UK's Department of Energy and Climate Change.[194] This new authority was scheduled to be formally established in January 2012. If such an initiative were realised, the authority could replace the existing weak temporary committee with a more powerful and resourceful formal authority. However, the new authority has not been discussed since its establishment, so it seems likely that the missionary climate change and energy committee will remain for the present.

E. Office of Energy and Carbon Reduction Since 2016

88. After the ruling party rotation in 2016, the new government merged the existing committees and created the Office of Energy and Carbon Reduction under the Executive Yuan.[195] The main mission of this office was to achieve the realisation of four policy initiatives and visions, including a nuclear-free homeland, energy security, a green economy, and environmental sustainability.[196]

F. NDC and Net Zero

89. As noted above, Taiwan promised to reach net-zero emissions by 2050 and the road map in late March 2022.[197] Therefore, under the same ruling government, an additional authority is added to the climate change policy formation, i.e., the NDC. The nature and the scope of the net-zero issues could easily fall into the domain of the NDC under the Organic Act of the National Development Council, specifically the overall planning and policy competence.[198]

---

194. GOV.UK, Department of Energy & Climate Change, available at: https://www.gov.uk/government/organisations/department-of-energy-climate-change.
195. Executive Yuan, Executive Yuan to set up energy and carbon office, 16 Jun. 2016, available at: https://english.ey.gov.tw/Page/61BF20C3E89B856/f5e3677e-a7df-4b99-b850-319482c49b8f.
196. Office of Energy and Carbon Reduction EY, Vision, available at: https://www.ey.gov.tw/oecr/C2CB1A9BE5491FEA.
197. Amid criticism, NDC chief insists 2050 net-zero goal realistic, 04/08/2022, available at: https://focustaiwan.tw/society/202204080008.
198. Article 2 of The Organic Act of the National Development Council: 'The NDC is charged with undertaking the following matters:

    (1) Overall planning, coordination, review and resource allocation for *national development policy*.
    (2) Overall planning, coordination, review and resource allocation for national development plans and coordination of mid- and long-term plan gender equality impact assessment.
    (3) Overall planning, coordination, review and resource allocation for *economic development policy*.

G. Other Authorities Relating to Climate Change Mitigation/Adaptation Works

90. As the climate change mitigation and adaptation works are cross-ministerial in nature, the wide involvement of different ministries in the central government is necessary.

91. Article 8 of the Greenhouse Gas Reduction and Management Act provided a unique design of distribution of authorities, i.e., Relevant central government agencies, that oversee the following projects:[199]

(1) Development of renewable energy and energy technology.
(2) Improvement of energy efficiency and energy conservation.
(3) Reduction in GHG emissions by industrial sectors.
(4) Transportation management, development of mass transit systems, and reduction in GHG emissions by other transportation sectors.
(5) Implementation of low-carbon energy transportation.
(6) Reduction and management of GHG emissions from buildings.
(7) Waste recycling and reuse.
(8) Forest resource management, biodiversity conservation, and strengthening of forests' carbon sequestration.
(9) Reduction and management of GHG emissions from agriculture and guarantee of food security.
(10) Green finance and GHG reduction incentive mechanisms.
(11) Assessment of impact of GHG reduction on the economy as a whole and planning of response measures.
(12) Establishment of GHG cap-and-trade scheme including allocation, auction, allowance sale, trade, and facilitation of international emission reduction cooperation mechanism.
(13) Research, development, and implementation of GHG reduction technologies.

---

(4) Overall planning, coordination, review and resource allocation for *social development policy*, and guidance and assistance to local governments for the implementation of main policy and mid- and long-term plans.
(5) Overall planning, coordination, review and resource allocation for industrial development policy.
(6) … .
(7) Overall planning, coordination, review and resource allocation for national land, regional and offshore island development and sustainable development policy.
(8) Overall planning, coordination, review and resource allocation for cultural and ethnic development policy.
(9) Overall planning, coordination, review and resource allocation for supervision and evaluation policy.
(10) Overall planning, coordination, review and resource allocation for administrative and regulatory reform policy, and coordination of regulatory impact assessments.
(11) Overall planning, coordination, review and resource allocation for other national development policy.'

199. Article 8(2) of the Greenhouse Gas Reduction and Management Act.

(14) Study of international GHG conventions and laws and participation in international conferences.
(15) Development and implementation of matters connected to climate change adaptation.
(16) Education and advocacy of climate change adaptation and GHG reduction.

92. These works are clearly related to the competence of difference authorities. For instance, the development of renewable energy (1) and the improvement of energy efficiency and energy conservation (2) are related to the authority of the Bureau of Energy, Ministry of Economic Affairs, while forest resource management (8) and the reduction and management of GHG emission from agriculture and guarantee of food security (9) would be under the authority of the Agricultural Council.

H. Local Governments Relating to Environmental Affairs

93. According to Articles 18 and 19 of the Local Government Act, environmental issues have been defined as part of local autonomy. Therefore, the local government should create a special agency in charge of related matters. Taking the capital of Taipei city as an example, it creates a structure similar to the EPA, including the following branches and divisions in its Department of Environmental Protection:[200]

– Division 1 was renamed the Air Quality and Noise Control Division.
– Division 2 was renamed the Water Quality and Vector Control Division.
– Division 3 was renamed the Environmental Cleaning and Maintenance Division.
– Division 4 was renamed the Waste Treatment Division.
– Division 5 was renamed the Resource Recycling Division.
– Division 6 was renamed the Occupational Safety Division

94. In addition to environmental issues, big cities have been keen to draft and adopt local actors for low-carbon cities (e.g., Taichung city, Tainan)[201] or low-carbon and green cities (e.g., Taoyuan).[202]

§6. Sources of Environmental Law

95. Taiwan's environmental law is derived from diverse legal sources. According to the tradition of legal precedence, international law and other related national law are the sources of energy law. Regarding international law, in spite of Taiwan's

---

200. https://english.dep.gov.taipei/cp.aspx?n=C1993281A5BA84F8.
201. Local Act on low carbon city of Taichung of 2014 and Tainan of 2020, available at: https://lawsearch.taichung.gov.tw/GLRSout/LawContent.aspx?id=GL002077; https://law01.tainan.gov.tw/glrsnewsout/EngLawList.aspx?id=GL000354.
202. Local Act on low carbon and green city of Taoyuan of 2021, available at: https://law.tycg.gov.tw/LawContent.aspx?id=GL000352.

ambiguous position as a sovereign state, Taiwan is keen to participate in the drafting of international laws. For instance, Taiwan became a formal member of the World Trade Organization in 2002. In this regard, its environmental subsidies and regulations should follow the normal rules under the General Agreement on Tariffs and Trade. Apart from Taiwan's compliance with international law as a member of international organisations, even though it is frequently excluded from international treaties, Taiwan voluntarily complies with several of them and participates in discussions about their formulation. For instance, Taiwan has participated in the Conference of Parties (COP) under the UNFCCC from its beginning and has drafted rules to achieve emission reduction targets. The adoption of the Renewable Energy Act in 2009 may have been related to the COP meeting in Copenhagen the same year, and the adoption of the GHG Reduction Act in 2015 may have been relevant to the COP meetings that took place in Paris in 2015. Under the international convention column of the EPA website, the role of the following conventions has been emphasised, and a special website to promote the related issues has been established:

- Paris Agreement.
- Basel Convention https://basel.epa.gov.tw/index.
- Convention on Mercury https://topic.epa.gov.tw/hg/mp-3.html.
- The Stockholm Convention on Persistent Organic Pollutants https://topic.epa.gov.tw/pops/mp-2.html.
- Montreal Protocol https://air.epa.gov.tw/EnvTopics/AirQuality_10.aspx.

96. In addition to international legal sources, the most important sources of environmental law are domestic law. The fundamental rights, such as living right and property rights, in constitutional law, may be relevant to the environmental rules. Moreover, the laws that are most relevant to environmental regulation are administrative, including the Administrative Procedural Act, Information Disclosure Act, Land Act, Urban Planning Act, and, specifically, the Environment Basic Act, Air Pollution Control Act, etc.

97. Finally, traditional laws, such as civil or criminal codes, can also become the source of energy law. For instance, Article 782 of the civil code intends to deal with the conflict and liability between private parties resulting from pollution,[203]

203. 'The owner of a land where water originates, or of a well, is entitled to claim compensation against another, who, owing to the works carried on by him, cuts off, reduces or pollutes the water of such land or well. If the water is necessary for drinking or for utilizing the land, the said owner is also entitled to claim to have the status quo ante restored. If it is impossible to have the status quo ante completely restored, then restoration shall be performed within the possible scope.
In the case of the preceding paragraph, if the damages are not caused by intentional acts or negligence, the court may reduce the amount of damages or exempt the liability.'

polluting water, air, soil,[204] and releasing radioactive material that pollutes the environment;[205] these parties may face criminal charges under the Criminal Code.

204. Article 190-1 of the Civil Code: 'A person who throws, abandons, drains, releases or uses other manner allowing a poisonous substance or any other substance that may harm health to pollute the air, soil, or rivers or other bodies of water and thereby causes harm shall be sentenced to imprisonment for no more than five years, detention, or a fine or combined with a fine no more than ten million dollars.'
205. Article 187-2 of the Civil Code: 'A person who endangers public safety by releasing nuclear energy or radioactivity that causes shall be sentenced to imprisonment of not more than five years.'

Part I. Pollution Control

Chapter 1. General Law

98. This chapter provides an introduction to three general laws on the framework act, education, and the EIA.

§1. Environment Basic Act of 2002

99. The basic act is a new type of legislation in Taiwan, and should not be confused with the basic act in Germany,[206] i.e., constitutional law, or the laws that govern special regions in a country, such as the Hong Kong Basic Law. In Taiwan, basic acts are used to govern special policy areas with national significance. So far, eight basic or fundamental acts exist in Taiwan:

(1) Basic Environment Act.
(2) Fundamental Communications Act.
(3) Educational Fundamental Act.
(4) Ocean Basic Act.
(5) The Indigenous Peoples Basic Law.
(6) Fundamental Science and Technology Act.
(7) Hakka Basic Act.
(8) Cultural Fundamental Act.

100. The use of the words basic or fundamental defines such acts because the related act is intended to legalise important doctrines that occur between policy and law. Thus, it may not be like ordinary acts that govern the rights and obligations of citizens or related parties directly. For instance, Article 28 of the EBA provided the ability to create the PPP and fee scheme: 'The central government shall establish a system in which those who pollute or destroy the environment pay. Pollution control or environmental restoration fees that are collected from those who pollute or destroy shall be used to preserve the sustainable use of the environment.' At the same time, this does not mean that the EPA can use this legal basis to create levies

206. 'Basic Law for the Federal Republic of Germany'. www.gesetze-im-internet.de.

on polluters; if it wished to do so, the EPA should use the legal basis in an ordinary act such as Article 16 of the Air Pollution Control Act, which provides details on levies.[207]

101. This act was developed in a special domestic and international atmosphere.[208] The change in party power in Taiwan in 2000 led to the pursuit of a nuclear-free homeland policy, which was inspired by German political ideas from 1998.[209] The 1997 Kyoto Protocol meetings in Japan also affected the neighbouring country of Taiwan. The climate change concerns are addressed in a soft manner in Article 21,[210] while the nuclear power issue is covered by a nuclear-free clause in Article 23.[211]

102. The official purpose of this Act was to raise environmental quality, advance citizen health and well-being, preserve environmental resources, and pursue SD by promoting environmental protection.[212] However, the more substantial, yet unmet, purposes were threefold: (1) to manage the environmental issues by coordinating affairs under the supervision of multiple competent authorities, (2) to provide a framework to guide the function of administrative branches, and (3) to serve the legal principles of the legislators.

---

207. Article 16 of the Air Pollution Control Act: 'Competent authorities at all levels may collect air pollution control fees from stationary and mobile pollution sources that emit air pollutants. The targets of air pollution control fees are as follows.

 1. Stationary pollution sources: Fees shall be collected from the owners of the pollution source based on the types and quantity of air pollutants emitted. Fees shall be collected from the actual user or manager if the owner of the source is not the user or manager. Fees shall be collected from the construction project owner if the pollution source is a construction project. For substances designated and officially announced by the central competent authority, fees may be collected from the vendor or importer based on the sales volume of the substance.

 2. Mobile pollution sources: Fees shall be collected from the vendor or user based on the types and quantity of air pollutants emitted, or from the vendor or importer based on the type, composition and quantity of fuel.'

208. *See* Anton Ming-zhi Gao, *An Alternative Way to Deal with Climate Change: A Comparative Study and Critical Review of Basic Acts and Bills on Climate Change and Energy in Japan, South Korea, and Taiwan*, Oil, Gas & Energy Law 9(2) (2011).

209. The plan to phase out nuclear power plants in 1998, *see*, e.g., Europe Slow Death for Nuclear Power, 15 Oct. 1998, available at: http://cdnedge.bbc.co.uk/1/hi/world/europe/194515.stm.

 However, the Federal government extended the lives of the seventeen reactors in September 2010 and faced the legal litigations from the State governments. *See* German states file legal complaint against nuclear phase-out reverse, 1 Mar. 2011, available at: http://www.powergenworldwide.com/index/display/articledisplay/3587681617/articles/powergenworldwide/nuclear/reactors/2011/03/german-states_file.html.

210. Article 21 of the Environmental Basic Act of 2002: 'Government entities at all levels shall actively adopt measures to control carbon dioxide emissions and establish related plans to mitigate the greenhouse effect.'

211. Article 23 of the Environmental Basic Act of 2002: 'The government shall establish plans to gradually achieve the goal of becoming a nuclear-free country. The government shall also strengthen nuclear safety management and control, protections against radiation, and the management of radioactive materials and monitoring of environmental radiation to safeguard the public from the dangers of radiation exposure.'

212. Article 1 of the Environmental Basic Act of 2002.

I. General Provisions

A. Legal Purposes

103. The EBA of 2002 adopted the general and specific goals of pursuing SD and environmental protection.[213]

B. Legal Definition

104. The EBA of 2002 provides a definition for 'environment' and 'sustainable development'.[214]

C. Basic Principles of Policy and Law

105. To achieve the goals outlined above and to link abstract goals to implement policies and action plans, basic acts and bills usually provide several principles. Energy and EBAs tend to adopt *simple* doctrines. The EBA of 2002 provided one principle of 'environmental priority'.[215]

D. Responsibility of Actors

106. Similar to the aforementioned guidelines for policy and action plans, a responsibility clause seeks to divide responsibility among different potential actors. Both can be seen as an *abstract* code of conduct for the actors involved.

107. EBA provides the following distribution of works among different authorities and actors (*see* Table 5).

213. *Ibid.*: 'This Act is formulated to raise the quality of the environment, advance the health and well-being of citizens, preserve environmental resources, and pursue sustainable development by promoting environmental protection. The regulations of other laws shall apply to those matters not regulated by this Act.'
214. Article 2(2) of Environmental Basic Act of 2002: '"Sustainable development" means satisfying contemporary needs without sacrificing the ability of future generations to satisfy their needs.'
215. Article 3 of the Environmental Basic Act of 2002: 'Economic, technological and social development shall equally emphasize environmental protection based on long-term national interests. However, in the event that economic, technological or social development has a seriously negative impact on the environment or endangers the environment, the protection of the environment shall prevail.'

Table 5 The Distribution of Works among Different Authorities and Actors in EBA

Responsible bodies		*Related provisions*
Government	Central government	For example, the central competent authority shall draft environmental protection laws and regulations, draw up national environmental protection plans, establish SD indicators and promote and implement such laws and regulations, plans and indicators. (Article 7)
		related Articles 7, 12, 13, 25, 26, 28, 30, 31, 33, 35, 36
	Government at all levels	Related articles, including Articles 4, 7, 8, 9, 10, 11, 15, 16, 17, 18, 19, 20, 21, 22, 25, 27, 32, 34, 36, 37, 38, 39, 40
		For example, Government entities at all levels shall incorporate environment first and SD concepts. (Article 8)
	Government	For example, Article 23: 'The government shall establish plans to gradually achieve the goal of becoming a nuclear-free country. The government shall also strengthen nuclear safety management and control, protections against radiation, and the management of radioactive materials and monitoring of environmental radiation to safeguard the public from the dangers of radiation exposure.'
	The Executive Yuan	For example, Article 29: 'The Executive Yuan shall establish a national sustainable development commission to be responsible for relevant strategies and policies on national sustainable development matters. Said strategies and policies shall be conferred to relevant cabinet-level agencies for execution. Said commission shall be comprised of one third each government representatives, academics and experts, and civic groups.'
	Local government	Related Articles of 7, 12, 25.
		For example, 7(2): 'Local governments, in view of the needs of natural and social conditions within the local jurisdiction, may draft autonomous laws and regulations and environmental protection plans, in accordance with the laws and regulations and national environmental protection plans in the foregoing paragraph, and promote and implement such laws and regulations and plans.'
	Court	Article 14: 'The courts may establish a dedicated court or designate dedicated personnel for environmental protection disputes.'
	Administrative court	Article 34(2)

Responsible bodies	*Related provisions*
Enterprises	Related articles of 4, 6, 13, 32, For example, Article 6: 'Enterprises shall plan for the phasing in of environmental protection concepts when carrying out their activities. Based on product lifecycles, enterprises shall promote clean production, prevent and reduce pollution, conserve resources and recycle and use recycled resources and other raw (or processed) materials or services that help lessen environmental impact with the purpose of achieving SD. Enterprises shall be responsible for assisting the government in implementing measures related to environmental protection.'
Citizens	Articles 4 and 5. For example, Article 5: 'Citizens shall uphold environmental protection concepts and lessen the environmental impact of daily life. In terms of consumer behaviour, citizens shall, as a principle, practice green consumption. In terms of daily life, citizens shall carry out waste disposal reduction, separation and recycling. Citizens shall actively carry out environmental protection and be responsible for assisting the government in implementing measures related to environmental protection.'

(*Source*: compiled by this author).

108. In summary, these clauses in the EBA try to distribute the responsibilities among the following main players:

- Responsibility of National and Central Governments.
- Responsibility of Local Government.
- Responsibility of Supply-Side Enterprises.
- Responsibility of Demand-Side Citizens.
- Cooperation among Responsible Bodies.

E. The Creation of Special Institutions

109. To address the issues in the EBA, Article 29 requested that The Executive Yuan establish a national SD commission that would be responsible for relevant strategies and policies on national SD matters. The Organization Ordinance for National Sustainable Development Council was created on 11 November 2021.[216]

216. Organization Ordinance for National Sustainable Development Council of 2021, available at: https://ncsd.ndc.gov.tw/Fore/nsdn/about/established.

The key works include the publication of National SD annual reports on the website,[217] tracking the implementation of Taiwan's own sustainable development goals (SDGs),[218] and conducting Taiwan's Voluntary National Review Implementation of the UN SDGs.[219]

110. The professional court for environmental matters is also a key concern for the EBA. Article 14 of the EBA provides that 'the courts may establish a dedicated court or designate dedicated personnel for environmental protection disputes'. To date, however, only special courts for Intellectual Property Rights and commercial courts have been established.[220]

F. Development of Special Comprehensive Strategies and/or Plans

111. Environmental matters that need to be resolved in a more consistent and long-term manner require additional planning and strategy. In the past, developments of comprehensive policy packages relied on the discretion of each government. However, to create a formal and regular requirement, the role of comprehensive strategy and planning is emphasised. Under the EBA, the central government is authorised to draw up national environmental protection plans,[221] i.e., the National Environmental Protection Plan, to address the needs of natural and social conditions within the local jurisdiction. Local governments may also draft local environmental protection plans in accordance with the aforementioned plans.[222] The Executive Yuan approved the current National Environmental Protection Plan of 2020 in early 2020.[223] Local governments have also adopted their own versions of annual environmental protection plans, such as I-lan,[224] Hualien,[225] and Kingmen county.[226]

217. National SD Annual Reports, available at: https://ncsd.ndc.gov.tw/Fore/nsdn/implement2/annualReport.
218. National SD status tracking report, available at: https://ncsd.ndc.gov.tw/Fore/nsdn/implement2/annualReport3.
219. *See*, e.g., Taiwan's Voluntary National Review Implementation of the UN Sustainable Development Goals Executive Yuan, Republic of China (Taiwan) September 2017, available at: https://ncsd.ndc.gov.tw/_ofu/download/Vhome/VNR.pdf.
220. Intellectual Property and Commercial Court Organization Act, Amended Date: 2020-01-15, available at: https://law.moj.gov.tw/ENG/LawClass/LawAll.aspx?pcode=A0010090.
221. Article 7(1) of the EBA.
222. Article 7(2) of the EBA.
223. National Environmental Protection Plan of 2020, available at: https://www.epa.gov.tw/DisplayFile.aspx?FileID=AE98DB8752AD358.
224. For example, Environmental Protection Plan of the I-lan County of 2018, available at: https://www.ilepb.gov.tw/Research/ResearchContent.aspx?id=140.
225. Environmental Protection Plan of Hualien county of 2014, available at: https://www.hlepb.gov.tw/cht/index.php?act=download&ids=666&path=../upload/cht/attachment/1d063d1963fa6a0d74dfd98e4b39df42.pdf.
226. For example, Environmental Protection Plan of Kingmen County, available at: https://ws.kinmen.gov.tw/Download.ashx?u=LzAwMS9VcGxvYWQvMzAyL3

G. Important Mechanism under EBA

112. As the environmental permit and emission standards have been regulated in respective pollution-oriented environmental legislations, the EBA tries to highlight the following aspects to reflect its basic feature.

H. Financial and Incentive Instrument

113. With the aim of rationally and effectively using resources and meeting environmental protection needs, Article 37 of the EBA requires that government entities at all levels adopt appropriate incentives, promotions, and compensation measures for the following activities:

(1) Protection of the natural, social and human environment.
(2) Research and development of clean production technologies, equipment or products for production cleaning.
(3) Research and development of resource recycling and reuse technologies.
(4) Promotion and application of renewable energy.
(5) Research and development of energy conservation technology and installation of products that conserve energy.
(6) Manufacture or installation of pollution control equipment.
(7) Moving for the purpose of protecting the environment.
(8) Provision of land or other resources to be used to protect the environment.
(9) Environmental reforestation and greenification.
(10) Other activities related to environmental protection.

I. International Cooperation

114. Even though international cooperation is a much softer approach than an incentivised scheme, its role in dealing with environmental issues may be underestimated. The very nature of environment requires that scientists study it across national boundaries;[227] the EBA therefore provide such a provision,[228] creating an essential element of successful international cooperation in terms of basic acts and bills.

JlbGZpbGUvMTAwMTAvMzU0Nzg3Lzkz5bm05bqm6YeR6ZaA57ij55Kw5aKD5L%2Bd6K236KiI55WrKOS%2FruiogikucGRm&n=OTPlubTluqbph5HploDnuKPnkrDlooPkv53orbfoqIjnlaso5L%2Bu6KiCKS5wZGY%3D&icon=..pdf.

227. Folmer, H. & Van Mouche, P., Transboundary Pollution and International Cooperation, *The International Yearbook of Environmental and Resource Economics, 2001*, 231–266 (2000).

228. Article 12 of the Environmental Basic Act of 2002: 'The central government shall promote international cooperation and technological assistance, engineering technology and experimental research related to global sustainable development and publish related information to facilitate its use by citizens and enterprises. Local governments may also carry out such work as deemed necessary.'

J. Educational and Information Campaign

115. To raise public awareness of the seriousness of environmental degradation and promote changes to people's daily behaviours, environmental education[229] is increasingly emphasised. Education also relates to the basic or fundamental aspect of dealing with environmental affairs and occurs in EBA.[230]

K. The Relationship among These Eight Issues

116. These issues noted above appear to be isolated and unrelated to each other. However, the important relationship between these issues is illustrated in Figure 2.

Figure 2 The Relationship Between the Main Issues of the EBAs

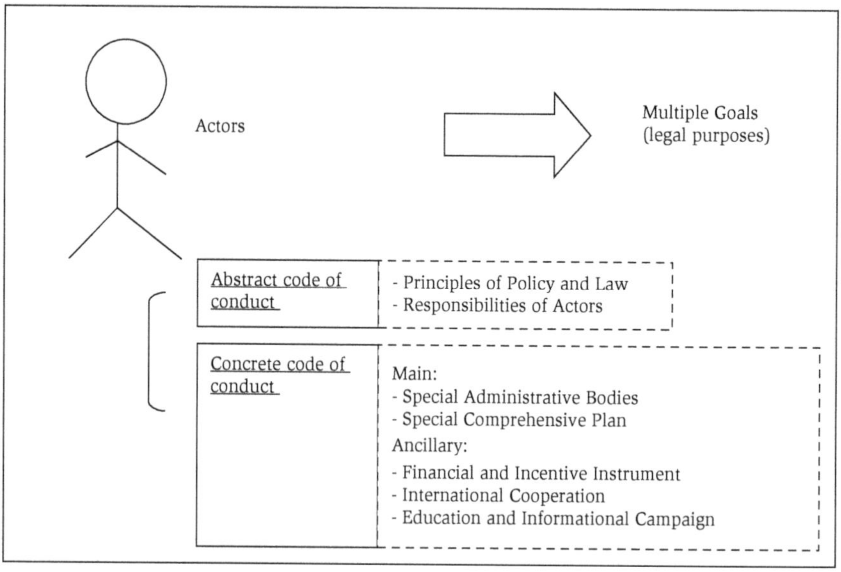

(*Source*: A.M. Gao; 'An Alternative Way to Deal with Climate Change: A Comparative Study and Critical Review of Basic Acts and Bills on Climate Change and Energy in Japan, South Korea, and Taiwan' OGEL 2 (2011), www.ogel.org URL: www.ogel.org/article.asp?key=3112).

229. For example, *see* EPA, Environmental Education Centre, available at: http://www.epa.gov/teachers/.

230. Article 9 of EBA: 'Government entities at all levels shall make widely available environment first and sustainable development education and study and strengthen public education to improve the environmental knowledge of citizens, establish environmental protection concepts and realize such concepts in daily life.'

117. How does the court treat these provisions, particularly the EBA's principle clause? The cornerstone principles concerning the legal effects of the EBA have been clarified in more than fifty cases.[231] These cases indicate that a judge's stance on the related provisions in the EBA, including Articles 2, 3, 4, 28 and 47, is that they only have the function of *policy declaration*. These provisions do not confer any *specific legal right* or *legal interests* on citizens,[232] nor do they give citizens any *legal right of claim*.[233] Thus, in order to claim the right to legal standing, the citizen is required to prove damages under not only the EBA but also some other substantive act.[234] A successful legal claim for compensation for loss of money, life, goods, or other property or right, in the form of money or other remedy, should not be based purely on the EBA.[235]

§2. Environmental Education Act

118. The Environmental Education Act (EEA) was promulgated on 5 June 2010 and designed to promote environmental education. It can be considered a specific legislation designed to implement the environmental education clause in the EBA.[236] The content of the EEA adopted a mixed approach of the basic and ordinary substantive acts.

119. One feature of the basic act is that it could indicate the special chapter (Chapter II Environmental Education Policy). This chapter shows how the EPA and local government are required to prepare for the National Environmental Education Framework[237] and the local government's action plan for national environmental education.[238]To perfect this framework and action plan, a special expert committee made up of the national environmental education review board, and the environmental education review board will be established.[239] Finally, the implementation

231. Gao, A.M.Z. & Juang, K.Y.C., The Effect of Basic Environmental Act on Environmental Governance in Taiwan: From the Aspect of Judicial Review, *Rule of Law for Good Environmental Governance*, 140, 2015.
232. High Administrative Court Ruling 2007/00095 (96年度停字第00095號); High Administrative Court Judgment 2004/23 (93年度訴更字第23號).
233. High Administrative Court Ruling 2007/00081 (96年度停字第00081號); High Administrative Court Judgment 2004/23 (93年度訴更字第23號); High Administrative Court Judgment 2003/374 (92年度訴字第374號).
234. High Administrative Court Ruling 2007/00081 (96年度停字第00081號); High Administrative Court Ruling 2007/01979 (96年度裁字第01979號).
235. Supreme Administrative Court Judgment 2005/729 (94年判字第 729 號).
236. Article 9 of the EBA.
237. Article 5(1) of the EEA.
238. Article 7(1) of the EEA.
239. Article 11 of the EEA: 'The competent central government authorities are to appoint experts, academics and relevant governmental agency (institution), organization representatives to launch a national environmental education review board to review, coordinate and advise on the national environmental education abstract and action plan.'; Article 12 of the EEA: 'The competent central-ruled municipality and county (municipal) municipality authorities are to appoint experts, academics and relevant governmental agency (institution), organization representatives to launch an

of such a framework and action plan would be subject to an annual review,[240] where the framework would undergo a comprehensive review at least once every four years.[241] The latest National Environmental Education Framework and Action plan can be found on the dedicated environmental education website under the EPA;[242] annual review reports from 2012–2020 can be downloaded from the same website.[243]

120. The substantive part of the EEA can be seen from the provisions relating to compulsory environmental education. 'Government agencies, state-run enterprises and institutions, school districts and non-profit organisations receiving the government's subsidy fund exceeding fifty percent' shall assign designated personnel to promote environmental education.[244] Institutions, state-run business institutions, high schools and secondary schools, and statutory bodies with over 50% of the funds sponsored by the government shall formulate environmental education programmes every year to promote environmental education. All employees, teachers, and students shall attend an environmental education programme for more than four hours.[245] If they do not comply, competent authorities shall command them to perform corrective actions before a deadline. If they fail to perform the corrective actions before the deadline, a fine of TWD 5,000–TWD 15,000 is levied, and the designated representative or the person responsible for the relevant environmental protection has to attend environmental protection seminars for between one and eight hours.[246] If offenders are unable to attend the seminar in a timely manner for a legitimate reason, they can apply for a single extension. Offenders who refuse to take the environmental seminar or do not complete it on time will be fined between TWD 5,000–TWD 15,000.[247] Individuals (whether a person, a representation or an organisation or an organisation itself) who violate the environmental protection laws or the obligations stated in the Administrative Law of Autonomous Act are suspended from construction and business operation or are fined for an amount more than TWD 5,000 by the disciplinary institution can also be required to attend environmental protection seminars lasting from one to eight hours.[248]

---

environmental education review board to review, coordinate and advise on a central-ruled municipality or county (municipal) municipality's environmental education action plan, with which to excel a jurisdiction's environmental education implementation and development.'

240. Article 6 of the EEA.
241. Article 5(2) of the EEA.
242. National environmental education Framework of 2019 (國家環境教育綱領(行政院1081122核定修正).pdf available at: https://eeis.epa.gov.tw/_res/get_attach.ashx?key=72125EA2331747ABD6351B46365F2EB1; National environmental education Action plan of 2020–2023 (國家環境教育行動方案(109年-112年)滾動修正版), available at: https://eeis.epa.gov.tw/front/resources/ResSearch/item.aspx?id=208.
243. Environmental Education Information System, available at: https://eeis.epa.gov.tw/front/resources/ResSearch/list.aspx?f=282.
244. Article 18 of the EEA.
245. Article 19 of the EEA.
246. Article 24 of the EEA.
247. Article 24-1 of the EEA.
248. Article 23 of the EEA.

121. A soft approach to encourage environmental education is also provided in the EEA; it was suggested that the EPA and could create a reward or incentive scheme for the following:

(i) The private sector groups that utilise public or private idle space or buildings to launch environmental education facilities and venues.
(ii) Citizens who voluntarily participate as environmental education volunteers.
(iii) Citizens who achieve excellent results with their environmental education.[249]

122. Solid finances and budgets are important to support these projects. Article 8(1) of the EEA urges the government to allocate budget for the required projects,[250] while Article 8(2) requires the EPA and local government to set up an 'environmental education fund' with stable funding resources.[251] These funds can be used to set up the following environmental education activities:

(i) Stage environmental seminars.
(ii) Stage environmental education campaign and activity.
(iii) Compile environmental education teaching materials, campaign literature and handbooks.
(iv) Conduct environmental education research and development.
(v) Promote environmental education, global exchange and cooperation.
(vi) Subsidise environmental education facilities or venues in staging environmental education activities.
(vii) Facilitate environmental education institutions and stage environmental education personnel training or environmental seminars.
(viii) Subsidise the stage of environmental education plans.
(ix) Train environmental education personnel.

---

249. Articles 20 and 21 of the EEA.
250. 'The competent government authorities of all levels and the competent central government authorities in charge of the designated enterprises shall allocate a budget as per the preceding three articles' national environmental education abstract, and environmental education action plan, with which to carry out environmental education-related measures.'
251. Article 8(2) of the EEA: 'The competent government authorities of all levels are required to set up an environmental education fund, and its funding sources are as follows,

I. From the environmental education fund set up by the competent government authorities of all levels, an expenditure budget amount of at least five percent is to be allocated per year, which is to be allotted as subsidy (donation) fund, except where there is no cumulative surplus on said fund.
II. From the proceeds the execution agency derives from executing the waste recycling work as per the Waste Cleanup Act, ten percent of the amount is to be allocated and allotted each year.
III. From the proceeds of penalty fines the competent government authorities of all levels have collected for breaching the environmental protection law or self-government acts, five percent of which is to be allocated and allotted each year.
IV. Fund interest gains.
V. Donations by the people, businesses or organizations.
VI. Other forms of income.'

123. The EEA also considers how to conduct the planning and implementation of environmental education in a professional manner. Article 13 requires that a department or person be appointed who is in charge of the planning, promotion, guidance, rewarding and assessment of environmental education. To implement the education programme, certification system for environmental education institutions and personnel should be established and run by the competent central government authorities.[252]

§3. Environmental Impact Assessment Act

I. Project EIA

124. EIA stands at the centre of Taiwan's environmental law before the construction of development projects begins. Unlike the pure procedural requirement of EIA in the countries and regions where the EIA originated, such as the US and European Union (EU),[253] the EIA in Taiwan combines substantive and procedural rules. The substantive feature is reflected in the so-called EIA veto function that is provided for in Article 14(1) of the EIA Act: 'The industry competent authority may not grant permission for a development activity prior to the completion of an environmental impact statement review or the authorisation of an environmental impact assessment report; permission granted in violation of this regulation shall be invalid.' Therefore, EIA permits become a priority for every development project. Projects which are granted EIA permits are seldom rejected during the follow-up process of acquiring development or other types of permits. Therefore, the EIA Act conferred a great deal of power and authority to the Environmental Impact Assessment Review Committee,[254] allowing it to define the fate of development activities when there is concern about the adverse impact on the environment, such as:[255]

---

252. Article 10 of the EEA.
253. Wood, C., *Environmental Impact Assessment: A Comparative Review* (2014); Glasson, J. & Therivel, R., *Introduction to Environmental Impact Assessment* (2013).
254. Article 3 of the EIA Act: 'Competent authorities at all levels shall establish an Environmental Impact Assessment Review Committee (herein referred to as 'the Committee') in order to review matters related to environmental impact assessment reports.

Terms for the members of the Committee in the foregoing paragraph shall be two years and experts and scholars may not account for less than two-thirds of the total number of committee members. When the industry competent authority is the developer, industry competent authority members shall withdraw from the voting process.

The Environmental Protection Administration, Executive Yuan, shall draft the organizational rules of the Committee established by the central competent authority and shall submit said rules to the Executive Yuan for approval and announcement.

Special municipality competent authorities shall draft the organizational rules of the Committees established by special municipality competent authorities and shall submit said rules to the authorized agency for approval and announcement.

County or city competent authorities shall draft the organizational rules of the Committees established by county or city competent authorities and shall submit said rules to the authorized agency for approval and announcement.'
255. Article 5(1) of the EIA Act.

(1) The establishment of a factory or the development of an industrial park.
(2) The development of a road, railway, mass rapid transit system, harbour, or airport.
(3) The extraction of soil and rock or the exploration and extraction of minerals.
(4) The development of water storage, water supply, flood control or drainage projects.
(5) The development or use of land for agriculture, forestry, fisheries, or livestock.
(6) The development of recreational areas, scenic areas, golf courses or sports fields.
(7) The development of cultural, educational, or medical facilities.
(8) The construction of new municipal districts, construction of tall buildings, or renovation of old municipal districts.
(9) The construction of environmental protection projects.
(10) The development of nuclear energy or other energies or the construction of radioactive waste storage or treatment facilities.

125. For projects that have a lower environmental impact, only the phase I EIA is required.[256] However, a phase II EIA should be conducted regarding concerns about a significant impact on the environment.[257] In this phase, developers and the government face more complex procedural rules (e.g., engagement with local people[258] and public hearings).[259]

126. Because of the EIA's importance in a project's pipeline, the lengthy process of acquiring an EIA also draws the attention of important foreign business associations like the American Chamber of Commerce Taiwan (Amcham) and the European Chamber of Commerce Taiwan (EECT). For instance, the EIA process is

256. Article 6 of the EIA Act.
257. Article 8 of the EIA Act.
258. *See* e.g., Art. 8(1) of the EIA Act: 'the developer shall perform the following matters:

1. Distribute the environmental impact statement to relevant agencies
2. Display or post the environmental impact statement at an appropriate location near the development site; this time period may not be less than thirty days
3. Publish in newspapers the name of the developer, the development site and the location where the review conclusion and the environmental impact statement are displayed or posted

The developer shall hold a public explanation meeting.'

Article 8(2) of the EIA Act.: 'The developer shall hold a public explanation meeting after the expiration of the time period for displaying or posting in the foregoing paragraph.'

259. Article 12 of the EIA Act: 'The industry competent authority shall, in conjunction with the competent authority, members of the Committee and other relevant agencies, invite together experts, scholars, groups and local residents to conduct an on-site inspection and hold a public hearing within thirty days after receipt of the draft environmental impact assessment report; records of the on-site inspection and public hearing shall be maintained and submitted to the competent authority within thirty days after the on-site inspection and public hearing.'

often considered an obstacle to Taiwan's larger plans by Amcham.[260] EECT even noted in its 2017 position paper that it is important to streamline the cumbersome EIA process and administrative procedures even for renewable energy projects;[261] this also leads to initiatives designed to facilitate the EIA process. In 2017, the former EPA minister indicated that the timeframe of the process depended on the complexity of the cases, but it aims to complete the EIA review within 180 days.[262]

127. Taiwan may seem an environmentally friendly nation, given the power of the EIA to scrutinise and decide the fate of a development project through its veto power. In reality, however, few projects have been vetoed by the EIA. By May 2016, 70% had passed the phase I review, and 92% had passed the Phase II review.[263] Most cases have been 'conditionally' passed, which have drawn criticism from environmentalists. In certain cases, there are many conditions that imply that the cases should not have been passed because of significant environmental concerns. Examining these conditions more closely, they may lack the rule of law to affect developers' rights and obligations. For instance, in 2010, there was no climate change law in Taiwan. Yet, a condition was imposed on Tai-power that it had to reduce emissions in its Da-Lin power plant renovation project.[264] Recently, even non-environmental factors, such as the failure to fishermen to settle down was considered to be a factor that will prevent a project from passing the EIA. However, this case was appealed by the developer and revoked by the Administrative Appealing Committee of the Executive Yuan due to the reason of lack of casual link between such condition and environmental protection.[265] This is a rare case that challenges the legitimacy and legality of the EIA conditions. In most cases, the developers follow conditions which are usually beyond the legal requirement. Therefore, the EIA Commission has the power to create 'new laws' that developers must follow during implementation. Such uncertainty led to the case where Bayer Dropped Planned Taiwan Plant passing the EIA review because of worries about uncertain obligations.[266]

---

260. Taiwan Business Topics, February 2018, Vol. 48, Issue 2, at p. 45, available at: https://amcham.com.tw/wp-content/uploads/2018/02/February-2018-Taiwan-Business-TOPICS.pdf.
261. ECCT releases 2017 Position Papers, 2016-11-10, available at: https://www.ecct.com.tw/ecct-releases-2017-position-papers/.
262. Minister of Environmental: you would know the results of EIA review within 180 days (環評過不過李應元：最快180天告訴你), 17 May 2017, available at: https://e-info.org.tw/node/204997.
263. EPA, An Overview on the draft amendment to EIA Act環境影響評估制度修正方向, 28 Jun. 2016, available at: https://www.slideshare.net/epaslideshare/ss-63515499.
264. The Controversial emission reduction review during the EIA process for Da-lin power plants (大林電廠環評 環保署槓上行政院溫室氣體減量將重新審查), 2010/07/28, available at: https://www.coolloud.org.tw/node/53434.
265. The offshore wind developer won a EIA case in the court (環評敗部復活 福海離岸風機過關), 20 Mar. 2019, available at: https://ctee.com.tw/news/policy/57366.html.
266. Bayer Drops Planned Taiwan Plant, Raising Concerns for Foreign Firms, available at: https://www.wsj.com/articles/SB882542228148757000.

128. Finally, it should be noted that even when the EIA is passed, there are additional requirements to fulfil. When a developer applies for modification of the contents of an environmental impact statement, assessment report, or review conclusion without the EIA being conducted again, the developer must submit an analysis report on how the environmental impact has changed.[267] For example, in one project related to Yunlin Technology Industrial Zone, there are thirteen analyses being reviewed by the EIA Committee.[268]

II. Policy EIA

129. A SEA is a systematic process designed to evaluate the environmental implications of a proposed policy, plan, or programme and provides the means to examine cumulative effects and appropriately address them at the earliest stage of decision-making alongside economic and social considerations.[269] The National Environmental Policy Act (NEPA) in the US was signed into law on 1 January 1970. NEPA requires federal agencies to assess the environmental effects of their proposed actions prior to making decisions.[270] As the Taiwan EIA Act is affected by NEPA, it includes SEA considerations; however, compared to the large number of legal provisions that regulate EIA, there is only a very abstract provision in the EIA Act. Article 26 of the EIA Act provides only very empty authorisation for the EPA to promulgate further rules.[271] The Ordinance on Policy EIA indicate the mandatory policies subject to SEA requirement as follows:[272]

– Industrial policy.
– Mine development policy.
– Water development policy.
– Land use policy.
– Energy policy.
– Animal husbandry Policy.
– Traffic transportation policy.
– Waste disposal policy.
– Policy on the disposal of radioactive nuclear waste.
– Other policies.

---

267. Article 37 of the Environmental Impact Assessment Enforcement Rules, Amended Date: 2018-04-11, available at: https://law.moj.gov.tw/ENG/LawClass/LawAll.aspx?pcode=O0090002.
268. For example, The 13th change of Yunlin industrial park development and EIA Review Report (110343A環保署雲林科技工業區開發計畫環境影響差異分析報告（第十三次變更）差異分析報告), available at: https://eiadoc.epa.gov.tw/EIAWEB/11.aspx?hcode=1110343A&srctype=0.
269. EU, Strategic Environmental Assessment, available at: https://europa.eu/capacity4dev/public-environment-climate/wiki/strategic-environmental-assessment.
270. US EPA, What is the National Environmental Policy Act?, available at: https://www.epa.gov/nepa/what-national-environmental-policy-act.
271. Article 26 of the EIA Act: 'The central competent authority shall separately determine the environmental impact assessment process for government policy for which there is concern of environmental impact.'
272. Article 3 of the Ordinance on Policy EIA.

130. The policies noted above may cover a wide range of policies. To provide clarity that can guide the government, the Ordinance on the Policy List of Must SEA is shown in Table 6.[273]

Table 6 Mandatory SEA Policies under Ordinance on the Policy of Compulsory SEA

Policy type	*Mandatory SEA policy*
Industrial policy	The establishment of industrial zone
	Energy-intensive industrial policy
Mine development policy	Sand and gravel development and supply
Water development policy	Water resources development policy
Land use policy	Golf course Changes in the scope of water quality and water quality protection zones Changes in the scope of drinking water source water quality protection areas New or expanded urban plan (applicable only to those with an area of 10 hectares or more) Municipal, county (city) regional planning
Energy policy	Energy Development Framework
Transportation policy	Major rail and road line
Waste disposal policy	Waste disposal policy, such as changing waste incinerators to regional biomass centres
Radioactive waste policy	Spent fuel reprocessing

(*Source*: Ordinance on Policy of Compulsory SEA).

131. However, for policies, programmes, or plans not listed in the above list, the government is free to voluntarily require the planning to follow the SEA. One example of this was the SEA report on the offshore wind power zonal development plan that was submitted to the EPA in December 2015 and approved in July 2016.[274]

273. Ordinance on the Policy of Compulsory SEA (101.10.17 應實施環境影響評估之政策細項), 17 Oct. 2012, available at: https://oaout.epa.gov.tw/law/LawContent.aspx?id=GL007321.
274. Chen, W.H., *EPA Approves SEA on Offshore Wind Energy Development*, Taipei, Times, 2016, http://www.taipeitimes.com/News/taiwan/archives/2016/07/14/2003651002. (Accessed 10 May 2022).

Chapter 2. Air Pollution

§1. Air Pollution Control

I. Air Quality Control Regions

132. The EPA shall delineate and officially announce each class of special municipality, county, and city control region based on the demands placed upon air quality by land use or air quality conditions.[275] Different zones can be divided into the following three classes:[276]

(1) Class 1 control regions: areas such as national parks and nature protection and conservation areas that are delineated in accordance with the law.
(2) Class 2 control regions: areas that meet air quality standards, with the exception of Class 1 control regions.
(3) Class 3 control regions: areas that do not meet air quality standards, with the exception of Class 1 control regions.

133. Further additional regulations have been introduced to different Class regions (*see* Table 7).

Table 7 Regulations in Different Air Quality Control Regions

Class 1 Control Regions	Stationary pollution sources shall not be newly installed or modified except for facilities that maintain the livelihoods of residents within the region, facilities necessary for the operation and management of national parks, and national defence facilities. (Article 6(1) of the Air Pollution Control Act)
Class 2 control regions	Newly installed or modified stationary pollution sources in which pollutant emissions reach a certain scale shall be required to perform modelling and simulation for their pollutant emissions to verify that these emissions will not exceed allowable pollutant increase limits within the control region where the pollution source is located or within adjacent control regions where air quality might also be affected. (Article 6(2) of the Air Pollution Control Act)

275. Article 5(1) of the Air Pollution Control Act.
276. Article 5(2) of the Air Pollution Control Act.

Class 3 control regions	Existing stationary pollution sources shall reduce pollutant emissions. Newly installed or modified stationary pollution sources in which pollutant emissions reach a certain scale shall employ the best feasible control technology. For specific large pollution sources, the minimum achievable emission rate control technology shall be adopted. Pollutant emissions from newly installed or modified stationary pollution sources shall perform modelling and simulation to verify that these emissions will not exceed allowable pollutant increase limits within the control region where the pollution source is located or within adjacent control regions where air quality might also be affected. (Article 6(3) of the Air Pollution Control Act)

(*Source*: compiled by this author).

II. Air Pollution Control Plan

134. EPA is obliged to draw up an air pollution control plan and review it every four years.[277] To implement this plan at the local government level, special municipality, county, and city competent authorities determine air pollution control plans and report them to the EPA to be approved and announced.[278] It is possible for more than two local governments to draft a joint plan.[279]

III. Cap-and-Trade Scheme

135. Based on topographical and meteorological conditions, the EPA may designate single or multiple special municipalities, counties, or cities where air pollutants might circulate as a *total quantity control zone*, determine plans for these zones, and officially announce and implement total quantity controls.[280] Further regulations would apply to a total quantity control zone that either does or does not meet air quality standards. For the former, newly installed or modified stationary pollution sources shall be required when pollutant emissions reach a certain scale to perform modelling and simulation for their pollutant emissions. This will help to prevent emissions from exceeding exceed allowable pollutant increase limits within

277. Article 7(1) of the Air Pollution Control Act.
278. Article 7(2) of the Air Pollution Control Act.
279. Article 7(3) of the Air Pollution Control Act: 'In drawing up the air pollution control scheme mentioned in the preceding article, special municipality, county or city competent authorities shall consider the fact that air pollutants are characterized by circulation, and shall determine the scheme in consultation with the competent authorities of adjacent special municipalities, counties or cities.'
280. Article 8(1) of the Air Pollution Control Act.

the zone.[281] The total quantity control plans for zones that meet air quality standards shall include allowable pollutant increase limits, measures to avoid reduction in air quality, principles for the approval of newly installed or modified stationary pollution sources, operational methods, and other matters.[282]

136. For zones that do not meet air quality standards, stringent rules must be applied to ensure air quality. An existing stationary pollution source shall apply to the special municipality, county, or city competent authorities for authorisation of its pollutant emissions and allow for reductions in accordance with the targets and deadlines that the central competent authority has designated based on air quality requirements. Newly installed or modified stationary pollution sources from which pollutant emissions reach a certain scale shall employ the most feasible control technology. In case of specific large pollution sources, the minimum achievable emission rate control technology shall be adopted. Newly installed or modified stationary pollution sources must reach emission quantities that are sufficient to offset pollutant emission increases.[283] The total quantity control plans for the total quantity control zones that do not meet air quality standards shall include pollutant types, quantity reduction targets, quantity reduction timetables, pollutant reduction quantities and timetables that must be implemented by the competent authorities of each special municipality, county and city within the control zone shall be required to implement, percentage of pollutants offset, along with principles for the approval of newly installed or modified stationary pollution sources, operational methods, and other matters.[284]

137. A trade scheme to create flexibility that can ensure air quality is introduced in Article 9 of the Act. The pollutant emission increases are offset by newly installed or modified stationary pollution sources, and the emission quantities are offset by existing stationary pollution sources that will be obtained from the following sources:

(1) The actual reduction difference banked by stationary pollution sources in accordance with regulations.
(2) Emission quantities obtained through trading or auction.
(3) Emission quantities reduced through improvement of mobile pollution sources.

138. The Air Pollution Control Plan prepared by the special municipality, county and city competent authority within total quantity control zones shall determine and amend air pollution control plans to take into account the need to improve air quality in the *total quantity control zones.*[285]

281. Article 8(2) of the Air Pollution Control Act.
282. Article 10(1) of the Air Pollution Control Act.
283. Article 8(3) of the Air Pollution Control Act.
284. Article 10(2) of the Air Pollution Control Act.
285. Article 11 of the Air Pollution Control Act.

IV. Air Quality Monitoring Stations

139. The EPA is required to establish air quality monitoring stations and regularly publicly report the state of air quality and its original data in cities, towns, and townships where petrochemical industrial areas are located and at appropriate points selected by competent authorities at all levels.[286] Moreover, Developers of special industrial parks must plan and install buffer zones within the boundaries of the parks and install air quality monitoring facilities in appropriate areas.[287] The status of reporting and its original data should be published by EPA periodically.[288]

V. Emergency Measures to Tackle Air Pollution

140. A general clause has been in place that authorises the government to adopt measures that can deal with emergent air pollution issues. Competent authorities at all levels and public and private premises shall promptly adopt emergency control measures when variations in meteorological conditions or other reasons cause concern about serious deterioration in air quality. When necessary, competent authorities at all levels shall issue air quality deterioration alerts and shall prohibit or restrict the use of transportation vehicles, the emissions of air pollutants by public and private premises, and activities at government agencies and schools.[289]

141. Special measures have been put in place to deal with emergency air pollution from power plants. To reduce coal-fired power generation, electricity generation enterprises may adjust the types of fuels used for power generation, and the fuels used by the enterprises for gas-fired power generation and air pollutant emissions may increase accordingly. The electricity enterprises may report increases to the central authority for its review and also submit them to the EPA for its approval. After approval, the limitations on both fuels used per year and emission quantities indicated on the permits are not applicable to electricity enterprises.[290]

142. The air pollutant emission quantities that increase due to the adjustment should be lower than the air pollutant emission quantities reduced because of the implementation of emergency control measures or reduction of coal-fired power generation;[291] this special measure is only valid until 31 December 2025.[292]

---

286. Article 13 of the Air Pollution Control Act.
287. Article 15(1) of the Air Pollution Control Act.
288. Article 15(3) of the Air Pollution Control Act.
289. Article 14(1) of the Air Pollution Control Act.
290. Article 14(2) of the Air Pollution Control Act.
291. Article 14(3) of the Air Pollution Control Act.
292. Article 14(5) of the Air Pollution Control Act.

VI. Air Pollution Control Fees and Funds

143. Stationary and mobile pollution sources that emit air pollutants are obliged to pay air pollution control fees to EPA,[293] except for construction projects, where fees are collected by special municipality, county, or city competent authorities.[294] Fund management committees may supervise the management and utilisation of these fees, and competent authorities at all levels may establish funds.[295] Fees collected will be used for matters related to the following purposes:[296]

(1) implementation of air pollution control work by competent authorities at all levels;
(2) inspection of air pollution sources and the auditing of the implementation and efficacy of such inspections;
(3) subsidies and incentives for the performance of air pollution abatement work by each category of pollution source;
(4) commissioning and subsidising of analysis laboratories for the performance of motor vehicle emissions testing;
(5) commissioning or subsidising of professional organisations for the performance of the testing, guidance and evaluation of stationary pollution sources;
(6) air pollution control technology research and development and strategy formulation;
(7) international environmental protection work involving air pollution;
(8) air quality monitoring and the auditing of the implementation and efficacy of such monitoring;
(9) expenses related to the collection of air pollution control fees;
(10) hiring personnel required for work related to air pollution control;
(11) air pollution health risk assessments and management;
(12) incentives for promoting the use of clean energy and related research and development;
(13) rewards for reporting air pollution.

144. Fees collected are shared between local and central government to help improve air quality; 60% of the funds collected by the EPA from stationary pollution sources are allocated to special municipalities, counties or cities where the pollution source is located, 20% collected from mobile pollution sources are allocated to the special municipalities, counties or cities where those affected by the mobile pollution sources live or where the oils and fuels are sold.[297] The local government therefore gains more funds to budget and manage pollution in their jurisdiction.

145. Those responsible for stationary pollution sources can apply to the special municipality, county, or city for incentives to effectively reduce pollutant emission

293. Article 16(1) of the Air Pollution Control Act.
294. Article 17(1) of the Air Pollution Control Act.
295. Article 18(2) of the Air Pollution Control Act.
296. Article 18(1) of the Air Pollution Control Act.
297. Article 17(1) of the Air Pollution Control Act.

quantities, while those who have already paid air pollution control fees related to Article 16(1) may apply to the competent authority of the special municipality, county or city to receive exemptions from fees.[298]

VII. Control Measures Applying to Public and Private Premises with Stationary Pollution Sources

146. [Emission standard] Public and private premises with stationary pollution sources that emit air pollutants have to comply with *emission standards.*[299] These standards are determined based on the evaluation of health risks and the feasibility of control technology.[300] Those responsible for the premises must effectively collect each type of air pollutant and maintain the normal operation of their air pollution control facilities and monitoring facilities. The maximum operating quantity of their stationary pollution sources may not exceed the maximum treatment capacity of their air pollution control facilities.[301]

147. [Permits] Public and private premises that possess stationary pollution sources shall, prior to installation or modification, submit air pollution control plans and apply for installation permits, then perform installation or modification based on those plans and the permit given.[302] *Reapplication* for permits is required when relocating or changing industry categories.[303]

148. Moreover, use permits are required for burning materials. First, fuels and auxiliary fuels that contain bituminous coal or other substances designated and officially announced by the central competent authority and that are also used by public or private premises have to meet the relevant standards for fuel types, ratio of fuels in combustion and fuel composition. Fuels can only be used after a permit has been applied for and acquired; records of the use of these substances must be maintained and reported to the special municipality, county or city competent authority in accordance with regulations.[304] Second, anyone who uses substances that tend to cause air pollution must prepare relevant documents and apply for a permit; the substances cannot be used until a permit is issued. Records of substance use must be maintained and reported according to regulations.[305]

149. [Ban] The EPA may prohibit or restrict substances that are: prone to causing air pollution and are controlled under international environmental protection conventions, as well as the manufacture, import, export, sale or use of products

298. Article 19(1) of the Air Pollution Control Act.
299. Article 20(1) of the Air Pollution Control Act.
300. Article 20(3) of the Air Pollution Control Act.
301. Article 23(1) of the Air Pollution Control Act.
302. Article 24(1) of the Air Pollution Control Act.
303. Article 25(1) of the Air Pollution Control Act.
304. Article 28(1) of the Air Pollution Control Act.
305. Article 29(1) of the Air Pollution Control Act.

manufactured from or filled with such substances.[306] *The EPA also prohibits several acts within class regions or total quality control zones, such as:*[307]

(1) Engagement in burning, melting, refining, grinding, casting, conveyance or other operation that causes the production of significant particulate pollutants that are dispersed into the air or onto the property of others.
(2) Engagement in construction projects, piling of powdered or granular materials, transportation of construction materials or waste, or other industrial processes without appropriate control measures that causes airborne dust or polluted air.
(3) Placement, mixing, stirring, heating or baking of substances, spontaneous combustion due to improper management, or engagement in other operations that causes odorous pollutants or toxic gases.
(4) Use, conveyance or storage of organic solvents or other volatile substances that causes odorous pollutants or toxic gases.
(5) Food preparation by the food and beverage industry that causes the dispersal of oily smoke or odorous pollutants.
(6) (Other obligation: duty to adopt emergency measures to deal with sudden air pollution); Public and private premises that have stationary pollution sources have several specific obligations:
   - First, they have a duty to adopt emergency measures to deal with sudden air pollution. When stationary pollution sources emit a large quantity of air pollutants due to a sudden accident, emergency response measures must be promptly activated, and the special municipality, county or city competent authority must be notified within one hour.[308]
   - Second, public and private premises that have been designated and officially announced by the central competent authority must establish dedicated air pollution control units or personnel positions.[309]
   - Third, reporting duty.[310]
   - Fourth, obligation to install automated monitoring facilities.[311]

306. Article 31 of the Air Pollution Control Act.
307. Article 32 of the Air Pollution Control Act.
308. Article 33 of the Air Pollution Control Act.
309. Article 34 of the Air Pollution Control Act.
310. Article 21(1) of the Air Pollution Control Act: 'Those public and private premises possessing stationary pollution sources designated and officially announced by the central competent authority shall report the quarterly air pollutant emissions of their stationary pollution sources for the previous quarter to the competent authority of the special municipality, county or city by the of the Air Pollution Control Act. end of January, April, July and October each year.'
311. Article 22 of the Air Pollution Control Act: 'Those public and private premises possessing stationary pollution sources designated and officially announced by the central competent authority shall complete the installation of automated monitoring facilities by the designated deadline in order to continuously monitor their operations or air pollutant emissions conditions, and shall apply to the competent authority of the special municipality, county or city for authorization. Those that have been designated and officially announced as being required to connect via the Internet shall complete the connection of their monitoring facilities via the Internet to the competent authority of the special municipality, county or city by the designated deadline, and shall be made public on the website of the special municipality, county and city competent authority.'

– Fifth, public or private premises are required to publish their permits and plans on their websites, such as air pollution control plans and air pollution control facility description; permits for the use of fuels and information reported in accordance with the Act; licence numbers and information of environmental engineering technicians, dedicated air pollution control personnel and environmental inspection and testing institutions; and emergency response measures and plans. However, information related to national defence and trade secrets that have been reported by public or private premises to special municipality, county or city competent authorities and then approved are not required to be published.[312]

VIII. [Mobile Pollution Sources] Control Measures That Apply to Mobile Pollution Sources

150. Air pollutants emitted by mobile pollution sources are required to meet emission standards.[313] To ensure compliance, every in-use vehicle, including both domestically made and imported vehicles, must have a complete individual inspection.[314] The users or owners of the mobile pollution sources shall maintain the effective operation of their vehicle's air pollution control equipment and may not remove or modify it.[315]

151. The operation of mobile pollution sources is subject to further regulation. As significant amounts of pollution result from idling, a vehicle is not allowed to idle for more than regulated times, which depend on the specific location and weather conditions.[316] Fuel sources must also meet the standard[317] and be approved by the EPA.[318] Mobile pollution sources should also follow the regulations in designed 'air quality maintenance zones',[319] including areas where specific motor

312. Article 35 of the Air Pollution Control Act.
313. Article 36(1) of the Air Pollution Control Act.
314. Article 36(3) of the Air Pollution Control Act.
315. Article 37(1) of the Air Pollution Control Act.
316. Article 38 of the Air Pollution Control Act.
317. Article 39(1) of the Air Pollution Control Act: 'The manufacture, import, sale or use of fuel supplied for use in mobile pollution sources shall comply with the composition standards for fuel types determined by the central competent authority. However, fuel supplied exclusively for export shall not be subject to this restriction.'
318. Article 39(2) of the Air Pollution Control Act: 'The fuel manufacturers in the preceding paragraph shall obtain permits issued by the central competent authority before the fuel they produce may be sold domestically; importers shall obtain permit documents issued by the central competent authority before they may apply to the competent authority governing the petroleum industry for import approval documents. Manufacturers or importers shall perform composition and property analysis on each batch (shipment) of fuel and maintain records which shall be reported to the central competent authority.'
319. Article 40(1) of the Air Pollution Control Act.

vehicles are prohibited or limited; and areas where the fuels, power types, and operation conditions of mobile pollution sources, status of operation, and access are prohibited or limited.[320]

152. [Motor vehicles] As a great deal of pollution from mobile pollution sources comes from motor vehicles, many regulations focusing on emissions have been introduced. For example, motor vehicles are required to obtain EPA-issued vehicle model exhaust testing compliance verification and EPA certification and authorisation before they may apply for licence plates.[321] Emissions are subject to periodic[322] and random[323] testing inspections. Additional laws have been created to facilitate random testing, such as the ability to perform irregular air pollutant emission testing or inspections of in-use mobile pollution sources at car parks or stations, at airports, on roadways, in port zones, on water bodies or at other appropriate locations, and may notify transportation vehicles when there is a concern of polluting that they must undergo testing at a designated location by a designated deadline.[324] Also, in-use motor vehicles where air pollutant emissions are determined through visual determination, visual inspection, or remote sensing that fail to meet the emission standards or the remote sensing screening standards must be repaired and undergo testing at a designated location by a given deadline.[325]

IX. Volatile Organic Compounds

153. The manufacture, import, and sale of chemicals that contain any volatile organic compounds (VOCs) designated and officially announced by the central competent authority must meet the composition standards for the volatile organic compounds contained in the chemicals. However, chemicals used exclusively for export are not subject to this requirement.[326]

X. Other Measures to Improve Enforcement

154. To ensure the site inspection of pollution sources, authorities at all levels may dispatch personnel bearing identification documents to inspect or appraise the air pollutant emissions, air pollution collection facilities, control facilities, and

320. Article 40(2) of the Air Pollution Control Act.
321. Article 42(1) of the Air Pollution Control Act.
322. Article 41(1) of the Air Pollution Control Act: 'For in-use motor vehicles that have undergone random testing of air pollutant emissions and that are determined to be unable to meet air pollution emission standards for mobile pollution sources due to poor design or assembly, the EPA shall order the manufacturer or importer to recall for repair within a limited time period all units of the model of the motor vehicle at issue that have already been sold.'
323. Article 43 of the Air Pollution Control Act: 'The central competent authority may commission other government agencies to periodically conduct the motor vehicle exhaust testing and pay a commission fee. The fee may be deducted from the fee of the motor vehicle exhaust testing.'
324. Article 45(1) of the Air Pollution Control Act.
325. Article 46(1) of the Air Pollution Control Act.
326. Article 47(1) of the Air Pollution Control Act.

monitoring facilities of public and private premises or mobile pollution sources, as well as the composition of fuel that is produced, stored or used and the composition of VOC containing chemicals manufactured, imported and sold by public and private premises or mobile pollution sources. They may order that relevant information be provided.[327]

155. To help the industry improve emissions, a soft approach is provided. Each competent authority in charge of the industry shall provide guidance to help improve all types of pollution sources. Relevant results from the guidance shall be published every year on websites designated by the central competent authority and reviewed periodically.[328]

156. To ensure the participation of NGOs in monitoring the enforcement of the rules in this act, it includes a public interest litigation clause. When public and private premises violate the act, or relevant orders that are determined to be related to the authorisation of the act and competent authorities at all levels are considered negligent in enforcement, victims or public interest groups may notify the authorities of this in writing. If regulations are still not enforced sixty days after the written notification is received, the victims or public interest groups may file a lawsuit directly with an administrative court and seek a ruling that orders the authorities to execute their duties.[329] Ordinary citizens can also contribute to the enforcement of this act. Citizens or groups may report any violation on the public or private premises of the provisions of the act or air pollutants that are emitted by in-use motor vehicles by submitting a description of facts or supporting information to the special municipality, county, or city competent authority.[330]

§2. Indoor Air Quality

157. To improve indoor air quality and to protect public health, the Indoor Air Quality Act was adopted on 23 November 2011. Indoor air pollution is generally defined as environmental pollutants that are normally dispersed in indoor air and which may directly or indirectly affect public health or the living environment after long-term exposure. These include carbon dioxide, carbon monoxide, formaldehyde, total volatile organic compounds, bacteria, fungi, airborne particles with a particle diameter of 10 micrometres or less (PM10), airborne particles with a diameter of 2.5 micrometres or less (PM2.5), ozone, etc.[331]

327. Article 48(1) of the Air Pollution Control Act.
328. Article 50 of the Air Pollution Control Act.
329. Article 93 of the Air Pollution Control Act.
330. Article 94 of the Air Pollution Control Act.
331. Article 3 of the Indoor Air Quality Act.

I. Premised at Stake

158. The following public and private premises may be subject to this Act:[332]

(i) Schools at the senior secondary level and below, and other premises that mainly provide child and youth education or child and youth activities.
(ii) Universities and colleges, libraries, museums, fine arts museums, cram schools or other cultural or social education institutions.
(iii) Premises that house medical institutions, nursing institutions, other medical care institutions, and social welfare institutions.
(iv) Office space of government agencies and public or private enterprises.
(v) Passenger carrying spaces and stations (terminals) of rail transportation enterprises, civil aviation enterprises, mass rapid transit system transportation enterprises and passenger transport services enterprises.
(vi) The business premises of financial institutions, post offices, and telecommunications enterprises.
(vii) Premises for physical education, sports, or fitness.
(viii) Classrooms, reading rooms, laboratories, performance halls, auditoriums, exhibition rooms and conference halls (rooms).
(ix) Opera houses, cinemas, KTV/MTV businesses, computer entertainment businesses, or other public recreational entertainment premises.
(x) Hotels, shopping malls, markets, restaurants, and other business premises for public consumption.

II. Measures

159. The following measures would apply to the above locations once they were designated. First, the indoor air quality of the premises must meet *indoor air quality standards.*[333] Moreover, owners, managers, or users of officially announced premises shall determine an indoor air quality *maintenance and management plan* and implement it accordingly.[334] The owners, managers, or users of officially announced premises then have to install dedicated personnel for indoor air quality maintenance and management to implement management and maintenance.[335] In addition, the owners, managers, or users of the officially announced premises shall commission analysis laboratories to regularly perform analyses of indoor air quality, make public the analysis results on a regular basis, and keep records.[336] Finally, the competent authority can dispatch personnel who will present verification of their duties

332. Article 6 of the Indoor Air Quality Act.
333. Article 7 of the Indoor Air Quality Act.
334. Article 8 of the Indoor Air Quality Act.
335. Article 9 of the Indoor Air Quality Act.
336. Article 10 of the Indoor Air Quality Act.

and perform on-site inspections, indoor air quality analyses or review testing (monitoring) records and may order that relevant data be provided. This cannot be evaded, obstructed, or refused by the owners, managers or users of the officially announced premises.[337]

160. This act also provides appropriate penalties. For instance, those who do not comply with the indoor air quality standard are ordered to make improvements by a specific deadline. If they fail to do so, they can be fined between TWD 50,000 and TWD 250,000. They may be ordered to make the improvements again with an updated timeline; if they miss the deadline again, fines may be imposed for each violation. In severe circumstances, the use of the relevant premises may be restricted or prohibited; when necessary, an order may be issued to terminate business.[338]

337. Article 12 of the Indoor Air Quality Act.
338. Article 15 of the Indoor Air Quality Act.

Chapter 3. Water Pollution

§1. Basic Measures

I. Principle

161. The fundamental principle in structuring this water pollution act is based on the concept that those who use a body of water to receive or convey effluent may not exceed its carrying capacity to avoid jeopardising the uses of the body of water.[339]

162. To appropriately manage water pollution, further works have been provided for authorities and enterprises, sewage systems or building sewage treatment facilities.

II. Public Authorities

163. The EPA is responsible for an overall planning duty. It is obliged to determine water pollution control programmes in consultation with the special municipality, county, and city competent authorities and report implementation progress to the Legislative Yuan annually.[340]

164. The detailed works that have been placed on the EPA include delineated water zones and determining classifications and quality standards for bodies of water that are dependent on the area's special characteristics and on-site conditions.[341] According to Article 6(1), total quantity control methods may be adopted by the special municipality, county or city competent authority to control water pollution.[342] Article 9(1) says that competent authorities at all levels must install water quality monitoring stations and issue official announcements of monitoring results at regular intervals and adopt appropriate measures.[343]

165. The polluter-pay principle has been adopted to improve water management. At the central government level, water pollution control fees may be levied by the EPA on enterprises and sewage systems (excluding public sewage systems and community sewage systems) that discharge wastewater or sewage into surface water bodies based on their discharge water quality and water volume or based on their discharge water quality and water volume as determined through the EPA's calculation method.[344] Local governments may collect water pollution control fees from households that are located in the sewage system zones and fail to discharge

339. Article 5 of the Water Pollution Control Act.
340. Article 12(2) of the Water Pollution Control Act.
341. Article 6(1) of the Water Pollution Control Act.
342. Article 9(1) of the Water Pollution Control Act.
343. Article 10 of the Water Pollution Control Act.
344. Article 11(1) of the Water Pollution Control Act.

sewage into sewage systems.[345] Different spending requirements for the funds collected by the EPA and the local government are specified in the act.[346]

III. Those Enterprises, Sewage Systems or Building Sewage Treatment Facilities

166. Those enterprises, sewage systems or building sewage treatment facilities that discharge wastewater or sewage into surface water bodies must comply with effluent standards.[347] Sludge produced through wastewater or sewage treatment must be properly treated and may not be arbitrarily stored or dumped.[348]

167. Sewage system infrastructure and wastewater treatment facilities must also comply with the requirements of water pollution control policies.[349]

§2. CONTROL MEASURES

I. Enterprises

A. *Plan and Permit*

168. Prior to establishment or modification, enterprises shall submit *water pollution control measure plans* and related documents for review and *approval* to the

---

345. Article 11(2) of the Water Pollution Control Act.
346. Article 11(3) of the Water Pollution Control Act: 'The water pollution control fees in the preceding two paragraphs shall be provided exclusively for national water pollution control matters; the disbursement items of these fees shall be the following.

I. Water pollution control fees collected in accordance with the provisions of Paragraph 1:
(1) Remediation of the pollution of surface water bodies and monitoring of water quality;
(2) Improvement of water quality in drinking water source quality protection areas;
(3) Improvement of water quality in water pollution total quantity control zones;
(4) Water pollution control technology research and development, acquisition and strategy research and development;
(5) Employment of personnel required for implementation of fee collection work; and
(6) Other relevant water pollution control work.

II. Water pollution control fees collected in accordance with the provisions of Paragraph 2:
(1) Construction of primary and secondary public sewage system main pipes;
(2) Construction of wastewater treatment plants and wastewater and sewage interception facilities;
(3) Construction of nightsoil dumping stations and nightsoil treatment plants;
(4) Construction of centralized treatment facilities for sludge produced by wastewater and sewage treatment facilities;
(5) Public sewage system operation and maintenance fees;
(6) Employment of personnel required for implementation of fee collection and management of public sewage system construction; and
(7) Other fees relevant to household sewage treatment work.

347. Article 7 of the Water Pollution Control Act.
348. Article 8 of the Water Pollution Control Act.
349. Article 12(1) of the Water Pollution Control Act.

special municipality, county or city competent authority or an agency commissioned by the central competent authority.[350] Afterwards, enterprises that discharge wastewater or sewage into surface water bodies must apply for a *discharge permit or simple discharge permit document* from the special municipality, county or city competent authority and obey the items registered on the document while discharging. Enterprises cannot change the indicated items unless they have permission from the special municipality, county or city competent authority.[351] The exception to this is enterprises that are connected to a sewage system; when they submit a water pollution control measure plan as noted above, then apply for a discharge permit and perform the registration modifications, the documents that they are required to possess shall be *signed by a legally registered and practising environmental engineer or other relevant professional engineer.*[352]

169. Those enterprises designated and officially announced by the central competent authority shall, prior to the registration of the application and modification of water pollution control measure plans, discharge permits or simple discharge permit documents, *disclose the concentration and quantity of the pollutants their discharged wastewater or sewage may contend.*[353] When the wastewater or sewage discharged by an enterprise causes pollutants beyond the effluent standard and the pollutant has been determined by the special municipality, county, or city competent authority to potentially endanger ecology or human health, the enterprise shall submit a *risk assessment and management report* as required by the central competent authority regulations to explain the risk of its wastewater or sewage on the ecology and human health and risk management measures that can be adopted.[354] Pollutants that are at stake, assessed and determined necessary by competent authorities at all levels, shall be added to the effluent standard.[355] Reports that are reviewed and approved by the special municipality, county, or city competent authority will also approve *the concentration or total quantity limit of their water pollution control measures plans, discharge permit, or simple discharge permit document.*[356]

---

350. Article 13(1) of the Water Pollution Control Act.
351. Article 14(1) of the Water Pollution Control Act.
352. Article 17(1) of the Water Pollution Control Act.
Those that meet one of the following circumstances may be exempt from obtaining the additional signature of an engineer pursuant to the foregoing paragraph:

(i) Those circumstances in which the items that require the signature of an engineer for a water pollution control measure plan that is required to be submitted when applying for a discharge permit pursuant to Art. 14 and for a water pollution control measure plan that has been previously reviewed and approved pursuant to Art. 13 have not been modified.
(ii) Those circumstances in which the items that require the signature of an engineer when applying for the extension of a discharge permit pursuant to Art. 15 have not been modified.

353. Article 14-1(1) of the Water Pollution Control Act.
354. Article 14-1(2) of the Water Pollution Control Act.
355. Article 14-1(4) of the Water Pollution Control Act.
356. Article 14-1(3) of the Water Pollution Control Act.

170. The validity period for discharge permits and simple discharge permit documents shall be five years. Those that still wish to continue to use their permits or permit documents after expiration shall, within the five-month period that starts six months prior to expiration, apply to the special municipality, county, or city competent authority for an extension. Extensions cannot exceed five years.[357] When there is concern regarding ecological or human health risks because of deteriorating water quality within the validity period of a discharge permit and the special municipality, county or city competent authority considers that the items in the permit cannot protect the bodies of water bodies or that the risks may be harmful to the public welfare, the authority shall *modify* permit items or cancel a permit or permit document.[358]

B. Regulations

171. The competent authority shall issue an official announcement for the cancellation of discharge pipes with unknown sources that are used for the discharge of industrial wastewater or sewage. For circumstances where no one has made a claim one week after the official announcement, the competent authority may seal or remove the indicated discharge pipelines.[359] Enterprises must also adopt water pollution control measures.[360]

II. Sewage Systems That Discharge Wastewater or Sewage

172. Sewage systems that discharge wastewater or sewage need to apply to the special municipality, county, or city competent authority for either a discharge permit or a simple discharge permit document and shall obey the items registered on the document while discharging. The items may not be changed without permission from the special municipality, county, or city competent authority.[361]

173. Discharge permits and simple discharge permit documents are valid for five years. Enterprises that wish to continue to use their permits or permit documents after expiration must apply for an extension at least five months prior to the expiration of the permit. An extension may not exceed five years.[362] When there is concern about the ecological or human health risks due to the deterioration of water quality within the validity period of a discharge permit or simple discharge permit

357. Article 15(1) of the Water Pollution Control Act.
358. Article 15(2) of the Water Pollution Control Act.
359. Article 16 of the Water Pollution Control Act.
360. Article 18 of the Water Pollution Control Act.
361. Articles 14 and 19 of the Water Pollution Control Act.
362. Articles 15(1) and 19 of the Water Pollution Control Act.

document, the special municipality, county or city competent authority may consider that if the items in the permit are not able to protect the bodies of water or may cause harm for public welfare, the authority shall modify permit items or cancel a permit or permit document.[363]

174. Sewage systems that discharge wastewater or sewage must adopt water pollution control measures[364]

III. Enterprises and Sewage Systems

A. Permit

175. An enterprise or sewage system must apply for permission to store or dilute wastewater and must obey all items on their permit. They may only apply for a permit to dilute wastewater only if there are no other alternative wastewater treatment facilities or methods.[365]

176. Enterprises or sewage systems that discharge wastewater or sewage shall follow an approved collection, disposal unit, and flow process, drain from an *approved and registered discharge point or from a discharge point authorised by the sewage management agency into a sewage system, and not reroute discharge.*[366] Wastewater or sewage that requires treatment before it can meet the designated control standards cannot be diluted with non-treated water that meets the relevant standards in this Act.[367]

177. If it is necessary to rescue personnel at a location that is regarded as a critical treatment facility, the special municipality, county or city competent authority must be notified within three hours to avoid restrictions on rerouting discharge and mixing diluting behaviours.[368]

178. Enterprises or sewage systems that have installed wastewater and sewage treatment/pre-treatment facilities must have adequate function and equipment and be maintained at a normal operation status.[369]

363. Articles 15(2) and 19 of the Water Pollution Control Act.
364. Articles 18 and 19 of the Water Pollution Control Act.
365. Article 20(1) of the Water Pollution Control Act.
366. Article 18-1(1) of the Water Pollution Control Act.
367. Article 18-1(2) of the Water Pollution Control Act.
368. Article 18-1(3) of the Water Pollution Control Act.
369. Article 18-1(4) of the Water Pollution Control Act.

B. Professional Personals

179. Enterprises or sewage systems must establish dedicated personnel or units that handle wastewater and sewage treatment.[370]

C. Reporting

180. Enterprises or sewage systems must appropriately report the operation of wastewater and sewage treatment facilities, analysis of effluent water quality and water volume, power consumption records, and other documents related to wastewater and sewage treatment to the special municipality, county, or city competent authority.[371]

D. Water Quality Analysis

181. An analysis laboratory that has been issued a permit by the central competent authority will be commissioned to perform the analysis of water pollutants, water quality, and water volume, except for in circumstances that have been approved by the central competent authority.[372]

E. Improvement Assistance

182. Each industry competent authority shall provide guidance and assistance to improve the treatment and discharge of the wastewater and sewage of enterprises and sewage systems.[373]

F. Emergency Measures

183. When there are concerns about serious endangerment of human health, agricultural or aqua cultural production, or drinking water sources due to the discharge of wastewater or sewage by an enterprise or sewage system, the statutory responsible person shall *adopt emergency response measures* promptly and notify the local competent authority within three hours.[374] Along with ordering that necessary control measures be adopted, the competent authority will also order the suspension of business or the partial or complete suspension of work.[375]

370. Article 21(1) of the Water Pollution Control Act.
371. Article 22(1) of the Water Pollution Control Act.
372. Article 23 of the Water Pollution Control Act.
373. Article 24 of the Water Pollution Control Act.
374. Article 27(1) of the Water Pollution Control Act.
375. Article 27(4) of the Water Pollution Control Act.

184. Maintenance and preventive measures will be adopted for circumstances where there are concerns about negligence causing leakage of pollutants or wastewater, or sewage into a body of water from the conveyance or storage equipment that was installed by an enterprise or sewage system. If leakage has been caused through negligence, *emergency response measures* must begin promptly, and the local competent authority must be notified within three hours of the occurrence of the accident. In those circumstances, the competent authority can also order the suspension of business or the partial or complete suspension of work.[376]

G. Automatic Monitoring System

185. In the following circumstances, an enterprise or sewage system that discharges wastewater or sewage into a body of water that has been delineated as a total quantity control water body must independently install an automatic monitoring system that will monitor effluent water quality and water volume:[377]

(i) If daily volume of wastewater or sewage discharges exceeds 1,000 cubic metres.
(ii) If the special municipality, county or city competent authority has determined the enterprise or sewage system to be a major water pollution source.

IV. Enterprises and Sewage Systems

186. The owners, users, and managers of building sewage treatment facilities need to either perform cleaning work internally or commission a clearance organisation to perform cleaning work.[378]

V. Administrative Inspection and Enforcement

187. Competent authorities at all levels may send identified personnel to the premises of an enterprise, sewage system, or building sewage treatment facility to perform any of the following verifications:[379]

(i) Inspect pollutant sources and wastewater and sewage treatment and discharge circumstances.
(ii) Request relevant information.
(iii) Take samples or flow measurements or document wastewater and sewage treatment and discharge circumstances with photographs.

376. Article 28(1) of the Water Pollution Control Act.
377. Article 31(1) of the Water Pollution Control Act.
378. Article 25(1) of the Water Pollution Control Act.
379. Article 26(1) of the Water Pollution Control Act.

When a competent authority at any level performs verification work in circumstances that may involve military secrets, military authorities will be consulted.[380]

Verification work may not be evaded, obstructed, or refused.[381] Inspection agencies and personnel must maintain confidentiality concerning inspected industrial, commercial or military secrets.[382]

VI. Water Pollution Control Zones

188. Depending on the water pollution conditions within the relevant jurisdiction, a special municipality, county, or city competent authority may delineate and announce water pollution control zones and shall report them to the central competent authority.[383] The central competent authority will complete this task for water pollution control zones that involve two or more special municipalities, counties, or cities.[384]

189. The following acts are prohibited within water pollution control zones:[385]

(i) The use of agricultural chemicals or chemical fertilizers that create concerns about pollution in bodies of water that are designated by the competent authority.
(ii) The dumping of garbage, night soil, sludge, acidic or basic liquid waste, construction waste, or other pollutants in bodies of water or within a designated distance from their shorelines.
(iii) The use of toxins, drugs or electric current to catch or kill aquatic organisms.
(iv) The raising of poultry or livestock in bodies of water that have been designated by the competent authority or within a designated distance from their shorelines.

VII. Underground Water and Soil

190. In general, wastewater or sewage *may not be injected* into groundwater bodies or discharged into soil. However, wastewater or sewage that has been treated to the extent that it complies with soil treatment standards and regulations, has been reviewed and *approved* by the special municipality, county or city competent authority, has received a permit and reported for approval may then be discharged into soil.[386]

380. Article 26(2) of the Water Pollution Control Act.
381. Article 26(3) of the Water Pollution Control Act.
382. Article 26(4) of the Water Pollution Control Act.
383. Article 29(1) of the Water Pollution Control Act.
384. Article 29(2) of the Water Pollution Control Act.
385. Article 30(1) of the Water Pollution Control Act.
386. Article 32(1) of the Water Pollution Control Act.

191. When an enterprise stores substances that have been officially announced and designated by the central competent authority, the enterprise must *instal facilities for preventing the pollution of groundwater bodies and monitoring equipment* and may apply for related usage matters *only after filing* said facilities and equipment for future reference with the special municipality, county, or city competent authority.[387]

§3. Public Interest Litigation Clause

192. When an enterprise or sewage system violates this Act or related orders pursuant to the authorisation of this Act, if the competent authority is negligent in enforcing the Act, then victims or public interest groups may notify the competent authority regarding the negligence. If competent authorities have not carried out the appropriate enforcement within sixty days after receipt of the written notification, the victims or public interest groups may name the competent authority at issue as a defendant and directly file a lawsuit with a high administrative court to seek a ruling that orders the competent authority to execute its duties.[388]

193. When issuing a verdict on the lawsuit in this way, the high administrative court may order the defendant agency to pay the appropriate lawyer fees, monitoring and appraisal fees, and other litigation costs to plaintiffs that have made specific contributions to the maintenance of the quality of bodies of water.[389]

387. Article 33(1) of the Water Pollution Control Act.
388. Article 72(1) of the Water Pollution Control Act.
389. Article 72(2) of the Water Pollution Control Act.

Chapter 4. Soil and Underground Water Pollution Remediation

§1. Introduction

I. Purpose

194. Due to the inability of the Water Pollution Act and other acts to prevent contaminated land or water, heavy intervention from the government has been proposed to deal with the issue of pollution, which led to the promulgation of the Soil and Groundwater Pollution Remediation Act ('Soil Act'). This ambitious act seeks to 'prevent and remediate soil and groundwater pollution, ensure the sustainable use of soil and groundwater, enhance the living environment, and protect public health'.[390] Thus, unlike traditional pollution legislation that focuses on prevention, this act also embraces remediation.

II. The Relationship Between This Act and the Water Pollution Act

195. The regulatory philosophy behind this Act differs from the Water Pollution Act, as does the regulated media. The relationship is illustrated in Table 8.

Table 8 Comparative Table of Regulated Media under the Water Pollution Act and Remediation Act

	Water Pollution Act	*Soil Act*
Similar	Underground water	Soil
Dissimilar	Surface water	Sediment (located at the lower level of surface water)
	Sludge produced through wastewater or sewage treatment by enterprises, sewage systems, and buildings' sewage treatment facilities	

(*Source*: compiled by the authors).

390. The Soil and Groundwater Pollution Remediation Act, Issue 6321, Presidential Office Gazette 15 (Office of the President, Republic of China (Taiwan), 2 Feb. 2000). Available at: http://www.president.gov.tw/Default.aspx?tabid=84&lctl=view&itemid=2295&ctid=96&q=%E5%9C%9F%E 5%A3%A4%E5%8F%8A%E5%9C%B0%E4%B8%8B%E6%B0%B4%E6%B1%A1%E6%9F%93%E6%95%B4%E6%B2%BB%E6%B3%95 (last visited 15 May 2022). Last amended by Issue 6905, Presidential Office Gazette 71 (Office of the President, Republic of China (Taiwan), 3 Feb. 2010). Available at: http://www.president.gov.tw/Portals/0/Bulletins/paper/pdf/6905.pdf (last visited 15 May 2022), at Art. 1.

III. Regulated Media or Materials

196. The regulated media in this Act, as its title indicates, mainly involves not only soil and groundwater pollution[391] but also includes regulation of 'sediment pollution'.[392]

IV. Responsibility Party

197. Since these pollutants[393] could have resulted from diverse sources or reasons, this Act seeks to urge the potential party that is the source of the problems to bear the responsibility to take appropriate measures. First, a 'polluter'[394] should bear the main responsibility for clean-up measures. However, other parties could also bear certain burdens, such as 'potential polluters' and 'interested parties of the polluted land'.[395]

V. Seven Regulatory Tools

198. To regulate the three types of polluters and regulated media, this act adopts seven regulatory tools. First, 'pollution monitoring standards'[396] and 'pollution

391. *Ibid.*, at Art. 2, para. 4, 'Soil Pollution means the introduction into soil of substances, biological organisms or forms of energy that alter soil quality, impact the normal use of the soil or endanger public health and the living environment.'; para. 5 'Groundwater Pollution means the introduction into groundwater of substances, biological organisms or forms of energy that alter soil quality, impact the normal use of the soil or endangers public health and the living environment.'
392. *Ibid.*, at Art. 2, para. 6, '"Sediment Pollution" means the introduction into sediment of substances, biological organisms or forms of energy that impact the ecological status of surface water bodies and the normal use of aquatic food or endanger public health and the living environment.'
393. *Ibid.*, at Art. 2, para. 7, 'Pollutant means a substance, biological organism or form of energy capable of causing soil or groundwater pollution through any of the following acts: leaking or discarding of pollutants; illegally discharging or injecting pollutants; brokering or allowing the leaking, discarding, illegal discharge or injection of pollutants; or failing to dispose of pollutants pursuant to applicable laws or regulations.'
394. *Ibid.*
395. *Ibid.*, at Art. 2, para. 16, 'Potential Polluter means a person who causes pollution to accumulate in the soil or groundwater resulting in soil or groundwater pollution due to the following actions: discharging, injecting, spreading of pollutants; or permitting or agreeing to the discharge of waste water into irrigation and drainage systems or irrigation and water catchment areas.'; para. 19, 'Interested Party of the Polluted Land means a person who is not a polluter of the land but is a user, administrator, or owner of the land when the land is declared a pollution control site or pollution remediation site.'
396. *Ibid.*, at Art. 2, para. 8, 'Soil Pollution Monitoring Standards means the determined pollutant concentrations at which soil pollution monitoring is required for the purpose of preventing soil pollution.'; para. 9, 'Groundwater Pollution Monitoring Standards means the determined pollutant concentrations at which groundwater pollution monitoring is required for the purpose of preventing groundwater pollution.'

control standards'[397] for soil and underground water lay the foundation for further regulatory tools, while 'sediment quality indicators' apply to sediment.[398] Once pollution reaches unacceptable levels, the site or zone regulations become active; site regulations apply to 'pollution control sites' and 'pollution remediation sites',[399] while zone regulations will apply to the 'pollution control areas'.[400] Finally, to remediate these sites or zones, goals for both soil and underground water will be set.[401] This article will further elaborate on the details of each regulatory tool; the tools and their application media are illustrated in Table 9.

Table 9 Seven Key Regulatory Tools under the Soil Act

	Soil	*Underground water*	*Sediment*
Pollution Monitoring Standards		O	
Pollution Control Standards		O	
Quality Indicators			
Pollution Control Site		O	
Pollution Remediation Site		O	
Pollution Control Area		O	
Pollution Remediation Goals		O	

(*Source*: Compiled by the authors).

§2. Multiple Authorities

199. In dealing with the soil and underground water pollution issues in Taiwan, the equal distribution of power among different authorities could play a crucial role.

397. *Ibid.*, at Art. 2, para. 10, 'Soil Pollution Control Standards means determined soil pollution control limits to prevent and control the worsening of soil pollution'. para. 11, 'Groundwater Pollution Control Standards means determined groundwater pollutant limits to prevent and control the worsening of groundwater pollution.'
398. *Ibid.*, at Art. 2, para. 12, 'Sediment Quality Indicators means categorized management or limits on use that have been determined in consideration of the special characteristics of pollution movement or biological availability and accumulation for the purpose of managing sediment quality.'
399. *Ibid.*, at Art. 2, para. 17, 'Pollution Control Site means a place where the source of soil or groundwater pollution has been clearly identified and the pollutants therein do not naturally exist in the environment but have occurred through scouring by rainwater, dispersal, deposition, or irrigation resulting in soil or groundwater pollution that meets the standards for control.'; para. 18, 'Pollution Remediation Site means a pollution control site which has been reviewed and declared by the central competent authority as a Pollution Remediation Site based on its preliminary assessment that the site is likely to seriously endanger public health and the living environment.'
400. *Ibid.*, at Art. 2, para. 20, 'Pollution Control Area means an area which has been delineated according to the scope or condition of soil or groundwater pollution of a pollution control site or pollution remediation site.'
401. *Ibid.*, at Art. 2, para. 13, 'Soil Pollution Remediation Goals means the limit on pollutants set according to the purpose of soil pollution remediation'; para. 14, 'Groundwater Pollution Remediation Goals means the limit on pollutants set according to the purpose of the groundwater pollution remediation.'

Following the tradition of prior environmental laws, this Soil Act creates a two-tier governing regime: the central government (e.g., EPA) and the municipality/local government (usually the Environmental Bureau).[402,403] EPA handles national or beyond local soil and underground water affairs, such as planning, drafting, supervision and implementation of national soil, sediment and groundwater pollution prevention and remediation policies, programmes, and plans.[404] The local government deals with similar issues but within its jurisdiction, such as planning, drafting and implementation of soil, sediment and groundwater pollution prevention and remediation action programmes and plans.[405]

200. However, not all affairs can be divided and distributed to different central/local authorities. Thus, *partial overlapping* is unavoidable. For instance, the EPA is in charge of 'supervision, assistance and approval of soil, sediment and groundwater pollution prevention, monitoring and remediation work by special municipalities, county or city competent authorities' under Article 4(4), while the municipality/local government takes care of similar issues regarding the 'implementation of soil and groundwater pollution prevention, monitoring and remediation work within their jurisdiction' under Article 5(3). Despite efforts to divide the work covered under the Soil Act, some of the duties it requires cannot be clearly defined and separated. Inevitably, the act has to require ambiguously 'all central and municipal' governments to address related matters, such as the 'continual monitoring and remedy duty'[406] and the administrative inspection/investigation power[407] in the prevention measures. This kind of legislative technique sometimes leads to a dangerous result where everybody's business becomes nobody's business.

402. For Example, Bureau of Environmental Protection, Kaohsiung City Government, available at: http://www.ksepb.gov.tw/WebSite/English (last visited 13 Dec. 2015).
403. The Soil and Groundwater Pollution Remediation Act, at Art. 3, 'The competent authority referred to in this Act means … the municipal government in special municipalities and the county or city government in counties or cities.'
404. *Ibid.*, at Art. 4 (e.g., 'drafting, deliberation and interpretation of soil, sediment and groundwater pollution remediation laws and regulations'; 'international cooperation, technology exchanges and personnel training related to soil, sediment and groundwater pollution remediation'; 'other national soil, sediment and groundwater pollution management, prevention and remediation matters'; etc.).
405. *Ibid.*, at Art. 5. Also, the issues such as: 'drafting and interpretation of the autonomous laws and regulations for soil, sedimentation and groundwater pollution remediation *within their jurisdiction*'; and 'soil, sediment and groundwater pollution prevention and remediation research, development and public awareness *within their jurisdiction*'.
406. *Ibid.*, at Art. 6, 'Competent authorities *at all levels* shall regularly monitor the quality of the soil and groundwater within their jurisdictions. When pollutant concentrations exceed the soil pollution or groundwater pollution control standards, the special municipality, county and city competent authorities shall take necessary measures to investigate the party responsible for the pollution and report to the central competent authority. When pollutant concentrations are lower than the soil or groundwater pollution control limits and meet soil or groundwater pollution monitoring standards, the special municipality, county and city competent authorities shall conduct regular monitoring, publicly announce the monitoring results and report such results to the central competent authority for reference.'
407. *Ibid.*, at Art. 7, 'Competent authorities at all levels may dispatch personnel bearing identification documents to enter public or private premises for the following verification work and may order site users, managers or owners to provide related data.'

201. In addition to the multilevel governmental design of environmental authorities, other *non-environmental authorities* may also be responsible for certain duties under the Soil Act, particularly at the preventive measures stage. The authorities in charge of the development of the zones[408] and water bodies[409] are required to fulfil certain duties and submit reports to the aforementioned central and local authorities. These authorities can be seen as 'supplementary authorities to the main central and local environmental authorities'.

§3. Key Measures under the Four Regulatory Stages

202. The tools used by authorities to manage soil and underground water can be divided into four categories according to the time span set forth in the Act. This article will elaborate on the tools used in the different stages as follows.

I. Phase I Preventive Measures

203. Among the measures available for the four stages, the preventive measures stage is unique in that the obligations and duties are mainly put on the related *government*, and only a limited burden is put on the special industries. As noted above, the planning, supervising, and monitoring duties are put on the central and municipal environmental authorities, while there are also supplementary authorities in place. Only certain industries under Articles 8 and 9 and their Ordinances are subject to the regime of related soil and land pollution investigation and evaluation reports to the related authorities.

---

408. *Ibid.*, at Art. 6, para. 3, 'The following local industry competent authorities shall regularly test soil and groundwater quality in accordance with the pollution potential in the area, and submit the resulting data to the special municipality, county or city competent authority for future reference:

(1) Industrial parks.
(2) Export processing zones.
(3) Science-based industrial parks.
(4) Environmental technology parks.
(5) Agricultural technology parks; and
(6) Other specially designated zones officially announced by the central competent authority.'

409. *Ibid.*, at Art. 6, para. 5, The industry competent authorities in charge of the following water bodies shall regularly test sediment quality, and submit the resulting data to the central competent authority for future reference after performing a comparative assessment of the sediment quality indicators, and publicly announce the state of the sediment quality:

(1) rivers;
(2) irrigation canals;
(3) lakes;
(4) reservoirs; and
(5) other specially designated surface water bodies officially announced by the central competent authority.

A. The Duty of Authorities under Articles 6 and 7

1. Three Main Regulatory Regimes

204. At this stage, the key regulatory tool is the establishment of Ordinances as follows (*see* Table 10).

Table 10 Main Ordinances at the Preventive Measures Stage

Regulatory Instrument	*Regulated Item*	*Related Ordinances*
Pollution Monitoring Standards	Soil	Ordinance on Pollution Monitoring Standards for Soil (31 January 2011)
	Underground Water	Ordinance on Pollution Monitoring Standards for Underground Water (10 February 2011)
	Underground Storage	Standard Operation Procedure (SOP) for Monitoring Soil and Gas of the Underground Storage (10 October 2006) SOP for Monitoring Underground Water of Underground Storage (18 October 2006) SOP for Monitoring the Underground Storage (18 October 2006) The Formats and Manuals for Application of Setting up Monitoring Equipment to Prevent Groundwater Pollution from Underground Storage (18 October 2006)
Pollution Control Standards	Soil	Ordinance of Soil Pollution Control Standards (31 January 2011)
	Underground Water	Ordinance of Groundwater Pollution Control Standards 10 February 2011)
Sediment Quality Indicators	Sediment	Ordinance on Sediment Quality Indicators (4 January 2012)

(*Source*: compiled by the authors).

2. Underground Water and Soil

205. In general, competent authorities at all levels are required to 'monitor' the quality of the soil and underground water in their jurisdiction.[410] The results of this

410. *Ibid.*, at Art. 6, para. 1, 'Competent authorities at all levels shall *regularly monitor* the quality of the soil and groundwater within their jurisdictions.'

process could trigger different regulatory processes. Meeting a higher threshold of soil and groundwater pollution control standards and a lower threshold of monitoring standards would oblige authorities to conduct different levels of intervention. The former standard would lead to the duty that 'the special municipality, county and city competent authorities shall *take necessary measures to investigate* the party responsible for the pollution and *report* to the central competent authority';[411] the latter standard would mean that 'the special municipality, county and city competent authorities shall *conduct regular monitoring, publicly announce* the monitoring results, and report such results to the central competent authority for reference'.[412]

206. As an example of the relationship between soil pollution monitoring standards and pollution control standards, more materials are provided under the Ordinance on soil pollution control standards (thirty-nine) than the one on soil pollution monitoring standards (eight).[413] The monitoring standards There are eight materials under the monitoring standards,[414] while there are thirty-nine items under the control standards.[415] There are eight overlapping items, as shown in Table 11.

Table 11 Overlapping Regulatory Items under the Monitoring Standards and Control Standards (Unit: Milligram/Kilogram)

	Monitoring Standards	*Control Standards*
Arsenic (As)	30	60

411. *Ibid.*, 'when pollutant concentrations exceed the soil pollution or groundwater pollution control standards … '.
412. *Ibid.*, at Art. 6, para. 1, 'When pollutant concentrations are lower than the soil or groundwater pollution control limits and meet soil or groundwater pollution monitoring standards, the special municipality, county and city competent authorities shall *conduct regular monitoring, publicly announce* the monitoring results and report such results to the central competent authority for reference.'
413. Ordinance on Pollution Monitoring Standards for Soil. TEPA, Huan-Shu-Tu-Tzu No. 1000008485 (31 Jan. 2011) (total six articles). Available at: http://ivy5.epa.gov.tw/epalaw/search/LordiDispFull.aspx?ltype=14&lname=0190 (last visited 15 May 2022).
414. *Ibid.*, at Art. 4, Ordinance on Soil 'pollution monitoring standards' includes 'Arsenic (As), Cadmium(Cd), Chromium(Cr), Cooper (Cu), Mercury (Hg), Nickel (Ni), Lead (Pb), Zinc (Zn).'
415. *Ibid.*, at Art. 5, 'Pollution Control Standards':

(1) Heavy Metals: Arsenic (As), Cadmium (Cd), Chromium (Cr), Cooper (Cu), Mercury (Hg), Nickel (Ni), Lead (Pb), Zinc (Zn).
(2) Organic compounds: Benzene, Carbon tetrachloride, Chloroform, 1,2-Dichloroethane, cis-1,2-Dichloroethylene, trans-1,2-Dichloroethylene, 1,2-Dichloropropane, 1,2-Dichlorobenzene, 1,3-Dichlorobenzene, 3,3'-Dichlorobenzidine, Ethylbenzene, Hexachlorobenzene, Pentachlorophenol, Tetrachloroethylene, Toluene, TPH (Total petroleum hydrocarbons), Trichloroethylene, 2,4,5-Trichlorophenol, 2,4,6-Trichlorophenol, Vinyl chloride, Xylenes.
(3) Pesticides: Aldrin, Chlordane, DDT, 4,4'-Dichlorodiphenyl-triichloroethane, Dieldrin, Endrin, Heptachlor, Toxaphene, Endosulfan.
(4) Other Organic compounds: Dioxins, Polychlorinated biphenyls.

	Monitoring Standards	*Control Standards*
Cadmium (Cd)	10 (Agriculture land for food purpose: 2.5)	20 (Agriculture land for food purpose: 5)
Chromium (Cr)	175	250
Cooper (Cu)	220 (Agriculture land for food purpose: 120)	400 (Agriculture land for food purpose: 200)
Mercury (Hg),	10 (Agriculture land for food purpose: 2)	20 (Agriculture land for food purpose: 5)
Nickel (Ni)	130	200
Lead (Pb)	1,000 (Agriculture land for food purpose: 300)	2,000 (Agriculture land for food purpose: 500)
Zinc (Zn)	1,000 (Agriculture land for food purpose: 260)	2,000 (Agriculture land for food purpose: 600)

(*Source*: Compiled by the authors).

207. A similar regulatory structure applies to the underground water regime. The two categories (heavy metals and general items) include fifteen items[416] under the Ordinance of pollution monitoring standards for underground water, while there are seven categories that include a total of forty items under the Ordinance on pollution control standards for underground water.[417] The overlapping items are related to the eight materials under heavy metals (*see* Tables 12 and 13).[418]

416. Ordinance on Pollution Monitoring Standards for Underground Water. TEPA, Huan-Shu-Tu-Tzu No. 1000010129 (10 Feb. 2011) (total six articles). Amended by TEPA, Huan-Shu-Tu-Tzu No. 1020109443 (18 Dec. 2013). Available at: http://ivy5.epa.gov.tw/epalaw/search/LordiDispFull.aspx?ltype=14&lname=0200 (last visited 15 May 2022).

417. The Ordinance on Ground Water Pollution Control Standards. TEPA, Huan-Shu-Shui-Tzu No. 0073680 (21 Nov. 2001) (total six articles). Amended by TEPA, Huan-Shu-Shui-Tzu No. 1020109478 (18 Dec. 2013). Available at: http://ivy5.epa.gov.tw/epalaw/search/LordiDispFull.aspx?ltype=14&lname=0130 (last visited 15 May 2022), at Art. 4.

418. For example, Arsenic (As), Cadmium (Cd), Chromium (Cr), Cooper (Cu), Lead (Pb), Zinc (Zn), Iron (Fe), and Manganese (Mn).

Table 12 Table for Monitoring Item and Value (Unit: Milligram/per Litre)

Monitoring Items	*Monitoring Value*	
	Type I	*Type II*
Heavy Metal		
Arsenic (As)	0.025	0.25
Cadmium (Cd)	0.0025	0.025
Chromium (Cr)	0.025	0.25
Cooper (Cu)	0.50	5.0
Lead (Pb)	0.025	0.25
Zinc (Zn)	2.5	25
Iron (Fe)	0.15	1.5
Manganese (Mn)	0.025	0.25
Ordinary Items		
Total hardness, calculated by $CaCO_3$	150	750
Suspended solid	250	1250
Chloride	125	625
Ammonium nitrogen	0.050	0.25
Nitrate, calculated by N	5.0	25
Sulphate calculated by SO_4^{2-}	125	625
Total organic carbon	2.0	10

Source: https://oaout.epa.gov.tw/law/EngLawContent.aspx?lan=E&id=160.

Table 13 The Regulated Pollutants and Regulatory Value (Unit: Milligram/per Litre)

Regulated Items	*Control Value (mg/L)*	
	Type I	*Type II*
Single ring aromatic hydrocarbons		
Benzene	0.0050	0.050
Toluene	1.0	10
Ethylbenzene	0.70	7.0
Xylenes	10	100
Polycyclic aromatic hydrocarbons		
Naphthalene	0.040	0.40
Chlorinated hydrocarbons		
Carbon tetrachloride	0.0050	0.050

Regulated Items	*Control Value (mg/L)*	
	Type I	*Type II*
Chlorobenzene	0.10	1.0
Chloroform	0.10	1.0
Chloromethane	0.030	0.30
1,4-Dichlorobenzene	0.075	0.75
1,1-Dichloroethane	0.85	8.5
1,2-Dichloroethane	0.0050	0.050
1,1-Dichloroethylene	0.0070	0.070
cis-1,2-Dichloroethylene	0.070	0.70
trans-1,2-Dichloroethylene	0.10	1.0
Phenols	0.014	0.14
Tetrachloroethylene	0.0050	0.050
Trichloroethylene	0.0050	0.050
Vinyl chloride	0.0020	0.020
Dichloromethane	0.0050	0.050
1,1,2-Trichloroethane	0.0050	0.050
Pesticide		
2,4-D	0.070	0.70
Carbofuran	0.040	0.40
Chlordane	0.0020	0.020
Diazinon	0.0050	0.050
Methamidophos	0.020	0.20
Paraquat	0.030	0.30
Parathion	0.022	0.22
Toxaphene	0.0030	0.030
Heavy metal		
Arsenic (As)	0.050	0.50
Cadmium (Cd)	0.0050	0.050
Chromium (Cr)	0.050	0.50
Cooper (Cu)	1.0	10
Lead (Pb)	0.050	0.50
Mercury (Hg)	0.0020	0.020
Nickel (Ni)	0.10	1.0
Zinc (Zn)	5.0	50

Regulated Items	*Control Value (mg/L)*	
	Type I	*Type II*
Ordinary items		
Nitrate calculated by N	10	100
Nitrite calculated by N	1.0	10
Other pollutants		
Total Petroleum Hydrocarbon as Diesel; TPH_d	1.0	10
Cyanide calculated by CN^-	0.050	0.50

Source: https://oaout.epa.gov.tw/law/EngLawContent.aspx?lan=E&id=161.

3. Sediment

208. A less rigid regime is applied to sediment. Article 6, paragraph 5 of the Soil Act says, 'the industry competent authorities in charge of the water bodies of rivers, irrigation canals, lakes, reservoirs, and other specially designated surface water bodies officially announced by the central competent authority' shall *regularly test sediment quality*, and *submit the resulting data* to the central competent authority for future reference after performing a *comparative assessment of the sediment quality indicators*, and *publicly announce the state of the sediment quality*. After that, the central competent authority will *determine classified management* of and use restrictions on the sediment quality indicators. The detailed rules concerning the content of the sediment quality, time of reporting, and documents required are provided in the Administrative Ordinance. According to Article 4 of the Ordinance on Sediment Quality Indicators,[419] the monitoring materials involve heavy metals,[420] organic compounds,[421] pesticides[422] and other organic compounds.[423] There is a range from the ceiling limit to the lowest limit for the indicator set for each material. For example, the indicator for '1,2-Dichlorobenzene' under organic compounds is 12.2 and 0.68 milligrams/kilogram, respectively.

419. The Ordinance on Sediment Quality Indicators. TEPA, Huan-Shu-Tu-Tzu No. 1000116349 (4 Jan. 2012) (total seven articles). Available at: http://ivy5.epa.gov.tw/epalaw/search/LordiDispFull.aspx?ltype=14&lname=0250 (last visited 15 May 2022), at Art. 4.

420. *Ibid.*, Arsenic (As), Cadmium (Cd), Chromium (Cr), Cooper (Cu), Mercury (Hg), Nickel (Ni), Lead (Pb), and Zinc (Zn).

421. For example, 1,2-Dichlorobenzene,1,3-Dichlorobenzene, Hexachlorobenzene, Fluoranthene, Fluorene, Dibenzo(a,h)anthracene, Indeno(1,2,3-cd)pyrene, Naphthalene, Phenanthrene, Pyrene, Acenaphthene, Acenaphthylene, Chrysene, Benzo(a)anthracene, Benzo(a)pyrene, Benzo(b)fluoranthene, Benzo(g,h,i)perylene, Benzo(k)fluoranthene.

422. For example, Aldrin, Chlordane, DDT, 4,4'-Dichlorodiphenyl- trichloroethane, Dieldrin, Endrin, Heptachlor, Toxaphene, and Endosulfan.

423. For example, Dioxins, (DEHP) [Di(2-ethylhexyl)phthalate], (DBP)(Di-n-butyl phthalate), DEP (Diethyl phthalate), BBP(Butyl benzyl phthalate), and Polychlorinated biphenyls.

4. Administrative Inspection Power

209. To acquire the necessary monitoring data, this Act also empowers competent authorities to enter public or private premises.[424] Once the pollution may affect human health, agricultural or aquacultural production, or drinking water sources, the authorities are also authorised to take appropriate remedial actions.[425]

II. The Behaviour Regulation of the 'Specified Industry' under Articles 8 and 9

210. To deal with the pollution issue in a more comprehensive manner, the main actor which may potentially cause pollution should also be included under the control regime. Under this act, the specified business/industry is required to provide soil pollution assessment investigation and test data or site soil pollution assessment investigation and test data.

211. According to Article 8, paragraph 1, if land used by a specified industry/business is *transferred*, the assignor is required to provide soil pollution assessment investigation and test data, which will then be reported to the special municipality, county, or city competent authority for future reference. The Ordinance defines a specified industry/business as detailed in Table 14.[426]

Table 14 Enterprises under Article 8, paragraph 1 of the Soil Act

Enterprise	
Factories where plant buildings, other associated facilities, and vacant land occupy an area of 100 square metres or greater	Leather and fur finishing industry
Petroleum and coal product manufacturing industry	
Basic chemical materials manufacturing industry	
Petrochemical raw materials manufacturing industry	
Synthetic resin and plastic manufacturing industry	
Synthetic rubber manufacturing industry	

424. The Soil and Groundwater Pollution Remediation Act, at Art. 7, para. 1, 'Competent authorities at all levels may dispatch personnel bearing identification documents to enter public or private premises for the following verification work and may order site users, managers or owners to provide related data.'

425. *Ibid.*, at Art. 7, para. 4, 'If a competent authority at any level discovers during the course of verification work that pollution of soil, sediment, or groundwater may affect human health, agricultural or aquacultural production, or drinking water sources, it may *adopt necessary response measures* in accordance with Art. 15, para. 1; and in order to mitigate the effect of pollution or prevent the expansion of pollution, it may *order* a polluter, potential polluter, or site user, manager, or owner to *implement the necessary response measures* in Art. 15, para. 1, subparas 3, 4, 7, and 8.'

426. *Ibid.*, at Art. 8, para. 1.

Enterprise	
Artificial fibre manufacturing industry	
Pesticide and environmental sanitation agent manufacturing industry	
Plastic sheets, panels, tubing, and imitation leather product manufacturing industry	
Steel refining industry	
Metal surface treatment industry	
Semiconductor manufacturing industry	
Printed circuit board manufacturing industry	
Battery manufacturing industry	
Electric power supply industry	
Gas station industry	
Waste disposal industry	
Factories where plant buildings, other associated facilities, and vacant land occupy an area of more than 100 square metres	Materials manufacturing industry
Fertilizer manufacturing industry	
Coating, dye and pigment manufacturing industry	
Steel casting industry	
Aluminium smelting industry	
Aluminium casting industry	
Copper smelting industry	
Copper casting industry	
Metal heat treatment industry	
Passive electronic components industry	
Materials and components industry	
Waste recycling and disposal industry	
Petroleum industry storage and transfer sites	

(*Source*: Official Announcement of Enterprises in Article 8, paragraph 1 of the Soil and Groundwater Pollution Remediation Act (1 March 2011)).

212. Under Article 9, a specified business that engages in any concerning behaviour[427] is required to 'submit site soil pollution assessment investigation and test data prior to the action in question, and shall request the special municipality,

427. For example, 'acquisition of an enterprise establishment license or registration, or application for a business license, in accordance with law'; 'change of business operator'; 'change of industry category (However, enterprises whose industry category before and after the change is one which has

county, or city competent authority, or an agency commissioned by the central competent authority, to perform review'. Another Ordinance further defines a specified business, as shown in Table 15.[428]

Table 15 Enterprises under Article 9 of the Soil Act

Enterprise	
Factories where plant buildings, other associated facilities, and vacant land occupy an area of 100 square metres or greater	Leather and fur finishing industry
Petroleum and coal product manufacturing industry	
Basic chemical materials manufacturing industry	
Petrochemical raw materials manufacturing industry	
Synthetic resin and plastic manufacturing industry	
Synthetic rubber manufacturing industry	
Artificial fibre manufacturing industry	
Pesticide and environmental sanitation agent manufacturing industry	
Plastic sheets, panels, tubing, and imitation leather product manufacturing industry	
Steel refining industry	
Metal surface treatment industry	
Semiconductor manufacturing industry	
Printed circuit board manufacturing industry	
Battery manufacturing industry	
Electric power supply industry	
Gas station industry	
Waste disposal industry	
Factories where plant buildings, other associated facilities, and vacant land occupy an area of more than 100 square metres	Materials manufacturing industry
Fertilizer manufacturing industry	
Coating, dye and pigment manufacturing industry	
Steel casting industry	

been officially announced by the central competent authority shall be exempt from this requirement)'; 'change of scope of operating site'; or 'implementation, in accordance with law, of termination of business, cancellation of operating permit or business license, termination of operation (shipping), plant (facility) closure, or discontinuation of production, manufacturing, or processing'.

428. The Soil and Groundwater Pollution Remediation Act, at Art. 9.

Enterprise
Aluminium smelting industry
Aluminium casting industry
Copper smelting industry
Copper casting industry
Metal heat treatment industry
Passive electronic components industry
Materials and components industry
Waste recycling and disposal industry
Petroleum industry storage and transfer sites

(*Source*: Official Announcement of Enterprises in Article 9 of the Soil and Groundwater Pollution Remediation Act (3 January 2011)).

III. Professionalism and Expertise Requirement

213. During the monitoring process, related data must be sound. To increase the credibility of the analysis, when soil, sediment, and groundwater pollution investigation or remediation work is performed, or soil and groundwater pollution test data is provided or submitted, the soil, sediment and groundwater pollutant testing shall be conducted by an *analysis organisation* that was approved by the central competent authority.[429] Further rules concerning the management of analysis organisation are provided in a special Ordinance.[430] Thus, only the professional analysis organisation identified in the Ordinance and approved by the EPA can be qualified to carry out the analysis.

214. In addition to the professional organisation requirement, there is also a requirement to maintain professional, skilled, and licensed staff. All documents provided or submitted in accordance with the Act, including *pollution control plans, pollution remediation plans, assessment investigation data, and pollution investigation and assessment plans*, must be certified by a *legally registered and practising environmental engineer, applied geological engineer, or other relevant professional engineer.*[431]

IV. Monitoring Wells and the Coordination of Information

215. Monitoring work requires the collection of related data on underground water and soil. Thus, there are additional regulations in detailed Ordinances on the siting, management, and decommissioning of related wells.[432]

429. *Ibid.*, at Art. 10.
430. Ordinance on the Management of Environmental Inspection Institutes (20 Mar. 2013).
431. The Soil and Groundwater Pollution Remediation Act, at Art. 11.
432. Ordinances on the siting of related wells for ground water monitoring. TEPA, Huan-Shu-Shuei-Tzu No. 0910091877 (27 Dec. 2002). Terminated by TEPA, Huan-Shu-Shuei-Tzu No. 1030016318

216. In fact, there are also other related authorities conducting monitoring work of soil and underground water. Therefore, under the Ordinance of Integration of Soil and Underground Water Information,[433] the EPA seeks to integrate the soil and underground water information of central and local environmental authorities, including the Industrial Agency of the Ministry of Economic Affairs, Management Agency of Scientific Parks under the National Science Council, the Environmental Science Park of the Municipal Government, and the Agriculture Technology Park of the Agriculture Council (AC) of the Executive Yuan, etc.

§4. INVESTIGATION AND ASSESSMENT MEASURES: REGULATIONS ON DESIGNATED 'CONTROL' AND 'REMEDIATION' SITES

217. After analysing the data collected during the previous phase, the authorities will intervene and require *potential polluters* to fulfil the appropriate requirements. At this stage, the role of the authorities is to identify the potentially polluted site[434] and designate it according to its pollution status. Following this, *the polluters or potential polluters* will bear the responsibility of drafting related plans to control or remedy the pollution.

I. Control Sites

218. Once there is a clear source of soil or groundwater pollution, and it is determined that the concentrations of pollutants *exceed* the relevant standards,[435] the special municipality, county, or city competent authority must publicly declare the site a soil and groundwater pollution *control site* (control site); further regulations on

(25 Feb. 2014). Available at: http://ivy5.epa.gov.tw/epalaw/search/LordiDispFull.aspx?ltype=06&lname=1400 (last visited 15 May 2022) and Ordinances on the siting and management of related wells for ground water monitoring. TEPA, Huan-Shu-Tu-Tzu No. 0990036323 (26 Apr. 2010). Available at: http://ivy5.epa.gov.tw/epalaw/search/LordiDispFull.aspx?ltype=14&lname=3200 (last visited 15 May 2022); and Ordinances on the decommission of related wells for ground water monitoring. TEPA, Huan-Shu-Tu-Tzu No. 0990036371 (26 Apr. 2010). Available at: http://ivy5.epa.gov.tw/epalaw/search/LordiDispFull.aspx?ltype=14&lname=3210 (last visited 15 May 2022).

433. Ordinance on Integration of Soil and Underground Water Information. TEPA, Huan-Shu-Tu-Tzu No. 0990109502 (2 Dec. 2010). Available at: http://ivy5.epa.gov.tw/epalaw/search/LordiDispFull.aspx?ltype=14&lname=3240 (last visited 15 May 2022).

434. The Soil and Groundwater Pollution Remediation Act, at Art. 12, para. 1, 'Competent authorities at all levels shall perform verification of sites suspected of having soil or groundwater pollution, and shall control pollution sources and investigate the state of environmental pollution in accordance with relevant environmental protection laws and regulations.'

435. The Soil and Groundwater Pollution Remediation Act, at Art. 12, para. 2.

this are provided in a detailed Ordinance.[436] After declaring a control site, the special municipality, county, or city competent authority must request that the land registration agency with local jurisdiction enter the site into the *land register.*[437] Following this, the *related plans and task controls* will come into play: the special municipality, county, or city competent authority, or central competent authority, will invite experts, scholars, and relevant agencies to help review and supervise the related *investigation plan, control plan, remediation plan, and health risk assessment and verification tasks.*[438]

II. Remediation Sites

219. If the site *severely endangers public health and the living environment*, the first step is to request approval from the central competent authority to publicly declare the site to be a soil and groundwater pollution remediation site (remediation site), and further regulations on this are provided in a detailed Ordinance.[439] The special municipality, county, or city competent authority also has similar duties to those of the *land register.*[440] Similar plans and task controls will also be introduced, including *investigation plans, control plans, remediation plans and health risk assessment and verification tasks.*[441]

220. In addition, an extra plan control regime is introduced due to the higher EHS (environment, health and safety) effects of this remediation site. Within three months of receiving a notification from the special municipality, county, or city competent authority, the remediation site polluter or potential polluter must submit a soil and groundwater pollution investigation and assessment plan and then implement the plan once it is approved.[442] If the remediation site polluter or potential polluter is not clearly known or has failed to comply with the actions, the special municipality, county, or city competent authority may notify *the interested party of the polluted land* to submit the plan.

221. Finally, for a remediation site, the government can enforce certain orders to *prohibit changing land ownership.*[443]

436. Ordinance on the Evaluation of the Designation of a Control Site for Soil and Ground Water Pollution. Terminated by TEPA, Huan-Shu-Tu-Tzu No. 1020031936F (24 Apr. 2013). Available at: http://ivy5.epa.gov.tw/epalaw/search/LordiDispFull.aspx?ltype=14&lname=0170 (last visited 15 May 2022).
437. The Soil and Groundwater Pollution Remediation Act, at Art. 12, para. 3.
438. *Ibid.*, at Art. 12, para. 13.
439. Ordinance on the Designation of Remediation Sites. TEPA, Huan-Shu-Tu-Tzu No. 0920031827 (7 May 2003). Available at: http://ivy5.epa.gov.tw/docfile/140160.pdf (last visited 15 May 2022).
440. The Soil and Groundwater Pollution Remediation Act, at Art. 12, para. 3.
441. *Ibid.*, at Art. 12, para. 13.
442. *Ibid.*, at Art. 14, para. 1.
443. *Ibid.*, at Art. 21 'Special municipality, county, or city competent authorities shall entrust registration competent authorities with local jurisdiction with registration of the prohibition of transactions regarding land that is a remediation site. When compulsory auction procedures have been implemented for the land, such procedures may be cancelled.'

222. Even if sites are not publicly declared to be remediation sites by the competent authorities, they may still be held to additional requirements or regulations. Mainly, a pollution control plan regime should be in place. The special municipality, county, or city competent authority can order the polluter or potential polluter to complete an investigation within six months and draft a *pollution control plan*, which is then to be implemented after being submitted to and receiving the approval of the special municipality, county, or city competent authority.[444] However, if the polluter or potential polluter is not clearly known or has failed to draft a pollution control plan, the special municipality, county, or city *competent authority* may take *appropriate measures*.[445]

§5. Regulatory Measures for Control Sites and Remediation Sites

223. After declaring a site to be a control or remediation site, the municipal competent authority is authorised to take certain actions to regulate them.

I. Competent Authorities

224. First, the competent authorities are empowered to *take action to alleviate the pollution situation*, including:[446]

(1) Ordering *polluters* to cease activities, suspend business activities, or partially or completely suspend work.
(2) Investigating groundwater pollution circumstances pursuant to the Water Pollution Control Act and identifying those who are liable for the pollution; if necessary, they may inform residents to stop using the groundwater or other polluted water sources and restrict the digging of wells to obtain groundwater.
(3) Providing necessary alternative drinking water or notifying tap water authorities to provide access to a tap water supply as a priority. (Special municipality, county, or city competent authorities may order the polluter, potential polluter, or interested party of the polluted land, or commission a third party, to implement the necessary response measures.).
(4) Erecting notification signs or fences. (Special municipality, county, or city competent authorities may order the polluter, potential polluter, or interested party of the polluted land, or commission a third party, to implement the necessary response measures).
(5) In conjunction with the agriculture and health competent authority, performing testing of agricultural or aquacultural products contaminated by or suspected of being contaminated by soil pollution and, when necessary, control or destroy contaminated products and provide appropriate compensation as well as restrict the use of agricultural land to the cultivation of specific crops.

444. *Ibid.*, at Art. 13, para. 1.
445. *Ibid.*, at Art. 13, para. 2.
446. *Ibid.*, at Art. 15, para. 1.

(6) Evacuating residents or controlling activities of the general public.
(7) Removing or disposing of pollutants. (Special municipality, county, or city competent authorities may order the polluter, potential polluter, or interested party of the polluted land, or commission a third party, to implement the necessary response measures).
(8) Other response measures as necessary. (Special municipality, county, or city competent authorities may order the polluter, potential polluter, or interested party of the polluted land, or commission a third party, to implement the necessary response measures).

II. Control Zone

225. Furthermore, within the declared Control and Remediation Site, the municipal authority can also further announce soil and groundwater pollution control zones (control zone).[447] In these zones, the municipal authority is authorised to take further aggressive measures to control and remedy the pollutants by designating the following:

(1) Prohibited behaviour in the soil and groundwater pollution control zones:[448] putting pollutants into soil; injecting wastewater and sewage into a groundwater body; discharging wastewater and sewage into soil; other controlled activities officially announced by the competent authority.
(2) Prohibited behaviour in the soil pollution control zones:[449] development actions prescribed in the Environmental Impact Assessment Act; new construction, extension, alteration, renovation, or demolition of buildings or facilities not required in a pollution control plan, pollution remediation plan, or other pollution improvement plans; other land use activities that have been designated by the central competent authority as affecting the health and living environment of residents.
(3) Prohibited behaviour in the groundwater pollution control zones:[450] a special municipality, county, or city competent authority may prohibit the drinking or use of groundwater, or utilisation as a drinking water source, within a groundwater pollution control zone.
(4) Prohibited agriculture-related behaviours in the zones.[451]

447. *Ibid.*, at Art. 16.
448. *Ibid.*, at Art. 17, para. 1.
449. *Ibid.*, at Art. 17, para. 2.
450. *Ibid.*, at Art. 17, para. 3.
451. *Ibid.*, at Art. 18, 'Special municipality, county, or city competent authorities shall jointly survey agricultural actions within pollution control zones in conjunction with agricultural and health agencies. When necessary, the special municipality, county, or city competent authority may prohibit the growing of edible crops, the raising of poultry or livestock, or the cultivating or harvesting of marine animals and plants within the pollution control zone.'

(5) The additional requirement of *clean-up or pollution prevention plans* for those engaging in the excavation, backfill, temporary storage, and transport of soil or groundwater extraction within a pollution control zone.[452]

III. Compensation Scheme

226. Finally, the rights of the interested party of the polluted land, i.e., the land user, manager or owner, may be limited in the soil and groundwater pollution control zones. They may request compensation from the polluter.[453]

§6. Remediation and Restoration Measures for Remediation Sites

I. Remediation Plan

227. As there are more EHS-related concerns generated by remediation sites than control sites, there are additional rules created to facilitate their remediation. The responsible authorities include mainly municipal authorities and land use authorities. The key regulatory tool at this phase is the remediation plan. The primary drafter of this plan is the *polluter or the potential responsible polluter* for the remediation site.[454] If there are multiple *polluters, potential polluters or interested parties of the polluted land*, they may jointly submit a soil and groundwater pollution remediation plan.[455]

228. However, if the identity of the remediation site polluter or potential polluter is not clear or if they have failed to comply with the actions, *the special municipality, county, or city competent authority* can draft a soil and groundwater pollution remediation plan that is intended to reduce pollution and prevent threats to citizens' health and living environment based on its financial status and the technical feasibility of remediation.[456] The responsible governmental authority must follow very stringent procedural rules to ensure the appropriateness of these plans.[457] When approving these types of soil and groundwater pollution remediation plans,

452. *Ibid.*, at Art. 19, para. 1.
453. *Ibid.*, at Art. 20.
454. *Ibid.*, at Art. 22, para. 1, 'A remediation site polluter or potential polluter shall submit a soil and groundwater pollution remediation plan pursuant to the investigation and assessment results in Article 14 within six months after notification by the special municipality, county, or city competent authority, and shall implement this plan after approval by the special municipality, county, or city competent authority.'
455. *Ibid.*, at Art. 22, para. 5.
456. *Ibid.*, at Art. 22, para. 2.
457. *Ibid.*, at Art. 23, 'Before granting the approval of a soil and groundwater pollution remediation plan described in the previous article, competent authorities at all levels shall display or post the soil and groundwater pollution remediation plan at a proper place for at least fifteen (15) days. Anyone who has comments on the plan set forth in the foregoing paragraph shall submit such comments in writing to the competent authorities at all levels within twenty (20) days after the display or posting of the plan as prescribed in the foregoing paragraph.'

competent authorities may, in accordance with the state of the environment, order *the remediation plan implementer* to submit *risk management methods* as well as *a soil and groundwater pollution control plan.*[458]

229. In terms of the content of these plans, it is essential that the 'soil and groundwater pollution "*remediation goal*" must be to reduce pollutant concentrations to less than soil and groundwater pollution control standards'.[459] If the remediation goals cannot reduce the concentrations to below the pollution control standards, a higher soil and groundwater pollution remediation goal is possible.[460] Similar to the procedural rules for the plans set by the municipal authorities, these goals are subject to rigid procedural rules (e.g., a mandatory public hearing requirement).[461]

230. The *developmental use of land* that has been designated as a remediation site may not be changed after approval of the remediation goals. Any changes in developmental use may be implemented only after requesting and obtaining the approval of the central competent authority in consultation with relevant agencies, and its changes must be in accordance with other laws and regulations.[462]

II. Ensuring the Plan Success

231. After this lengthy process, the plan and target will be finalised and proposed. To implement the plan, the polluters, potential polluters, interested parties of the polluted land or the user, administrator or owner of the land within the soil pollution or groundwater pollution control area shall cooperate to implement the plan.[463] To confirm compliance, competent authorities at all levels may conduct administrative inspections by dispatching identified personnel to the site to investigate or order that any necessary materials be produced. Evasion, obstruction or refusal is prohibited.[464]

---

458. *Ibid.*, at Art. 24, para. 7.
459. *Ibid.*, at Art. 24, para. 1.
460. *Ibid.*, at Art. 24, para. 2, 'With regard to the soil and groundwater pollution remediation plan in the foregoing paragraph, if factors such as the geological conditions, pollutant characteristics, or pollution remediation technologies preclude remediation until pollutant concentrations are less than soil and groundwater pollution control standards, soil and groundwater pollution remediation goals based on environmental impact and health risk assessment results may be submitted after requesting and obtaining the central competent authority's approval.'
461. *Ibid.*, at Art. 24, para. 5 & para. 6, 'Competent authorities must hold public hearings before approving remediation plans containing goals that are not less than control standards. In the foregoing paragraph, the central competent authority shall determine hearing holding procedures and relevant binding matters.' For further detailed rules, *see* the Ordinance on Public Hearings of Soil and Ground Water Pollution Site Remediation. (Amended on 2 Feb. 2012).
462. *Ibid.*, at Art. 24, para. 4.
463. *Ibid.*, at Art. 25.
464. *Ibid.*

232. If the plan is successfully implemented and the concentrations of soil and groundwater pollutants at a control site or remediation site are less than the control standards as a result of the adoption of appropriate measures or the implementation of a control plan or remediation plan, *the implementer of the appropriate measures or plan* shall *request* that the special municipality, county, or city competent authority or central competent authority grant approval.[465] Subsequently, because there are fewer EHS concerns about the remediation sites, the competent authority must return the land use to its original status in a less regulated manner.[466]

§7. Other Regulatory Measures

I. Financial Mechanisms

233. Since the prevention measures and related control and remediation measures require a great deal of financial support to perfect, a sound funding scheme is necessary. In the act, a special fund called the Soil and Groundwater Pollution Remediation Fund is created by levying soil and groundwater pollution remediation fees on *manufacturers and importers in accordance with the amounts of officially announced chemical substances* that have been *manufactured and imported by such enterprises.*[467] The official use of such funds is to improve the soil and groundwater

465. *Ibid.*, at Art. 26, para. 1.

466. *Ibid.*, at Art. 26, para. 2, 'The following matters shall be performed after the special municipality, county, or city competent authority, or central competent authority, grants its approval:

(1) Publicly announce the cancellation of the control or regulatory listing of the control site or remediation site implemented pursuant to Article 12, paras 2 and 3, and cancellation of reading.
(2) Officially announce the removal or modification of the delineation of the soil pollution or groundwater pollution control area as set forth in Article 16; and
(3) Request the land registration agency with local jurisdiction to revoke the control site or remediation site registration implemented pursuant to Article 12, para. 3 and registration of prohibition of transactions regarding the land implemented pursuant to Article 21'.; *See also*, Article 26, para. 4 of the Soil Act: 'For land that has been remediated, land use industry competent authorities shall, according to actual land use needs, carry out land use restoration matters.'

467. *Ibid.*, at Art. 28, para. 1, 'There are also other supplementary funding sources provided in Article 29:

(1) The amounts paid by polluters, potential polluters, and interested parties of the polluted land pursuant to Article 43 and Article 44.
(2) Payments from land developers pursuant to Article 51, para. 3
(3) Accrued interest income generated by the Fund.
(4) Funds appropriated through the budget process as determined by the central competent authority.
(5) Funds from the partial appropriation of relevant environmental protection funds.
(6) Funds from the partial appropriation of criminal and administrative fines for environmental pollution; and
(7) Other related income.'

quality.[468] The funding management is managed by a special funding management commission.[469] Further rules are provided in the administrative ordinances.[470]

---

468. *Ibid.*, at Art. 28, para. 3, 'The fund in the first paragraph shall be used for the following purposes:

(1) Expenditures made by competent authorities at all levels for verification, adoption of necessary response measures, supervision, and plan determination, review, investigation, assessment, implementation, and change pursuant to Article 7, para. 1 and 5; Article 12, para. 1, para. 5, 6, 8 through 10, and 13; Article 13, para. 1 and 2; Article 14, para. 1 and 3; Article 15; Article 22, para. 1, 2, and 4; Article 24, para. 3 through 5; and Article 27, para. 1 and 2.
(2) The fund's claims for relevant compensation and legal expenses.
(3) The fund's relevant personnel and administrative management expenses, personnel expenses incurred by soil and groundwater pollution prevention and remediation work.
(4) Expense of soil and groundwater pollution control work performed by competent authorities at all levels.
(5) Expense of audit of soil and groundwater pollution verification and implementation effectiveness.
(6) Expense relevant to international environmental protection work involving soil and groundwater pollution.
(7) Expense relevant to audits of soil and groundwater quality monitoring and implementation effectiveness.
(8) Expense relevant to levying soil and groundwater pollution remediation fees.
(9) Expense relevant to soil and groundwater pollution health risk assessment and management.
(10) Expense of researching, promoting, developing, and creating incentives for soil and groundwater pollution remediation technology.
(11) Matters concerning subsidies for soil and groundwater pollution prevention work; and
(12) To cover other costs in connection with soil pollution or groundwater pollution remediation approved by the central competent authority.'

469. *Ibid.*, at Art. 30, 'In the foregoing article, a fund management committee shall be established for the Soil and Groundwater Pollution Remediation Fund (termed management committee) to bear responsibility for fund management and use. The management committee may establish work and technical subcommittees to meet the following needs:

(1) Remediation site review pursuant to Article 12, para. 3.
(2) Assessment and clean-up priority ranking pursuant to Article 14 or Article 27.
(3) Review of expenses and costs for essential response measures.
(4) Review and approval of pollution remediation plan or remediation goals pursuant to Article 22, Article 24, or Article 27; and
(5) Other relevant matters regarding the review of appropriations from the Fund.'

470. Ordinance on the Collection and Spending of Soil and Groundwater Pollution Remediation Funds. Executive Yuan, Shiao-Shuo-San-Tzu No. 05020 (11 Jun. 2001). Amended by Executive Yuan,Yuan-Shuo-Chu-Shiao-Tzu No. 1000006957A (9 Nov. 2011). Available at: http://ivy5.epa.gov.tw/epalaw/search/LordiDispFull.aspx?ltype=14&lname=0100 (last visited 15 May 2022); and the Ordinance on Setting Soil and Groundwater Pollution Remediation Charge. TEPA, Huan-Shu-Shuei-Tzu No. 00687227 (29 Oct. 2001) (total ten articles). Amended by TEPA, Huan-Shu-Tu-Tzu No. 1000016896 (7 Mar. 2011). Available at: http://ivy5.epa.gov.tw/epalaw/search/LordiDispFull.aspx?ltype=14&lname=0110 (last visited 15 May 2022).

II. Liability of the Soil and Groundwater Polluters

A. The Responsibility for Clean-up Costs

234. When land is polluted, the involved authorities pay for certain costs first, and these payments pass on to the responsible parties later. According to Article 31, paragraph 1 of the act, joint payment responsibility is incurred if 'an interested party of the polluted land fails to demonstrate due diligence as a good manager'. This joint payment is the responsibility of the interested party as well as the polluter and/or the potential polluter.[471]

235. As the interested party of the polluted land may not be held liable for the pollution in certain cases, the act also allows the interested party to claim compensation from the polluter and/or the potential polluter.[472] Ultimately the duty to pay should be on the polluter; thus, the potential polluter can also seek compensation from the polluter.[473]

B. The Liability for Damage

236. The liability regime for damage is similar to the aforementioned clean-up cost regime. In general, there is joint liability for compensation by polluters, potential polluters and 'an interested party of the polluted land who has committed major negligence'.[474] However, the act allows the party mentioned to seek compensation from the polluter or potential polluter.[475]

237. Finally, this act may apply retrospectively in certain cases. When Polluters, potential polluters, and shareholders who have a controlling interest or more than half the shares of a company cause soil or groundwater pollution, they may be held liable in certain cases that occurred before this act was effective.[476]

---

471. The Soil and Groundwater Pollution Remediation Act, at Art. 31, 'If an interested party of the polluted land fails to demonstrate due diligence as a good manager, that party shall bear responsibility for expenditures made by competent authorities at all levels pursuant to Article 13, para. 2; Article 14, para. 3; Article 15; Article 22, para. 2 and 4; and Article 24, para. 3, and the polluter and potential polluter shall bear joint payment responsibility.'
472. *Ibid.*, at Art. 31, para. 2, 'An interested party of the polluted land may seek compensation from the polluter or potential polluter for the settlement costs in the foregoing paragraph and the expenditures in Article 14, para. 2 and Article 22, para. 3.'
473. *Ibid.*, at Art. 31, para. 3, 'The potential polluter may seek compensation for the expenditures in the foregoing paragraph from the polluter.'
474. *Ibid.*, at Art. 52, para. 1, 'When soil and groundwater pollution causes a third party to suffer damage, and there are *multiple polluters or potential polluters, the polluters or potential polluters* shall have joint liability for compensation for damages, likewise in the case of *an interested party of the polluted land who has committed major negligence*.'
475. *Ibid.*, at Art. 52, para. 2.
476. *Ibid.*, at Art. 53, 'Article 7, Article 12 to 15, Article 22, Article 24, Article 25, Article 37, Article 38, and Article 43, para. 1 to 3, para. 5, and para. 7 to 9 of the Act shall apply to polluters, potential polluters, and shareholders with a controlling interest or more than half the shares of a company causing soil or groundwater pollution that has occurred prior to the effective date of this Act.'

III. Public Benefit Litigation Clause

238. This act allows *victims or public interest groups* to launch lawsuits against the competent authorities to facilitate the enforcement of related provisions as long as the public or private premises violate the act or violate a legal order determined to be related to the authorisation of this act and that the competent authority is negligent in its enforcement.[477] A reimbursement regime is also applicable for the costs incurred by the victims or public interest groups to help create incentives to bring such lawsuits. The reimbursement includes the appropriate attorneys' fees, detection and appraisal fees and other litigation costs to plaintiffs that have made specific contributions to soil or groundwater pollution remediation.[478]

477. *Ibid.*, at Art. 54, para. 1, 'When public or private premises violate this Act or a legal order determined pursuant to the authorization of this Act and the competent authority is negligent in enforcement, victims or public interest groups may notify the competent authority in writing concerning the details of the negligent enforcement. When a competent authority has failed to carry out enforcement in accordance with the law within 60 days after receipt of the written notification, the victims or public interest groups may name the competent authority at issue as a defendant and file a lawsuit directly with an administrative court based on the negligent behaviour of the competent authority in the execution of its duties in order to seek a ruling ordering the competent authority to implement its duties.'

478. *Ibid.*, at Art. 54, para. 2.

Chapter 5. Marine Pollution Control

239. To control marine pollution, protect the marine environment, maintain its ecology, safeguard public health and sustainably use marine resources, the Marine Pollution Control Act (Marine Act) was promulgated on 1 November 2000 and revised once in 2014.[479] The marine area applied in this act refers to the intertidal zones, internal waters, territorial seas, contiguous zones, exclusive economic zones and waters superjacent to the continental shelf under the jurisdiction of the ROC.[480] But it can be expanded to cover circumstances in which the discharge of hazardous substances occurs in marine areas outside of the aforementioned areas.[481]

§1. Competent Authorities

240. The main competent authority of this Act is similar to other environmental legislations, i.e., EPA and local government.[482] The following authorities may also come into play under certain circumstances:

(1) The coast guard authority and military, customs or other government agency: The coast guard authority performs interdiction, collection of evidence or enforcement referral tasks implemented pursuant to this act. They may also request the assistance of the military, customs or other government agency in the performance of tasks.[483]
(2) Port management authorities and port industry competent authorities: All categories of port management authorities adopt measures in accordance with this act and other related regulations in order to prevent, eliminate and mitigate pollution in the port zones under their jurisdiction. They also provide guidance for pollution abatement in the port zones under their jurisdiction.[484]
(3) Financial Supervisory Commission: The central competent authority works with the Financial Supervisory Commission to determine the amount of the letter of financial guarantee or the maximum compensation liability of the liability insurance policy relating to the public or private premises that engage in oil conveyance, marine projects, marine dumping, marine incineration, or other activities.[485]
(4) Each industry competent authority may *restrict the use of a marine area.*[486]

241. Finally, to handle major marine pollution incidents, a special task force may be created in the cabinet. The Executive Yuan may also establish a major

479. Marine Pollution Control Act, Announced Date: 2000-11-01, Amended Date: 2014-06-04, available at: https://law.moj.gov.tw/ENG/LawClass/LawAll.aspx?pcode=O0040026.
480. Article 2(1) of the Marine Pollution Control Act.
481. Article 2(2) of the Marine Pollution Control Act.
482. Article 4(1) of the Marine Pollution Control Act.
483. Article 5 of the Marine Pollution Control Act.
484. Article 11 of the Marine Pollution Control Act.
485. Article 13(1) and (3) of the Marine Pollution Control Act.
486. Article 9(1) of the Marine Pollution Control Act.

marine pollution incident handling task force, and the EPA may establish a marine pollution incident handling work group.[487]

§2. Basic Measures

I. General Measures

242. The EPA considers marine conditions when they make determinations about *marine environment categories and marine environment quality standards.*[488] To protect the marine environment or meet the needs of the industry competent authority for special marine environments, the EPA may, in accordance with marine environment categories, quality standards, and characteristics, *delineate marine control zones and determine marine environment control standards*. They also issue official announcements and perform implementation after zone implementation plans and *pollution control measures* based on these zones and standards have been determined.[489] The pollution control measures announced and published by the EPA include the discharge of pollution, the use of toxicants or chemicals to catch or kill aquatic organisms, and other acts.[490]

243. Competent authorities at all levels, in accordance with marine environment categories, *instal marine environment monitoring stations or facilities* in their respective marine jurisdictions, publish official monitoring results at regular intervals, and adopt appropriate *control measures*; when necessary, each industry competent authority may *restrict the use of a marine area.*[491] Interfering with or damaging monitoring stations or facilities installed by competent authorities is prohibited.[492]

244. The marine polluter *bears responsibility for the clean-up* of marine environment pollution. The industry competent authority or competent authority may first adopt emergency measures and, when necessary, may perform clean-up and disposal work on behalf of the polluter. The polluter has to bear responsibility for all expenses generated by emergency measures or clean-up and disposal work.[493]

II. Major Marine Pollution Accident

245. The Executive Yuan has the ability to establish a *major marine pollution incident handling task force* to handle major marine pollution incidents; the EPA can establish a marine pollution incident handling work group to address general marine

487. Article 10(1) of the Marine Pollution Control Act.
488. Article 8(1) of the Marine Pollution Control Act.
489. Article 8(2) of the Marine Pollution Control Act.
490. Article 8(3) of the Marine Pollution Control Act.
491. Article 9(1) of the Marine Pollution Control Act.
492. Article 9(2) of the Marine Pollution Control Act.
493. Article 14(2) of the Marine Pollution Control Act.

pollution incidents.[494] The EPA also drafts *marine oil pollution emergency response plans* to handle major marine oil pollution emergencies and then submits these plans to the Executive Yuan for approval.[495]

III. Harbour Pollution

246. All categories of port management authorities shall adopt *measures to prevent, eliminate, and mitigate pollution in the port zones*[496] and all categories of port industry competent authorities shall provide guidance for *pollution abatement* in the port zones under their jurisdiction.[497]

IV. Ocean as the Final Disposal Site

247. Marine dumping fees are based on the category and quantity of the substance to be dumped and are collected from groups that receive EPA approval to use the sea as a final disposal site. Fees are placed in a special fund for management and use and are then given to be used to control, monitor, and dispose of marine pollution, restore the marine ecology and complete other marine environment protection tasks along with the associated research and training.[498]

V. Emergency Plan, Financial Guarantee or Insurance

248. Public or private premises that have been designated by the EPA and engage in oil conveyance, marine projects, marine dumping, marine incineration, or other activities that create pollution concerns are required to submit an *emergency response plan that is* sufficient to prevent and handle marine pollution as well as a *letter of financial guarantee or liability insurance policy* for the compensation of pollution damages. Only once these are done and they have received EPA approval may they engage in such activities.[499] Competent authorities at all levels may *demand that the public or private premises or other marine-related enterprises provide pollution handling equipment and professional technical personnel to assist with handling* when an emergency pollution incident occurs on the sea; the marine polluter shall bear responsibility for all necessary expenses. When necessary, the fund described above may be used to pay expenses and provide compensation that is sought from the marine polluter.[500]

---

494. Article 10(1) of the Marine Pollution Control Act.
495. Article 10(2) of the Marine Pollution Control Act.
496. Article 11(1) of the Marine Pollution Control Act.
497. Article 11(2) of the Marine Pollution Control Act.
498. Article 12(1) of the Marine Pollution Control Act.
499. Article 13(1) of the Marine Pollution Control Act.
500. Article 13(4) of the Marine Pollution Control Act.

IV. Exemption from Sanction

249. Groups that cause pollution through one of the circumstances listed below are not punished:[501]

(1) Fleeing disaster or insuring the safety of a ship, aircraft, seawall or other major structure.
(2) Acts involving national defence, natural disasters, war, or other acts performed in accordance with regulations or orders.
(3) Acts performed with the permission of the EPA to prevent, eliminate, or mitigate pollution, protect the environment, or complete special research.

§3. The Prevention of Pollution from Pollution Sources on Land

250. Public or private premises that fail to receive the permission of the EPA *may not discharge* wastewater or sewage into the sea or the following areas adjacent to the sea:[502]

(1) Nature reserves or ecological conservation areas.
(2) Ecological protection areas, significant scenic areas or recreation areas of national parks.
(3) Wildlife preserves.
(4) Aquaculture resource conservation areas.

251. Public or private premises are required to *adopt measures* to prevent, eliminate or mitigate pollution and to *promptly notify* competent authorities at all levels as well as industry competent authorities when serious marine pollution has occurred or may be occurring through marine discharge pipes, discharge points, waste dumps, or waste disposal sites.[503] The local competent authority then *completes necessary response measures*. When necessary, the EPA can adopt these measures directly; the public or private premises at issue shall bear *responsibility for all expenses* generated by response and handling measures.[504]

§4. The Prevention of Pollution from Marine Projects

252. Public or private premises that use marine facilities to engage in the exploration or extraction of oil, the conveyance of oil or chemical substances, or the discharge of wastewater or sewage shall first submit marine pollution control plans that specifically state the contents of marine pollution control tasks, marine monitoring, and emergency response measures, and other matters designated by the EPA, and

501. Article 14(1) of the Marine Pollution Control Act.
502. Article 15(1) of the Marine Pollution Control Act.
503. Article 16(1) of the Marine Pollution Control Act.
504. Article 16(2) of the Marine Pollution Control Act.

must receive its approval before they may engage in these activities.[505] The public or private premises have to continuously perform marine monitoring and regularly share their monitoring records with the EPA.[506] Those public or private premises that use marine facilities to engage in the exploration or extraction of oil or the conveyance of oil shall maintain records of exploration, extraction, or conveyance.[507]

253. Public or private premises may not discharge, spill, leak, or dump wastewater or sewage, oil, waste, hazardous substances or other polluting substances that have been designated and officially announced by the central competent authority into the sea.[508] The premises that have received permission to do so must maintain records of discharges[509] and keep them on file for at least ten years.[510]

254. Public or private premises that engage in marine projects that either cause serious marine pollution or create concerns about serious pollution have to promptly adopt measures designed to prevent, eliminate or mitigate pollution and share them with competent authorities and industry competent authorities.[511] In the circumstance noted in the previous paragraph, the competent authority can order that specific response measures occur and can handle them directly if necessary. The public or private premises at issue bear responsibility for all expenses generated by response and handling measures.[512]

§5. The Prevention of Pollution from the Disposal of Waste at Sea

255. Public or private premises that use ships, aircraft, marine facilities or other methods to engage in marine dumping or marine incineration have to apply for permission from the central competent authority.[513]

256. Marine dumping and marine incineration can only be performed in zones designated by the central competent authority. The central competent authority shall delineate and announce the marine dumping and incineration zones based on marine environment categories, quality standards, and water quality conditions.[514]

257. The central competent authority shall announce categories A, B, and C based on the impact on the marine environment.[515]

505. Article 17(1) of the Marine Pollution Control Act.
506. Article 17(2) of the Marine Pollution Control Act.
507. Article 17(2) of the Marine Pollution Control Act.
508. Article 18(1) of the Marine Pollution Control Act.
509. Article 18(2) of the Marine Pollution Control Act.
510. Article 18(3) of the Marine Pollution Control Act.
511. Article 19(1) of the Marine Pollution Control Act.
512. Article 19(2) of the Marine Pollution Control Act.
513. Article 20 of the Marine Pollution Control Act.
514. Article 21 of the Marine Pollution Control Act.
515. Article 22 of the Marine Pollution Control Act.

- Category A substances may not be dumped in the sea; permission must be obtained from the central competent authority each time.
- Category B substances are to be dumped.
- Category C substances may be dumped only during the specified time period and within the total quantity limits permitted by the central competent authority.

258. The managers of ships, aircraft, or marine facilities that engage in marine dumping or incineration shall keep records of their activities. These must be regularly reported to the central competent authority, and they must allow for verification.[516]

259. Public or private premises that cause serious marine pollution or concern of serious pollution because of their activities must adopt measures to prevent, eliminate or mitigate pollution and promptly notify competent authorities and industry competent authorities of these measures.[517] In the circumstance noted in the previous paragraph, the competent authority may order that necessary response measures be taken and may handle them directly; the public or private premises at issue will bear responsibility for all expenses generated by response and handling measures.[518]

260. The above regulations shall apply, where appropriate, to dumping in the sea by ships, aircraft, marine facilities, and other man-made structures.[519]

§6. The Prevention of Sea Pollution by Ships

261. Ships must be equipped with pollution prevention equipment and may not pollute the sea.[520] The wastewater or sewage, oil, waste and other polluting substances of a ship shall remain on board or be emitted into on-shore reception facilities unless the law allows them to do otherwise. All categories of port management authorities are required to instal reception facilities for the pollutants and may collect necessary handling expenses.[521] Ships loading, unloading, or transporting oil, chemical goods or other cargo that might cause sea pollution have to adopt appropriate emissions prevention measures.[522]

262. The port management authority may prohibit ships from sailing or setting sail if there is concern that the ship may cause pollution of the marine environment.[523] When necessary, the port management authority or enforcement authority

516. Article 23 of the Marine Pollution Control Act.
517. Article 24(1) of the Marine Pollution Control Act.
518. Article 24(2) of the Marine Pollution Control Act.
519. Article 25 of the Marine Pollution Control Act.
520. Article 26 of the Marine Pollution Control Act.
521. Article 29 of the Marine Pollution Control Act.
522. Article 30 of the Marine Pollution Control Act.
523. Article 27 of the Marine Pollution Control Act.

may, in conjunction with the central competent authority, examine the marine pollution prevention certificates or verification documents, operation manuals, oil, cargo records, and other designated documents of domestic and foreign ships.[524]

263. For those circumstances in which the construction, repair, demolition, salvage, or tank or cargo hold cleaning of a ship causes marine pollution or the concern of pollution, the following measures shall be adopted and polluting substances cleaned up:[525]

(1) Set up appropriate equipment for the containment or removal of floating oil on the surface of the waters surrounding work areas.
(2) Provide appropriate reception facilities in work areas for waste oils, wastewater or sewage, waste and other hazardous substances.
(3) Prevent the emission into the sea of oils, waste oils, wastewater or sewage, waste, residue and hazardous substances.
(4) Adopt other measures designated by the central competent authority.

264. When a ship suffers a maritime disaster or other accident which causes marine pollution or concern of pollution, the shipmaster and shipowner shall promptly adopt measures to prevent, eliminate or mitigate pollution and notify the local navigation and aviation competent authority, port management authority and local competent authority.[526] The competent authority may order that necessary response measures be taken, and when required, they may directly handle the response. The owner of the ship at issue shall bear responsibility for all expenses generated by response and handling measures.[527]

§7. Liability for Damage Compensation

265. The shipowner shall bear liability for compensation for the damage caused by the sea pollution caused by a ship.[528] If a ship has a gross tonnage of over 400 tonnes or of an oil tanker or chemical tanker with a gross tonnage of over 150 tonnes, the shipowner must purchase liability insurance or provide a guarantee based on the gross tonnage of the ship; this may not be suspended or terminated.[529] The designated shipowner includes the owner, lessee, agent, and operator of a ship.[530]

524. Article 28 of the Marine Pollution Control Act.
525. Article 31 of the Marine Pollution Control Act.
526. Article 32(1) of the Marine Pollution Control Act.
527. Article 32(2) of the Marine Pollution Control Act.
528. Article 33(1) of the Marine Pollution Control Act.
529. Article 33(2) of the Marine Pollution Control Act.
530. Article 33(4) of the Marine Pollution Control Act.

266. Claimants for compensation for pollution damage may seek compensation directly from the liability insurer or seek to secure the guarantee as compensation.[531]

267. The port management authority can prevent the ship and its crew from leaving the country before their liability obligations are fulfilled or if there is concern that they will not be fulfilled. This restriction does not apply to those who provide a guarantee.[532]

§8. Public Interest Litigation Clause

268. When public or private premises violate this act or related orders that are considered relevant to its authorisation, if the competent authority is negligent in enforcement, victims or public interest groups may notify the competent authority in writing regarding the details of the negligence. If enforcement, according to the law, has not been completed within sixty days after the complaint is received, the victims or public interest groups may name the competent authority as a defendant and directly file a lawsuit with an administrative court based on their negligent behaviour. The lawsuit can be designed to request that the competent authority carry out enforcement.[533] When issuing a verdict on such a lawsuit, the administrative court can order the defendant competent authority to reimburse the plaintiffs for the appropriate lawyer fees, detection and appraisal fees and other litigation costs.[534]

531. Article 34 of the Marine Pollution Control Act.
532. Article 35 of the Marine Pollution Control Act.
533. Article 59(1) of the Marine Pollution Control Act.
534. Article 59(2) of the Marine Pollution Control Act.

Chapter 6. Waste Disposal

§1. Definition of Waste

269. Waste legislation in Taiwan, i.e., the Waste Disposal Act (Waste Act), underwent a major revision in January 2017. Taiwan borrowed the ideas from the EU Waste Directive and changed the definition of waste, greatly expanding it. This caused the act to have a wider scope of applicability.

'Waste' means any movable solid or liquid substance or object:[535]

I. Which is discarded;
II. Whose original purpose is weakened, given up, no longer existing, or unclear;
III. Which results from construction, manufacturing, processing, repairing, selling, or other activities and is not deliberately created;
IV. Which results from a production process with no feasible technology existing and is of no economic or market value;
V. Which is announced as 'waste' by a central competent authority.

270. As there is an open clause ('which is announced as "waste" by a central competent authority') in this act, it is possible for its applicability to be uncertain. In addition, Article 2-1 of this act further expands the scope of waste, saying that: any product coming from industry activities shall be determined as waste when it is under any of the following circumstances:[536]

(i) The product is determined to have no economic or market value by the central competent authority and is intended to be disposed of illegally or harmful to the environment and human health.
(ii) The product is not lawfully stored or used and is intended to be disposed of illegally or to cause pollution.
(iii) The reuse product is not used in accordance with this act and is intended to be disposed of illegally or to cause pollution.

271. In this regard, waste may become an uncertain concept which may be affected by market uncertainty, legal status, etc.

272. There are two types of waste in this act:[537] (i) General waste refers to waste that is not industrial waste. (ii) Industrial waste refers to waste that is produced from industry activities (but excluding waste generated by the employees themselves), including both hazardous and general industrial waste. Hazardous industrial waste

535. Article 2(1) of the Waste Disposal Act.
536. Article 2-1 of the Waste Disposal Act.
537. Article 2(2) of the Waste Disposal Act.

is produced by an industry and is toxic or dangerous with a concentration or volume sufficient to influence human health or pollute the environment. General industrial waste is waste produced by an industry that is not hazardous.

§2. Competent and Enforcement Authority

273. The institutional design to deal with waste management is very different from ordinary environmental law and general administrative law. Usually, one ministry, i.e., the EPA, bears the main responsibility, and it may be assisted by the environmental bureau of the local government. The competent authority clause of this act follows this idea by saying that: 'Competent authority' as referred to in this act means the EPA, Executive Yuan, at the central government level, the municipal government in special municipalities and the county or city government in counties or cities.[538]

274. However, in Article 5 of this act, the unique concept of '*Enforcement authority*' is created. Enforcement authority, as referred there, means the environmental protection bureau of a special municipality government, of a county or city government, or the public office of a rural township, urban township, or city.[539] The enforcement authority can establish dedicated units for the performance of recycling, clearance, disposal, and waste investigation work for general waste.[540] The enforcement authority is also responsible for planning what land will be used for recycling, clearance, and disposal of general waste and shall coordinate with and grant preference to the relevant agencies for the land acquisition.[541] The recycling, clearance, and disposal of general waste shall be performed by the environmental protection bureau of the special municipality government in special municipalities and by the environmental protection bureau of the provincial city in provincial cities. In counties, the recycling and clearance of general waste shall be performed by the public office of a rural township, urban township, or city, and the disposal of general waste shall be performed by the environmental protection bureau of the county. When necessary, the county may commission the public office of a rural township, urban township, or city to perform disposal work.[542]

275. A wide range of administrative inspection powers has been conferred to competent enforcement authorities to improve the enforcement of the Waste Act. The competent authority may, on its own or through a commissioned enforcement authority, dispatch personnel bearing identification documents to *enter public or private premises* or intercept waste or surplus earth and gravel clearance equipment to perform inspection or sampling of waste storage, clearance, disposal or reuse circumstances and order the provision of relevant information. Waste or surplus earth

538. Article 4 of the Waste Disposal Act.
539. Article 5(1) of the Waste Disposal Act.
540. Article 5(2) of the Waste Disposal Act.
541. Article 5(3) of the Waste Disposal Act.
542. Article 5(4) of the Waste Disposal Act.

and gravel clearance equipment must carry vehicle verification documents that record the production source and disposal site of the waste or surplus earth and gravel and allow for these to be inspected.[543] If a competent authority or the commissioned enforcement authority performs an inspection and finds one of the circumstances listed below, they may *detain the clearance or disposal facilities or equipment* and may *order their owner or user* to perform clearance or disposal by a specific deadline. When necessary, the property or real estate of the owner may be used or have its use restricted, or the necessary tap water, electricity, or other power source of the place of business may be cut off as punishment:[544]

(i) There is a concern about serious pollution from the waste, surplus earth and gravel, clearance equipment or disposal facilities, or the equipment on public or private premises.
(ii) There is a concern about serious pollution from the waste or surplus earth and gravel carried by clearance equipment.

§3. The Disposal of General Waste

I. Distribution of Cleaning Responsibility

276. With the exception of general waste that shall be cleared pursuant to the following regulations, general waste in designated clearance areas shall be cleared by the enforcement authority:[545]

(i) For land or buildings related to public sanitation, the owner, manager, or user shall perform clearance.
(ii) For covered walkways or sidewalks connected to land or buildings, the owner, manager, or user of the land or building at issue shall perform clearance.
(iii) For roadways or public spaces that are used for special purposes, the user shall perform clearance.
(iv) For general waste abandoned and left on site by the owner after the occurrence of a fire or disaster, the building owner or manager shall perform clearance; for those lacking the capacity to perform clearance, the enforcement authority must complete it for them.
(v) For general waste left after the demolition of a building, the original owner, manager, or user shall perform clearance.
(vi) For the excrement and urine of livestock or poultry on roadways or other public premises, the owner or manager shall perform clearance.
(vii) For the sludge matter of septic tanks, the owner, manager, or user shall perform clearance.

543. Article 9(1) of the Waste Disposal Act.
544. Article 9(2) of the Waste Disposal Act.
545. Article 11 of the Waste Disposal Act.

(viii) For the road surfaces and drainage gutters of public lanes or alleys with widths of four metres or less, the households on opposite sides or adjacent sides shall each clear half.
(ix) For roadway traffic islands, greenbelts, parks and other public premises, the management organisation shall perform clearance.

II. Regulations

277. The *transport, sorting, storage, discharge, methods, equipment and reuse of general waste recycling, clearance and disposal* shall comply with the regulations of the central competent authority.[546] The enforcement authority may, based on the special characteristics of designated clearance areas, add general waste sorting, storage, and discharge regulations, and shall report these to the higher competent authority for future reference.[547]

278. Enforcement authorities at all levels shall, based on actual needs, *instal general waste recycling and storage equipment* at appropriate locations and public premises.[548] The enforcement authority shall be responsible for *the clearance of general waste* and shall perform appropriate *sanitary disposal.* However, for general waste produced outside of households, the enforcement authority may designate clearance methods and disposal premises.[549]

III. Recycle

A. Regulated Objects

279. For articles and the packaging and containers thereof that, after consumption or use, are sufficient to produce general waste that possesses one of the following characteristics and causes concern that they may create serious environmental pollution, the manufacturer or importer of the articles and the packaging and containers thereof, or the manufacturer or importer of the raw materials bears responsibility for recycling, clearance, and disposal, and the vendor bears responsibility for recycling, clearance work that is:[550]

(i) Difficult to clear or dispose of.
(ii) Contains a component that does not readily decompose over a long period.
(iii) Contains a component that is a hazardous substance.
(iv) Is valuable for recycling and reuse.

546. Article 12(1) of the Waste Disposal Act.
547. Article 12(2) of the Waste Disposal Act.
548. Article 13 of the Waste Disposal Act.
549. Article 14 of the Waste Disposal Act.
550. Article 15(1) of the Waste Disposal Act.

B. Regulation

280. For general waste that is produced after the consumption or use of the articles or the packaging and containers are officially announced (herein referred to as 'regulated recyclable waste'), *recycling, storage, clearance, and disposal* shall comply with the regulations of the central competent authority.[551]

281. A responsible enterprise designated and officially announced by the central competent authority must *mark articles or the packaging and containers* thereof with relevant recycling labels.[552] A vendor of articles or the packaging and containers that are designated and officially announced by the central competent authority must, in accordance with the regulations of the central competent authority, *instal resource recycling facilities and perform recycling work.*[553]

282. For those articles or the packaging and containers for which there is a concern of serious pollution to the environment, the central competent authority may *officially announce the prohibition of use or the restriction of manufacturing, import, sales and use.*[554]

283. The central competent authority may designate and officially announce categories of regulated recyclable waste to be recycled through *recycling incentive methods* and the monetary amounts of recycling incentives.[555] A vendor shall pay consumers in accordance with the officially announced monetary amounts of recycling incentives and *may not refuse* to do so.[556]

C. Fee and Fund

284. The enterprises responsible for recycling, clearance, and disposal (herein referred to as the responsible enterprises) shall register with the competent authority. A manufacturer, based on the manufacturing volume for the current quarter, and an importer, based on the import volume reported to customs, have to pay *recycling, clearance and disposal fees* within fifteen days after the reporting and payment of business taxes every quarter. Fees are calculated according to rates approved by the central competent authority; these fees shall be used for the Resource Recycling Management Fund, and a financial institution shall be commissioned for the collection and safekeeping of the fees.[557]When an importer reports its import volume to customs, it has to also report container materials and other specifications of articles and containers as designated by the central competent

551. Article 18(1) of the Waste Disposal Act.
552. Article 19(1) of the Waste Disposal Act.
553. Article 19(2) of the Waste Disposal Act.
554. Article 21 of the Waste Disposal Act.
555. Article 22(1) of the Waste Disposal Act.
556. Article 22(2) of the Waste Disposal Act.
557. Article 16(1) of the Waste Disposal Act.

authority.[558] For fee rates, the Resource Recycling Fee Rate Review Committee established by the central competent authority shall perform reviews *based on materials, volumes, weights, impacts on the environment, reuse values, recycling, clearance and disposal costs, recycling, clearance and disposal ratios, auditing and collection costs, fund financial conditions, monetary amounts of recycling incentives, and other relevant factors* and submit its review to the central competent authority for approval and official announcement.[559]

285. The Resource Recycling Management Fund shall be used for the following purposes:[560]

(i) The payment of recycling, clearance and disposal subsidies.
(ii) The provision of subsidies and incentives for recycling systems and reuse.
(iii) The covering of expenses when the enforcement authority performs disposal on behalf of others.
(iv) The covering of auditing and certification expenses of the impartial auditing and certification group selected and commissioned by the central competent authority.

IV. Implementation of the Clearance and Disposal of General Waste by Special Municipality, County, or City Competent Authority

286. For the implementation of the clearance and disposal of general waste, a special municipality, county or city competent authority shall, based on clearance and disposal costs, *collect fees* from households and other non-industrial sources within designated clearance areas.[561] The special municipality, county or city competent authority may, in consideration of actual operational requirements, a*dd fee collection regulations other than those above and fee collection verification labels.*[562]

287. Costs related to general waste clearance and disposal include management costs, labour costs, land use costs for disposal sites and plants, compensation expenses, operational and maintenance costs and average annual procurement costs based on usage limits for all clearance and disposal machinery, equipment and facilities, and restoration costs, and shall deduct income from general industrial waste clearance and disposal work performed on behalf of others and other income.[563] Such fees are collected based on the actual costs, but fees for machinery, equipment, facilities and restoration costs have been collected annually since

558. Article 16(2) of the Waste Disposal Act.
559. Article 16(5) of the Waste Disposal Act.
560. Article 17(1) of the Waste Disposal Act.
561. Article 24(1) of the Waste Disposal Act.
562. Article 24(3) of the Waste Disposal Act.
563. Article 25(1) of the Waste Disposal Act.

2001.[564] The special municipality, county, or city competent authority shall collect fees annually from 2001 for the per kiloton construction costs and restoration costs of privately owned or operated general waste incinerators.[565]

V. Designated Clearance Areas

288. 'Designated clearance area' means a clearance area officially announced and designated by the enforcement authority based on environmental sanitation needs.[566]

289. The following acts are strictly prohibited within designated clearance areas:[567]

(i) Spitting phlegm, betel nut juice, or fibre, or the discarding of wastepaper, cigarette butts, chewing gum, fruit or the skin, pit or juice thereof, or other general waste.
(ii) Polluting the ground, pools of water, drainage gutters, walls, beams or pillars, utility poles, trees, roadways, bridges, or other fixed structures.
(iii) Sunning or piling of articles that hinder sanitation and orderliness on roadsides, outside of houses, or on roofs.
(iv) Collecting items from waste clearance, disposal or storage tools, equipment or sites of articles that have been discarded; however, the collection of general waste recycling items designated pursuant to Article 5, paragraph 6 is not restricted in this way.
(v) Discarding hot ashes or embers, dangerous chemical substances or products, explosive substances, or products within waste storage equipment.
(vi) Discarding animal corpses in places other than waste storage equipment.
(vii) Urinating or defecating in non-designated locations.
(viii) Discarding articles in drainage gutters.
(ix) Raising of poultry or livestock that hinders nearby environmental sanitation.
(x) Posting or painting of advertisements that pollutes fixed structures.

§4. Disposal of Industrial Waste

I. Waste Disposal Hierarchy

290. The disposal of industrial waste, except for reuse methods, shall be performed in accordance with the following methods:[568]

564. Article 26(1) of the Waste Disposal Act.
565. Article 26(2) of the Waste Disposal Act.
566. Article 3 of the Waste Disposal Act.
567. Article 27 of the Waste Disposal Act.
568. Article 28 of the Waste Disposal Act.

(i) Self-clearance and disposal.
(ii) Joint clearance and disposal, where enterprises apply to the industry competent authority for permission to establish a joint waste clearance and disposal organisation to clear and dispose of the relevant category of waste.
(iii) Commissioned clearance and disposal.[569]
(iv) Other methods that receive permission from the central competent authority.

II. Regulated Enterprise and Public Entities

291. Enterprises of a certain scale that are designated and officially announced by the central competent authority shall perform the following task within a certain time period as demanded by the official announcement:[570]

(i) Operations may begin only after the review and approval of *an industrial waste disposal plan* that has been submitted to the special municipality, county, or city competent authority or the organisation commissioned by the central competent authority. This regulation shall also apply to the modification of matters related to the production and disposal of industrial waste.
(ii) In accordance with the format, items, content, and frequency stipulated by the central competent authority, *report* to the special municipality, county, or city competent authority via the Internet the *circumstances regarding the production, storage, clearance, disposal, reuse, export, import, transit and transshipment of the waste at issue.* However, those circumstances in which the central competent authority allows the submission of written reports shall not be subject to this restriction.
(iii) Industrial waste clearance and transport machinery that is designated and officially announced by the central competent authority must install and maintain *real-time tracking systems* in accordance with the specifications designated by the central competent authority.

---

569. A. Commission a public and private waste clearance and disposal organization that has received competent authority permission for the clearance and disposal of the category of waste at issue to perform clearance and disposal.

B. Commission the enforcement authority to perform clearance and disposal after receiving enforcement authority's consent.
C. Commission a clearance and disposal facility installed by the industry competent authority itself or through its guidance to perform clearance and disposal.
D. Commission a waste clearance and disposal facility installed by a public enterprise designated by the competent authority to perform clearance and disposal.
E. Commission a clearance and disposal facility installed by a private organization that has signed an investment contract with the sponsoring authority pursuant to the Promotion of Private Participation in Infrastructure Projects Act to perform clearance and disposal.
F. Commission a waste disposal facility of an enterprise receiving permission pursuant to the management regulations prescribed by Article 29, Paragraph 2 to perform disposal.

570. Article 31(1) of the Waste Disposal Act.

292. The industry competent authority, development unit, or management unit of a newly-established industrial park or science park shall plan and install industrial waste disposal facilities within or outside of the park. The industrial park or science park may begin operations only after the industrial waste disposal facilities have completed installation.[571] The industry competent authority, development unit, or management unit of an existing industrial park or science park shall complete the installation of industrial waste disposal facilities within six months after the promulgation of revisions to the Waste Act; after receiving central industry competent authority approval, the installation shall be completed no later than 31 December 2004.[572]

III. Regulation

293. Enterprises designated and officially announced by the central competent authority shall employ professional technical personnel.[573]

294. Facilities that operate to clear and dispose of general waste or general industrial waste cannot clear or dispose of hazardous industrial waste at the same time.[574]

295. When there is surplus disposal capacity in an industrial waste disposal facility, it may be used by other enterprises with the permission of the competent authority with local jurisdiction.[575]

296. Methods and facilities for storage, clearance and disposal of industrial waste shall meet regulations designated by the central competent authority.[576]

IV. Distribution of Responsibility

297. When an enterprise commissions clearance and disposal of its waste, it must share liability with the commissioned agency. If the commissioned agency fails to properly clear the waste and the commissioning enterprise does not exercise due diligence, the commissioning enterprise and agency will be liable for joint environmental clearance and improvement in terms of the waste.[577]

---

571. Article 32(1) of the Waste Disposal Act.
572. Article 32(2) of the Waste Disposal Act.
573. Article 28(2) of the Waste Disposal Act.
574. Article 28(6) of the Waste Disposal Act.
575. Article 29(3) of the Waste Disposal Act.
576. Article 36(1) of the Waste Disposal Act.
577. Article 30(1) of the Waste Disposal Act.

V. Unable to Perform the Disposal of Industrial Waste

298. When an enterprise is unable to perform the disposal of industrial waste it has produced, and there is no industrial waste disposal organisation that can be commissioned for disposal, the enterprise must properly store the industrial waste it has produced. When necessary, the industry competent authority may collect fees from an enterprise to instal industrial waste disposal facilities or perform temporary storage, either independently or with appropriate guidance.[578]

299. When an enterprise is unable to manage self-generated industrial waste, and when there is no industrial waste management organisation that can be commissioned for management, the industry competent authority may work with the central competent authority to officially announce that enterprises in designated areas can send their industrial waste to industrial waste management facilities that are established by or through the guidance of the industry competent authority.[579]

VI. Import and Export Requirement and Import Ban

300. The import, export, transit, and transshipment of industrial waste may commence only if permission is granted by the special municipality, county, or city competent authority; for hazardous industrial waste, additional approval from the central competent authority is necessary. However, waste that is officially categorised as industrial raw material by the central competent authority after consultation with the industry competent authority is not subject to this provision.[580]

301. Industrial waste shall be *banned from importation* if one of the following circumstances apply:[581]

(i) Evidence exists that the waste will severely endanger human health or the living environment.
(ii) No appropriate treatment technology and equipment is domestically available for the waste.
(iii) The waste is to be directly solidified, landfilled, incinerated, or disposed of at sea.
(iv) The waste cannot be properly disposed of domestically.
(v) The waste is an obstruction to domestic waste management.

578. Article 33 of the Waste Disposal Act.
579. Article 34 of the Waste Disposal Act.
580. Article 38(1) of the Waste Disposal Act.
581. Article 38(4) of the Waste Disposal Act.

VII. Hazardous Industrial Waste

302. Hazardous industrial waste is prioritised for domestic treatment and recycling and can only be exported to Organisation for Economic Cooperation and Development member countries or countries which have signed a bilateral agreement with the ROC for transboundary movement of hazardous industrial waste in accordance with international convention or other states/regions that are announced by the central competent authority. The waste disposal organisations of the state of import must be capable of performing follow-up treatment and recycling in an environmentally sound manner.[582]

303. The operation and monitoring of methods and facilities for storage, clearance and disposal of industrial waste shall be *recorded* in detail and maintained for at least three years for future reference.[583]

304. For hazardous industrial waste that requires special treatment technology, the competent authority may, in consultation with the central industry competent authority, *instal appropriate facilities* and store, clear or dispose of them and *collect essential fees*.[584]

VIII. Reuse

305. Reuse of industrial waste shall be processed in accordance with the regulations stipulated by the central industry competent authorities or central competent authority.[585]

306. The central industry competent authority shall be responsible for the whereabouts of the reuse products which are designated by the central competent authority and shall conduct environmental monitoring when necessary when:[586]

(i) The reuse products are used in sea or land reclamation.
(ii) The reuse products are used improperly and are likely to endanger the environment or human health.
(iii) The central competent authority considers it necessary to strengthen the control of such reuse products.

582. Article 38(2) of the Waste Disposal Act.
583. Article 37(1) of the Waste Disposal Act.
584. Article 35 of the Waste Disposal Act.
585. Article 39(1) of the Waste Disposal Act.
586. Article 39-1 of the Waste Disposal Act.

IX. Emergency Measures

307. When an enterprise endangers human health or agricultural or fishery operations while storing, clearing, or disposing of industrial waste, the competent authority shall promptly order it to make improvements and adopt emergency measures. When necessary, orders may be issued for the suspension of work or suspension of business.[587]

§5. The Management of Public and Private Waste Clearance and Disposal Organisations and Waste Analysis Laboratories

308. Enterprises that engage in waste clearance or disposal are required to submit public or private waste clearance and disposal organisation permission applications to the special municipality, county, or city competent authority or organisation commissioned by the central competent authority. They may not perform duties until their permission is granted.[588]

309. Analysis laboratories may perform testing as noted in this act only after obtaining permission from the central competent authority.[589]

§6. Incentives to Improve the Waste Management

I. Reward to Report (An Offence) to the Authority by the Citizens

310. For acts that violate this Act, the public may provide detailed information or submit proof to inform the local enforcement authority or competent authority.[590]

311. For the informing action, if the competent authority or enforcement authority verifies that the information is true and imposes fines, as the fines reach specific amounts, they may allot a specific percentage of the actual collected fines as rewards for the informants.[591] When the competent authority or enforcement authority conducts verification of the foregoing case, the informants identifying information will be kept confidential.[592]

II. Tax Credit

312. Enterprise expenses incurred from waste clearance are tax deductible.[593]

---

587. Article 40 of the Waste Disposal Act.
588. Article 41(1) of the Waste Disposal Act.
589. Article 43(1) of the Waste Disposal Act.
590. Article 67(1) of the Waste Disposal Act.
591. Article 67(2) of the Waste Disposal Act.
592. Article 67(4) of the Waste Disposal Act.
593. Article 68(1) of the Waste Disposal Act.

III. Rewards

313. Enterprises that are in compliance with relevant regulations of this Act and that have excellent performance in the area of waste clearance, reduction, recycling, and reuse shall be rewarded.[594]

314. Funds gained by the enforcement authority for selling recycled waste shall be spent according to specific purposes relevant to waste recycling, and a specific percentage may be allotted as rewards for waste recycling operators.[595]

§7. Public Interests Litigation

315. When a public or private premise violates this act or related orders that are found to be relevant to its authorisation and the competent authority is negligent in enforcement, victims or public interest groups may provide written notifications of the details of the lack of enforcement. If the authorities have not carried out enforcement within sixty days, the victims or public interest groups may name the competent authority as a defendant and directly file a lawsuit with a high administrative court based on the negligent behaviour of the competent authority to seek a ruling that will order the competent authority to execute its duties.[596]

316. When issuing a verdict on this type of lawsuit, the high administrative court, pursuant to its authority, may order the defendant agency to pay the appropriate lawyer fees, monitoring and appraisal fees, and other litigation costs to plaintiffs that have made specific contributions to the effective clearance and disposal of waste.[597]

594. Article 68(2) of the Waste Disposal Act.
595. Article 69(1) of the Waste Disposal Act.
596. Article 72(1) of the Waste Disposal Act.
597. Article 72(2) of the Waste Disposal Act.

Chapter 7. Noise Pollution Control

317. As Taiwan has a very high population density in urban areas and the use of mobile transportation, like scooters, is common, there is a serious level of noise pollution. Noise control is mainly governed by the Noise Control Act of 2021 ('Noise Act'). The original Noise Act of 1983 has fourteen articles, but after revisions in 1992, 1999, 2003, and 2008, there are now a total of thirty-seven articles. There was also a minor revision concerning military airports in 2021.[598]

§1. Competent Authorities: EPA and Beyond

318. Based on the general clause for competent authority in environmental legislation, there is a division of powers between the central government (EPA) and local government.[599] Unlike other environmental legislations, however, the Noise Act provides more detailed tasks for the EPA and local government in Article 4[600] and Article 5 of the Noise Control Act.[601]

598. Amended and promulgated Arts 15 and 17 by Presidential Order No. 11000004221 on 20 Jan. 2021.

599. Article 2 of the Noise Control Act.

600. 'I. Planning, determination and implementation of national noise control policies, programs and plans

II. Discussion, deliberation and interpretation of national noise control laws and regulations
III. Determination of national noise monitoring matters and research and development of control technologies
IV. Determination of noise control standards
V. Supervision, guidance and approval of noise control work
VI. Coordination and implementation of noise control work that involves two or more special municipalities, counties or cities
VII. Delineation of noise control zones that involve two or more special municipalities, counties or cities
VIII. Coordination for major noise disputes
IX. Training of professional noise control personnel
X. Management of noise analysis laboratories
XI. Noise testing of motorized vehicles
XII. Public awareness work for noise control
XIII. International cooperation related to noise control
XIV. Inspection and appraisal of noise sources.'

601. 'I. Planning and implementation of special municipality, county or city noise control programs

II. Research and development for special municipality, county or city noise control
III. Coordination for special municipality, county or city noise disputes
IV. Delineation of noise control zones within the jurisdiction areas of special municipalities, counties or cities
V. Special municipality, county or city noise monitoring
VI. Public awareness work for special municipality, county or city noise control
VII. Inspection and appraisal of noise sources.'

319. Other authorities may play a role in noise control. First, *police authorities* are required to address individuals who produce sounds that are intermittent or difficult to measure but are sufficient to jeopardise the quietness of others' lives, as required by law.[602] Second, *the industry competent authority* bears responsibility for providing assistance during the improvement of all types of noise.[603] Beyond that, the *Ministry of National Defense* can be required to collaborate with the EPA in determining noise control regulations for premises, construction projects, and facilities, as well as equipment like motor vehicles and aircraft, for military authorities and their subordinate units.[604] *The military aviation competent authority* is authorised to determine aircraft noise abatement plans and adopt appropriate control or compensation measures.[605] Finally, the Ministry of Transportation and Communications may have input into setting motor vehicle and civil aircraft noise control standards[606]

§2. Noise Control Zone

320. Special municipality, county, and city competent authorities may delineate and officially announce each class of *noise control zone* based on noise conditions within their areas of jurisdiction and shall perform evaluations at regular intervals to delineate and officially announce new noise control zone classes.[607] Once designated, engaging in the following activities that impair the tranquillity of others' lives is prohibited at times and in the places or premises that have been officially announced:[608]

(i) Igniting fireworks.
(ii) Holding folk activities like god alter worship, temple festivals, weddings, and funerals.
(iii) Conducting activities like food and beverage preparation, laundering and dyeing, printing, or other commercial activities that use power machinery.

321. In addition, sounds emitted by the following locations, construction projects, or facilities within noise control zones may not exceed noise control standards:[609]

602. Article 6 of the Noise Control Act.
See also Art. 21 of the Noise Control Act: 'The police authorities shall promptly notify the special municipality, county or city competent authority to handle the situation when they obtain knowledge of any violations of Article 9, Paragraph 1 during the course of investigations conducted as prescribed in Article 6.'
603. Article 22 of the Noise Control Act.
604. Article 33 of the Noise Control Act.
605. Article 17(1) of the Noise Control Act.
606. Article 11(1) of the Noise Control Act.
607. Article 7(1) of the Noise Control Act.
608. Article 8(1) of the Noise Control Act.
609. Article 9(1) of the Noise Control Act.

(i) Factory plants or sites.
(ii) Entertainment premises.
(iii) Business premises.
(iv) Construction projects.
(v) Public address facilities.

322. Finally, within designated control zones, for construction projects and other uses of public or private premises that have been officially announced and designated by the central competent authority as facilities prone to generate noise, the direct contractor of the construction project or the facility owner or operator of other public or private premises shall apply to the special municipality, county, or city competent authority for a *permit* before installation or operation may begin, and must engage in installation or operation in accordance with permit content.[610]

§3. Motor Vehicles and Civil Aircraft

323. Sounds generated by motor vehicles and civil aircraft may not exceed motor vehicle and civil aircraft *noise control standards*.[611] Motor vehicles for domestic use are required to meet these noise control standards before they may be imported, manufactured, or used.[612]

324. A licensing scheme has been introduced to ensure compliance with standards. Domestically manufactured and sold motor vehicles shall obtain *vehicle model noise inspection compliance certificates* before they may apply for licence plates. Both passenger vehicles that have a gross weight in excess of 3,500 kilograms and imported motor vehicles shall obtain vehicle model exhaust testing compliance certificates issued and receive the central competent authority's certification and authorisation before applications may be submitted for licence plates.[613] Even after motor vehicles have passed this vehicle model noise inspection, the central competent authority may perform *random noise testing*.[614] In addition, regarding aircraft noise and other transportation from civil/military airports under the jurisdiction of civil airports and civil control towers, after the special municipality, county, or city competent authority has performed monitoring and found that noise exceeds environmental sound level standards, the operating or management agency (organisation) shall determine *a noise improvement plan* for that area or road section. This must be done within 180 days of notification by the special municipality, county, or city competent authority and may determine an amelioration plan when improvements cannot be made.[615]

610. Article 10(1) of the Noise Control Act.
611. Article 11(1) of the Noise Control Act.
612. Article 11(2) of the Noise Control Act.
613. Article 12(1) of the Noise Control Act.
614. Article 12(2) of the Noise Control Act.
615. Article 14(1) of the Noise Control Act.

325. Citizens can play a role in noise control as well. Citizens may *report* noise impairing public tranquillity from in-use motor vehicles to the competent authority. Vehicles which have been reported and notified by the competent authority shall undergo testing at a designated location by a designated deadline.[616]

§4. AIRPORT

326. The land use and development plan could play a front role in control noise pollution. Special municipality, county, and city governments shall, in accordance with the following principles, carry out a review and planning of *existing land use and development plans within each class of aircraft noise control zone:*[617]

(i) Class 1 aircraft noise control zones: existing land use and development plans shall be evaluated.
(ii) Class 2 aircraft noise control zones: new schools, libraries and medical institutions may not be constructed.
(iii) Class 3 aircraft noise control zones: new schools, libraries and medical institutions may not be constructed; Class 3 zones may not be delineated as residential zones.

327. A noise improvement plan is used to deal with noise pollution from aircraft noise and other transportation from civil/military airports. When aircraft and other airport transportation are found to exceed environmental sound level standards by appropriate monitoring, the operating or management agency (organisation) shall determine a *noise improvement plan* for that area or road section within 180 days of notification by the special municipality, county or city competent authority, and may determine an amelioration plan when improvement cannot be made.[618] In addition, regarding aircraft noise from civil/military airports that are under the jurisdiction of military control towers, the military aviation competent authority, in consultation with the civil aviation operating or management agency (organisation) and special municipality, county, or city competent authority shall determine *aircraft noise improvement plans* based on the level of impact of the aircraft noise in each zone class. The military aviation competent authority and civil aviation operating or management agency (organisation) must *adopt appropriate control or compensation measures*.[619] The military aviation competent authority, in consultation with the special municipality, county or city competent authority, is also required to determine *aircraft noise abatement plan*s and adopt *appropriate control or compensation measures* based on the impact level in airfields used exclusively for the take-off and landing of military aircraft.[620]

616. Article 13 of the Noise Control Act.
617. Article 18(1) of the Noise Control Act.
618. Article 15(1) of the Noise Control Act.
619. Article 15(2) of the Noise Control Act.
620. Article 17(1) of the Noise Control Act.

328. To monitor noise pollution, airfields controlled by the central competent authority shall install *automatic monitoring equipment* for the continuous monitoring of aviation noise conditions in the environs of that airport.[621] Records of monitoring results must be *maintained and reported* to the local competent authority.[622]

§5. Administrative Inspection Clause

329. Competent authorities at all levels are authorised to dispatch personnel carrying identifying documents or distinguishing markings to enter public or private premises from which noise has been emitted or for which there is evidence sufficient to determine there is concern about noise emission to inspect and appraise noise conditions.[623] No one may, for any reason, evade, obstruct, or refuse the inspections and appraisals.[624] The regulations apply, where appropriate, when the competent authority inspects motor vehicle or civil aircraft noise conditions.[625]

330. Furthermore, police may be required to report to the local government. They must *promptly notify* the special municipality, county, or city competent authority regarding any situation in their regular exercise of duty where they become aware of potential sound violations within noise control zones.[626] This allows the local competent authorities to trigger the administrative inspection process.

§6. Soft Approach

331. The industry competent authority bears responsibility for providing assistance during the improvement of all types of noise.[627]

621. Article 16(1) of the Noise Control Act.
622. Article 16(2) of the Noise Control Act.
623. Article 19(1) of the Noise Control Act.
624. Article 19(2) of the Noise Control Act.
625. Article 19(3) of the Noise Control Act.
626. Article 21 of the Noise Control Act.
627. Article 22 of the Noise Control Act.

329b24 Hot and cold and dry and wet are said of things, some in virtue of their being capable of acting, others in virtue of their being capable of being affected.

He says this not because both the contrarieties are capable of acting and being affected in that each pair acts and is affected, but, there being two oppositions, he is calling that of the hot and cold 'capable of acting' and that of the wet and dry 'capable of being affected'. And he supports these claims by defining each of them: hot, he says, is what aggregates things which are of the same kind but segregates things that are of different kinds, whereas cold is that which aggregates things which are of the same kind and things that are not of the same type. And 'that which aggregates' and 'that which segregates' are names of activities.[287] And again, he says that the wet is that which is bounded with difficulty by its own boundary, but easily bounded by that of something else, and dry what is easily bounded by its own boundary but bounded with difficulty by that of something else. And 'bounded with difficulty' and 'easily bounded' signify affections.

But someone might reasonably be led to object to this account by attending to the facts. For hot and cold are not only capable of acting but capable also of being affected (for what is hot is affected by what is cold, and the latter by what is hot), nor in turn are wet and dry capable of being affected only, but also capable of acting. For if all the elements change into one another, wet and dry are bound to act upon one another; for it is he himself who says that earth changes into water, which makes it necessary that what is wet should be active with reference to what is dry, and similarly water into earth, where what is dry is manifestly active with reference to what is wet. Why, then, does he here make an absolute distinction,[288] saying that hot and cold are capable of acting, whilst wet and dry are capable of being 217,1
affected?

This difficulty, then, we can solve by appealing to things that are said in Book 4 of *Meteorology*, claiming that this is said in connection with the coming-to-be of composite bodies. For these are found around the central place of the universe, I mean around the earth, as would be expected of things which share some portion of earth; for they could not be composed of this alone. For earth by itself is loose and easily dispersed, so it is held together by water binding and moistening it, just as the water is circumscribed by it. But when these are mixed they hold each other together, though they cannot by themselves achieve a perfect fusion, but require heat and cold to fuse them together and endow them with form,[289] wet and dry presenting the role of substratum and matter, heat and cold being analogous to form.

Chapter 8. Ionising Radiation Protection

332. To protect against the detriment of ionising radiation and to maintain the health and safety of our citizens, the Ionizing Radiation Protection Act ('Radiation Act') was adopted on 30 January 2002.[628] As ionising radiation is unavoidable in modern society, this act adopts a realistic approach. In Article 1, the act identifies an 'all in accordance with the ALARA (As Low As Reasonably Achievable) principle'.[629] This approach can also be found in the related articles, such as exceptions for Natural Radiation and exemption clause. The former stipulates that: '[t] he provisions of the Act do not apply to naturally occurring radioactive material, background radiation, and their exposure herein, unless there is a threat to public safety',[630] while the latter states that '[w]hen a radiation source poses no radiation safety hazard, it is exempted from this Act'.[631]

§1. Competent Authority: Atomic Energy Council

333. The main government body in charge of ionising radiation protection is not the EPA but an authority named the Atomic Energy Council (AEC).[632] The AEC is the authority which oversees safety related to atomic energy in Taiwan. In addition to strictly enforcing nuclear safety regulation, nuclear emergency preparedness and response, radiation protection, environmental radiation monitoring, and properly planning the management of radioactive waste, the AEC also actively promotes scientific and technological research and innovation in the field of nuclear energy. The AEC also maintains the spirit of 'profession, activeness, innovation, and service' to implement the nuclear-free homeland policy. It is committed to the regulation and supervision of nuclear energy and radiation safety, enhancing the capability of handling nuclear emergency response, and positively facing the issues of nuclear power plant decommissioning and radioactive waste safety management.[633]

334. The core purpose of radiation protection administration is the use of regulatory control and inspection to protect people and the environment from ionising radiation. The objects of regulatory control encompass radioactive materials and equipment capable of producing ionising radiation which are used or will be used by nuclear facilities, medical units, academic institutions, industrial entities, and/or agricultural units, etc. Those objects that require protection are radiation practitioners, people receiving radiological diagnoses or radiation therapy, the general public, and the environment. To ensure the safety of radiation applications, the Department of Radiation Protection of AEC introduced a graded-approach programme for licensing and permitting designed to conduct regulatory control of

628. Ionizing Radiation Protection Act, Announced Date: 2002-01-30, available at: https://law.moj.gov.tw/ENG/LawClass/LawAll.aspx?pcode=J0160009.
629. Article 1 of the Ionizing Radiation Protection Act.
630. Article 4 of the Ionizing Radiation Protection Act.
631. Article 53(1) of the Ionizing Radiation Protection Act.
632. Article 3 of the Ionizing Radiation Protection Act.
633. About AEC, 27 Jan. 2022, available at: https://www.aec.gov.tw/english/About-AEC-1.html.

radioactive materials, as well as equipment capable of producing ionising. Associated radiation practices such as production, sale, import, export, installation, use, tentatively disuse, transfer and permanently disuse, etc., as well as radiation practitioners and radiation protection personnel, are also affected. The Department of Radiation Protection also assists in strengthening users' self-management ability, reducing the dose of radiation for workers ALARA, improving the medical exposure quality as well as facilitating services of online application system, and enhancing administrative service quality and domestic radiation safety.[634]

335. The authority of the ionising radiation project is mostly held by the central government in the form of the AEC rather than the local governments, but other central authorities might play a role. For instance, central government health authorities, i.e., the *Ministry of Health and Welfare*, may assist AEC in formulating the examination items in the special physical check-ups (health checks)[635] and the standards for Medical Exposure Quality Assurance governing (1) the establishment of a medical exposure quality assurance team, (2) the assignment of specialists, and (3) the commissioning of jobs to relevant organisations.[636] Also, for radioactive material and equipment capable of producing ionising radiation in possession of a military agency, the regulations are formulated by the AEC and the *Ministry of Defence*.[637]

§2. AEC's Role

336. Safety Standards: To limit radiation exposure from radiation sources or practices, the AEC shall refer to the latest standards of the International Commission on Radiological Protection to define the *Safety Standards for Protection against Ionising Radiation* and, if warranted, to formulate the relevant guides so as to regulate the levels of radiation protection practice and personal dose limits.[638] Such rules should include the Safe Transport of Radioactive Material. These regulations, including the standardisation for packaging, shipment, transport, and storage of radioactive material and their authorisation, should also be completed by AEC.[639]

337. To ensure compliance, this act grants the AEC broad powers for administrative inspections and sanctions. For instance, the AEC is authorised to *inspect* the practice and workplace of the facility at any time to check the compliance of facility operators. If any non-compliance occurs, the AEC can order the facility operator to fix the situation by a specific deadline. If they fail to do so, the AEC can order a partial or complete termination of practice. In serious situations, the AEC may

634. Radiation Protection, Last Update: 28 Jun. 2022, available at: https://www.aec.gov.tw/english/Radiation-Protection-4.html.
635. Article 16(6) of the Ionizing Radiation Protection Act.
636. Article 17(3) of the Ionizing Radiation Protection Act.
637. Article 54 of the Ionizing Radiation Protection Act.
638. Article 5 of the Ionizing Radiation Protection Act.
639. Article 6 of the Ionizing Radiation Protection Act.

revoke the permit of the facility operator.[640] When the AEC becomes aware of a radiation hazard at any public or private location, it dispatches properly identified officers to inspect the site and measure ionising radiation. It may also require the site's owner, the user, the operator, or any other representative to provide related information.[641]

338. In addition, the AEC is required to conduct environmental radiation monitoring at properly designated locations, where radiation monitoring facilities are set up, samples are taken, and the results are made available to the public.[642]

339. The AEC has been authorised to deal with public radiation hazards. When either a public radiation hazard or the possibility of a hazard other than a nuclear accident occurs, thereby posing a danger to public health and safety, the AEC collaborates with relevant agencies to take intervention measures; when deemed necessary, the authorities may restrict the movement or order the evacuation of people and vehicles in the area.[643] The AEC can recuperate its costs once it establishes who is responsible for the damage.[644] Organisations cannot evade, interfere, or refuse to comply with the intervention measures.[645]

340. Finally, to achieve the regulatory goal of this Act, the competent authority may require facility operators, employers, or radiation protection service providers to file periodic reports detailing their radiation protection activities.[646]

§3. The Duty of the Facility Operators

341. For radiation protection, the facility operator is required to create a radiation protection plan in advance and then submit it for approval from the AEC. No operations may be carried out unless the plan is approved.[647] The facility operator shall, on the basis of the scale and nature of its practice, establish an organisation for radiation protection or designate personnel to implement radiation protection for its practice.[648] The facility operator shall then ensure that, in the areas outside the radiation workplace, the level of radiation caused by its practice, as well as the concentration of radioactive material in water, air, and sewerage, does not exceed the limits of the Safety Standards for Protection against Ionising Radiation.[649] The

640. Article 11 of the Ionizing Radiation Protection Act.
641. Article 20(1) of the Ionizing Radiation Protection Act.
642. Article 19 of the Ionizing Radiation Protection Act.
643. Article 27(1) of the Ionizing Radiation Protection Act.
644. Article 27(3) of the Ionizing Radiation Protection Act.
645. Article 27(4) of the Ionizing Radiation Protection Act.
646. Article 28(1) of the Ionizing Radiation Protection Act.
647. Article 7(2) of the Ionizing Radiation Protection Act.
648. Article 7(1) of the Ionizing Radiation Protection Act.
649. Article 8(1) of the Ionizing Radiation Protection Act.

facility operator may not discharge any waste gas or waste water containing radioactive material until after a radiation safety assessment is conducted and submitted to the AEC and approval has been granted.[650]

342. The facility operator is required to create a *plan* that designates areas in the workplace and implements control measures and radiation monitoring, then submit the plan to the Competent Authority for *approval*. No activities can be performed without plan approval.[651] Based on the facility type, the characteristics of practice, and the level of radiation exposure in the workplace, the facility operator shall divide its radiation workplace into *controlled areas and supervised areas*. Control measures are to be adopted inside the controlled areas, necessary radiation monitoring is carried out inside the supervised areas, and environmental radiation monitoring is conducted outside the radiation workplace.[652]

343. [Accident or emergency] When there is a serious radiation accident in the radiation workplace, and in case of emergency, the facility operator may take emergency exposure measures to prevent the occurrence or worsening of a disaster and to protect public health and safety.[653] Emergency exposure refers to the acceptance of voluntary systematic exposure to rescue people in danger and prevent a situation from getting worse or other emergencies that occur during or after an accident.[654]

344. When any of the following accidents occur, the facility operator must take the necessary protective measures and notify the AEC immediately:[655]

(1) the dose of radiation received by a worker exceeds the limits of the Safety Standards for Protection against Ionising Radiation;
(2) the radiation level in areas outside radiation workplaces or the concentration of radioactive material contained in water, air or sewerage exceeds the limits of the Safety Standards for Protection against Ionising Radiation;
(3) radioactive material is missing or has been stolen.

345. When notified of an accident, the AEC dispatches its officers for an inspection and may order the facility operator to stop part or all of its practice connected with the accident.[656] After an accident occurs, the facility operator, in addition to its responsibility for cleaning up in accordance with the relevant provisions, is required to shall investigate, analyse, and record the accident and then submit the report to

650. Article 9 of the Ionizing Radiation Protection Act.
651. Article 10(2) of the Ionizing Radiation Protection Act.
652. Article 10(1) of the Ionizing Radiation Protection Act.
653. Article 12 of the Ionizing Radiation Protection Act.
654. Article 2 of the Ionizing Radiation Protection Act.
655. Article 13(1) of the Ionizing Radiation Protection Act.
656. Article 13(2) of the Ionizing Radiation Protection Act.

the AEC within a limited period of time.[657] Finally, the facility operator, in addition to adopting necessary protective measures, may not alter or destroy the scene without the approval of the AEC.[658]

§4. The Regulation on Personnel and Employers

I. Age Limits, Pregnancy and Accident Training

346. There is an age limit on the persons engaged in or participating in ionising radiation work, but those who participate in practice should be at least 18 years old.[659] However, when required for teaching or occupational training purposes, those who are under 16 but over 18 years old can participate in practice.[660] No one under 16 years old can be engaged in or participate in practice.[661]

347. There is an additional limit on pregnancy. The employer, upon being informed of a worker's pregnancy, shall immediately review working conditions to ensure to the embryo or foetus does not exceed the limits specified in the provisions of the Safety Standards for Protection against Ionising Radiation. When there is concern about possible overexposure, working conditions or duties must be adjusted by the employer.[662]

348. Employers are required to train their employees. For radiation workers on active duty, the employer shall, on a regular basis, conduct necessary education and training for protection against and prevention of radiation accidents and maintain relevant records.[663] This education and training are obligatory.[664]

349. In addition, employers are required to regularly monitor radiation exposure for workers. Upon assessment, if it is estimated that the worker's estimated annual cumulative exposure is unlikely to exceed the relevant proportion of the dose limit, the employer may monitor the operating environment or personal doses through sampling.[665] The measurement and assessment of the monitored dose shall be administered by a personnel dose assessment organisation accredited by the Competent Authority.[666] The employer must document and maintain files of the results of personnel dose monitoring and inform radiation workers involved.[667] At the same time, employers have an obligation to medical surveillance. The employer must (1)

657. Article 13(3) of the Ionizing Radiation Protection Act.
658. Article 13(4) of the Ionizing Radiation Protection Act.
659. Article 14(1) of the Ionizing Radiation Protection Act.
660. Article 14(1) of the Ionizing Radiation Protection Act.
661. Article 14(2) of the Ionizing Radiation Protection Act.
662. Article 14(3) of the Ionizing Radiation Protection Act.
663. Article 14(4) of the Ionizing Radiation Protection Act.
664. Article 14(5) of the Ionizing Radiation Protection Act.
665. Article 15(1) of the Ionizing Radiation Protection Act.
666. Article 15(3) of the Ionizing Radiation Protection Act.
667. Article 15(4) of the Ionizing Radiation Protection Act.

require physical examinations when hiring radiation workers; and (2) routinely perform physical check-ups on current radiation workers and take appropriate measures in response to the results.[668] When a radiation worker receives a dose of more than 50 mSv due to one-time accidental exposure or emergency exposure, the employer shall administer special medical surveillance, including:[669]

(1) a special physical check-up,
(2) dose assessment,
(3) decontamination,
(4) necessary treatment, and
(5) other appropriate measures.

350. After special medical surveillance is completed, the employer is required to consult with physicians, radiation protection personnel, or other experts regarding the results, exposure history, and physical condition of the exposed workers and make appropriate job adjustments.[670]

351. The employer must bear all costs related to physical check-ups and special medical surveillance.[671] They must also create and maintain documentation of (1) the physical examinations and check-ups and (2) the special medical surveillance[672] Finally, the physical check-ups and the special medical surveillance are obligatory for radiation workers.[673]

§5. Regulation on Hospitals

352. To improve the quality of radiological diagnosis and treatment and to reduce the radiation exposure received by patients, whenever healthcare organisations use: (1) radioactive material, (2) equipment capable of producing ionising radiation, or (3) related facilities that the competent authority has declared to require a medical exposure quality assurance programme, health care organisations must: (i) create a medical exposure quality assurance plan based on the Standards for Medical Exposure Quality Assurance, and (ii) the plan must be approved by the competent authority.[674] When there is concern about excessive exposure for patients receiving radiological diagnosis and treatment, healthcare organisations shall inform patients of such concerns in advance and give proper radiation protection.[675]

---

668. Article 16(1) of the Ionizing Radiation Protection Act.
669. Article 16(2) of the Ionizing Radiation Protection Act.
670. Article 16(3) of the Ionizing Radiation Protection Act.
671. Article 16(4) of the Ionizing Radiation Protection Act.
672. Article 16(5) of the Ionizing Radiation Protection Act.
673. Article 16(7) of the Ionizing Radiation Protection Act.
674. Article 17(1) of the Ionizing Radiation Protection Act.
675. Article 18 of the Ionizing Radiation Protection Act.

§6. Product Regulation

353. No radioactive material shall be added to commercial products unless approved by the AEC,[676] and the added amount cannot exceed the limits approved by the AEC.[677] When a commercial product exposes the human body to radiation at a dose level that raises concern about a public health risk, the AEC will conduct radiation inspection or measurement in collaboration with relevant agencies.[678] If the result from the inspection or measurement indicates a violation of standards or a public risk, the AEC will make public announcements of each product's name and related information and require the manufacturer, distributor or owner to take specific measures.[679]

§7. Construction and Building Regulations

354. To avoid using construction material contaminated with radiation, the AEC may, when necessary, require relevant suppliers to (1) conduct radiation inspection and measurement of raw material and products, or (2) issue 'proof of absence of radioactive contamination'.[680]

355. The radiation inspection and measurement of material and products, as well as the issuance of 'proof of absence of radioactive contamination', is to be conducted in compliance with the AEC's regulations or commissioned to organisations, schools or groups accredited by the AEC.[681]

356. Regarding steel bars or beams that will be used in a construction project, the local government construction authorities may require the project contractor, in collaboration with the construction supervisor, to submit 'proof of absence of radioactive contamination'.[682] When the AEC becomes aware of radioactive contamination in a building or construction project, it must immediately inform the residents and owner(s) of that building or project.[683] When the radiation dose of the building reaches a certain level, the competent authority is required to document the situation and file the records with the local government land administration authorities to be included in a database for public access.[684]

676. Article 21(1) of the Ionizing Radiation Protection Act.
677. Article 21(2) of the Ionizing Radiation Protection Act.
678. Article 22(1) of the Ionizing Radiation Protection Act.
679. Article 22(2) of the Ionizing Radiation Protection Act.
680. Article 23(1) of the Ionizing Radiation Protection Act.
681. Article 23(2) of the Ionizing Radiation Protection Act.
682. Article 24(1) of the Ionizing Radiation Protection Act.
683. Article 24(2) of the Ionizing Radiation Protection Act.
684. Article 24(3) of the Ionizing Radiation Protection Act.

357. To protect lives and property, when there is a possibility of radioactive contamination, title transfer of such buildings shall be accompanied by certified radiation measurement reports.[685] Regarding buildings with a possibility of radiation contamination, the AEC shall make public announcements every year and whenever deemed necessary by circumstances.[686]

§8. Regulation on Radiation Protection Service

358. Business related to radiation protection service may not be conducted until an application to do so is submitted to and approved by the AEC.[687] When conducting such businesses, the radiation protection service shall conduct its work in good faith and abide by its duty to be truthful.[688]

§9. Management of Radioactive Material, Equipment Capable of Producing Ionising Radiation

I. Licence and/or Notification

359. [Permits or Registration for Work, Practice and Facilities] Radioactive material, as well as equipment capable of producing ionising radiation and practice, shall require, as designated by the AEC, a *permission or registration.*[689] Practice designated as requiring permission shall not proceed until applications have been filed with the AEC and permission has been granted, or permits have been issued.[690] Radiation work designated as requiring registration shall not proceed until the appropriate documentation has been filed and approval has been granted by the AEC.[691]

360. [Production Permits and Requirements] Businesses may not produce radioactive material, construct production facilities, or manufacture equipment capable of producing ionising radiation until after the competent authority reviews the application and issues a permit.[692]

361. During the period of validity of permits, facility operators shall conduct measurement at least once a year on (1) the radioactive material, (2) the equipment capable of producing ionising radiation, or (3) the facility, and file the certified measurement report with the competent authority.[693]

685. Article 25(1) of the Ionizing Radiation Protection Act.
686. Article 25(2) of the Ionizing Radiation Protection Act.
687. Article 26(1) of the Ionizing Radiation Protection Act.
688. Article 26(3) of the Ionizing Radiation Protection Act.
689. Article 29(1) of the Ionizing Radiation Protection Act.
690. Article 29(2) of the Ionizing Radiation Protection Act.
691. Article 29(3) of the Ionizing Radiation Protection Act.
692. Article 30(1) of the Ionizing Radiation Protection Act.
693. Article 32(3) of the Ionizing Radiation Protection Act.

II. Qualified Personnel and Training

362. In the case of high-intensity radiation facilities that contain high-activity radioactive material or high-energy equipment capable of producing ionising radiation, the operation must be conducted by *qualified personnel*,[694] as must the operation of facilities that produce radioactive material.[695]

363. [Training of Handling and Operating Personnel] The personnel to handle radioactive material or operate equipment capable of producing ionising radiation must receive training as specified by the competent authority and obtain radiation safety certificates or licences.[696] However, (1) persons with radiation-related certificates that are accredited by the competent authority, or (2) persons being trained under supervision of qualified personnel for instructional purposes are not bound by this requirement.

III. Change of Nature in Registration

364. If there is any change to the items recorded on the permission, permit, or registration, facility operators are required to apply *for revision of registration* with the competent authority within thirty days following the change.[697]

365. When the safety conditions that are required for (1) the usage of radioactive material and equipment capable of producing ionising radiation, or (2) the operation of its production and manufacturing facilities deviate from what was previously approved, facility operators shall apply to the competent authority for approval to cease usage or operation and keep the material or equipment enclosed and stored in accordance with approved means.[698] Regarding the preceding suspended material, equipment or facilities, neither (1) the usage of radioactive material or equipment capable of producing ionising radiation nor (2) the operation of production facilities may be resumed until approval is obtained from the competent authority.[699]

IV. Permanent Suspension

366. [Procedures for Permanent Suspension] Regarding radioactive material, equipment capable of producing ionising radiation, or their production/manufacturing facilities under permanent suspension, facility operators shall file with the competent authority records of all material or equipment in possession and (1) return the goods to the original manufacturer or seller, (2) transfer them to

694. Article 29(4) of the Ionizing Radiation Protection Act.
695. Article 30(2) of the Ionizing Radiation Protection Act.
696. Article 31(1) of the Ionizing Radiation Protection Act.
697. Article 33(1) of the Ionizing Radiation Protection Act.
698. Article 34(1) of the Ionizing Radiation Protection Act.
699. Article 34(2) of the Ionizing Radiation Protection Act.

another owner, (3) dispose of them as radioactive waste, or employ a handling method specified by the competent authority. The time for such handling shall not exceed three months. However, the transfer or return may extend beyond the deadline pending the competent authority's approval.[700] Within six months after the permanent suspension of (1) production/manufacturing facilities or (2) high-intensity radiation facilities, facility operators must submit to the competent authority a *clean-up plan* for facility decommissioning and complete the plan's implementation within three years after the permanent suspension begins.[701] During the execution of the clean-up plan, the competent authority may dispatch officers to perform on-site inspection at any time; facility operators must report to the competent authority for inspection upon completion of the plan.[702]

367. [Criteria for de facto Permanent Suspension] Radioactive material, ionising radiation equipment, or their production/manufacturing facilities will be regarded as being permanently suspended if any of the following occurs and shall be handled in accordance with the above measures:[703]

(1) failure to apply for approval with the Competent Authority to cease usage or operation and the situation lasts for more than one year;
(2) suspension of usage or operation has been approved, yet it has been deemed by the competent authority to pose a threat to the environment or human health and be beyond salvage or repair; or
(3) the permit has been terminated by the competent authority.

700. Article 35(1) of the Ionizing Radiation Protection Act.
701. Article 35(2) of the Ionizing Radiation Protection Act.
702. Article 35(3) of the Ionizing Radiation Protection Act.
703. Article 36 of the Ionizing Radiation Protection Act.

Chapter 9. Toxic Chemical Substances Control

368. TCSCA is the most important chemical control law in Taiwan. It has undergone six amendments since its promulgation in 1986; most recently, an amendment was promulgated by Presidential Order on 11 December 2013 and came into full force on 11 December 2014. The revised TCSCA introduces many concepts of EU REACH regulation in Taiwan. Under the new act, enterprises manufacturing or importing new substances or a given quantity of existing chemical substances shall register them with the EPA. Enterprises that manufacture or import new substances or existing toxic chemical substances without the approval of the EPA will be liable to fines in the range of TWD 200,000–TWD 2 million for manufacturers or TWD 30,000–TWD 300,000 for importers. TCSCA also requires enterprises that handle certain controlled toxic chemical substances to apply for permits, registration, or approval and comply with relevant management measures. Here 'handling' refers to activities such as the manufacture, import, export, sale, transport, use, storage, or discarding of chemical substances.[704]

369. An important revision to TCSCA occurred in 2019. The title of the act was changed to the TCCSCA.[705] Under TCCSCA, the regulation of existing and new chemicals in Taiwan has been named 'Regulation of New and Existing Chemical Substance', which was updated in 2019. Specifically, for an existing chemical, if manufacture or import activity in Taiwan includes more than 100 kilograms/year, unlike EU REACH, Phase 1 registration shall be processed within six months after the activity occurs. Annex 6 of this regulation includes a list of 106 existing chemical substances that make up the first batch of priority existing chemical substances. Beginning in 2020, manufacturers or importers in Taiwan should consider processing full registration if their substance is listed in Annex 6.[706]

§1. Competent Authority

370. This act authorises the EPA and environmental protection division of the local government as the main competent authority.[707] In addition, a clear division of work has been provided for the EPA[708] and the local government.[709]

704. Taiwan Toxic Chemical Substance Control Act (TCSCA), 2015-12-31, available at: https://www.chemsafetypro.com/Topics/Taiwan/Taiwan_Toxic_Chemical_Substance_Control_Act_TCSCA.html.
705. Toxic and Concerned Chemical Substances Control Act, Amended Date: 2019-01-16, available at: https://law.moj.gov.tw/ENG/LawClass/LawAll.aspx?pcode=O0060012.
706. Bryan Zhou, Chemical regulatory updates in Taiwan, 2 Dec. 2020, available at: https://www.european-coatings.com/articles/chemical-regulatory-updates-in-taiwan.
707. Article 2 of the Toxic and Concerned Chemical Substances Control Act.
708. Article 4 of the Toxic and Concerned Chemical Substances Control Act: 'The matters designated as the responsibility of the central competent authority:

    I. Drafting of nationwide toxic and concerned chemical substances management policies, programs, and plans.

371. To coordinate inter-department chemical substances risk assessment and management measures, the Executive Yuan must establish the *National Chemical Substance Management Board*, and the Premier of the Executive Yuan shall convene relevant government departments and assemble experts, scholars, and group representatives to strengthen the responsibility of relevant national chemical substance decision-making and coordination. They will then hand responsibility over to the relevant agencies for implementation by designating a board member or minister to serve as executive of the National Chemical Substance Management Board. The central competent authority shall be responsible for staff matters.[710] Resolutions of this board shall be implemented by relevant ministries. The Executive Yuan

---

II. Drafting, review, and interpretation of nationwide toxic and concerned chemical substances management laws and regulations.
III. Oversight of nationwide toxic and concerned chemical substances transport management.
IV. Supervision, guidance, and approval of toxic and concerned chemical substance management by special municipalities or counties/cities.
V. Coordination of management of toxic and concerned chemical substances in cases involving relevant agencies, two or more counties and cities, a special municipality and county/city, or two special municipalities.
VI. Training of nationwide toxic and concerned chemical substances management research, development, and implementation personnel.
VII. International cooperation and scientific/technological interchange concerning toxic and concerned chemical substances.
VIII. Awareness of nationwide toxic and concerned chemical substances management.
IX Oversight of mutual aid groups for nationwide toxic and concerned chemical substances.
X. Management and oversight of chemical substance registration and reporting tasks.
XI. Other matters concerning the nationwide management of toxic chemical and concerned substances.'

709. Article 5 of the Toxic and Concerned Chemical Substances Control Act: 'The responsibilities of special municipality, county and city competent authorities are as follows:

I. Planning and implementation toxic chemical substance and chemical substance of very concern management implementation programs and plans within its area of jurisdiction.
II. Implementation of toxic chemical substance and chemical substance of very concern management laws and regulations implement and drafting, interpretation, and implementation of autonomous management laws and regulations within its area of jurisdiction.
III. Toxic chemical substance and chemical substance of very concern management research and development and awareness within its area of jurisdiction.
IV. Investigation and analysis of the transport and dispersion of toxic chemical substances and chemical substances of very concern within its area of jurisdiction.
V. Investigation of toxic chemical substance and chemical substance of very concern management and statistical data production and reporting within its area of jurisdiction.
VI. Oversight of regional toxic and concerned chemical substances' mutual aid groups within its area of jurisdiction.
VII. Oversight of toxic chemical substance and chemical substance of very concern transport and handling within its area of jurisdiction.
VIII. Implementation and audit of chemical substance registration implementation and reporting matters.
IX. Other relevant toxic chemical substance and chemical substance of very concern management matters within its area of jurisdiction.'

710. Article 7(1) of the Toxic and Concerned Chemical Substances Control Act.

will regularly monitor their oversight and make reports to the public, and *annually report policies and objectives to the Legislative Yuan.*[711]

372. To ensure enforcement, assistance from private and public sectors is vital. The competent authority may appoint a subordinate agency or commission another agency or group to implement relevant management research, personnel training, hazard assessment, and prevention matters related to toxic chemical substances and concerned chemical substances.[712] The competent authority may commission an administrative corporation, legal person, juridical organisation, or relevant professional group to implement environmental accident response consulting and related matters regarding toxic chemical substances and concerned chemical substances and certify their professional competence.[713]

§2. Assessment, Prevention and Management of Toxic Chemical Substances

I. Four Classes

373. This act defines four types of toxic chemical substances:[714]

(1) Class 1 toxic chemical substances are substances that tend not to decompose in the environment or that pollute the environment or endanger human health due to bioaccumulation, bioconcentration, or biotransformation.
(2) Class 2 toxic chemical substances are substances that cause tumours, infertility, teratogenesis, genetic mutations, or other chronic diseases.
(3) Class 3 toxic chemical substances are substances that endanger human health or the lives of biological organisms immediately upon exposure.
(4) Class 4 toxic chemical substances are substances that have endocrine disruptor properties or are environmental pollutants or chemicals which endanger human health.

374. The central competent authority shall officially *announce toxic chemical substances as Class 1, Class 2, Class 3 or Class 4* when the toxicological characteristics of chemical substances conform to the above toxic chemical substance classification. (8(1)) The central competent authority may *restrict or prohibit the handling of Class 1, 2, and 3* toxic chemical substances.[715] Handlers may apply for the removal of restrictions or prohibitions when they can prove that prevention and control methods employed in the toxic chemical substance use process can prevent or avoid pollution of the environment or the endangerment of human health. The

711. Article 7(2) of the Toxic and Concerned Chemical Substances Control Act.
712. Article 6(1) of the Toxic and Concerned Chemical Substances Control Act.
713. Article 6(2) of the Toxic and Concerned Chemical Substances Control Act.
714. Article 3(1) of the Toxic and Concerned Chemical Substances Control Act.
715. Article 8(2) of the Toxic and Concerned Chemical Substances Control Act.

applicant may submit an appeal when an application is rejected, but only once.[716] Prior to handling *Class 4* toxic chemical substances, toxicity and relevant information about the toxic chemical substances must be *reported to* special municipality, county, or city competent authorities. Handling must be performed with the *permission* of the competent authorities in compliance with authorised items.[717]

375. When it is verified through either scientific techniques or field testing and research of a toxic chemical substance that was originally announced as a management item later fails to meet requirements, the central competent authority shall *promptly issue an official announcement of modification or cancellation.*[718]

II. Records and Disclosure

376. The handler shall *produce reports and regularly report records* concerning the handling of toxic chemical substances and their release quantities; such records shall be maintained for future reference.[719] The competent authority shall provide the *release quantities records online* to the public for reference on a stage-by-stage basis.[720]

III. Operation

377. The central competent authority may control the handling of Class 1 and Class 2 toxic chemical substances by means of *total release quantity control methods.*[721] Unless other regulations apply, the handling of toxic chemical substances shall be conducted in compliance with *methods officially announced or approved by the central competent authority.*[722] The central competent authority may, based on management requirements, officially announce *control concentration standards and graded handling quantity* for toxic chemical substances.[723]

378. The handler shall mark toxicity and pollution control items in compliance with regulations on *chemical substance containers, packaging,* and *handling premises and facilities* and shall keep safety data sheets for the toxic chemical substances in question on hand.[724]

---

716. Article 8(3) of the Toxic and Concerned Chemical Substances Control Act.
717. Article 8(4) of the Toxic and Concerned Chemical Substances Control Act.
718. Article 12 of the Toxic and Concerned Chemical Substances Control Act.
719. Article 9(1) of the Toxic and Concerned Chemical Substances Control Act.
720. Article 9(2) of the Toxic and Concerned Chemical Substances Control Act.
721. Article 10 of the Toxic and Concerned Chemical Substances Control Act.
722. Article 11(1) of the Toxic and Concerned Chemical Substances Control Act.
723. Article 11(2) of the Toxic and Concerned Chemical Substances Control Act.
724. Article 17 of the Toxic and Concerned Chemical Substances Control Act.

379. An enterprise that manufactures, uses, stores, or transports Class 1, 2, and 3 toxic chemical substances is required to *employ professional technical management personnel* based on regulations about the performance of toxic chemical substance pollution control and risk prevention.[725]

380. Toxic chemical substance handlers *may not sell or transfer* such toxic chemical substances to enterprises that have not obtained a permit, completed registration, or obtained approval. However, the case shall not be subject to this restriction if the situation has been reported to and received the approval of the special municipality, county, or city competent authority in advance.[726] The selling or transfer may not involve *mail orders, online shopping, or other transaction platforms* where the identities of the parties involved in the transaction cannot be established.[727]

IV. Permission and Registration

381. A manufacturer, importer or seller of Class 1, 2, or 3 toxic chemical substances shall apply to the special municipality, county, or municipal competent authority for a *permit*, and their operations must be in compliance with the content of the permit.[728] An enterprise using or storing Class 1, 2, or 3 toxic chemical substances shall apply to the special municipal, county, or city competent authority *for registration* and must operate in compliance with the content of the registration document.[729] An enterprise disposing of or exporting Class 1, 2, or 3 toxic chemical substances shall apply to the special municipality, county or city competent authority *for registration* by the batch or shipment and may only begin handling after doing so.[730] When toxic chemical substances that have not been approved or permitted by a special municipality, county, or city competent authority are imported, the customs authority shall order the taxpayer to *return said shipment* within a limited period of time.[731]

382. The competent authority may *modify or cancel the above permit, registration document, or approval* when necessary to prevent Class 1, 2, 3, and 4 toxic chemical substances from polluting the environment and endangering human health.[732] If a toxic chemical substance handler's permit, registration, or approval has been cancelled or revoked pursuant to the regulations of this Act, or if the handler has been ordered to terminate operation, the handler may not apply for a handling permit, registration, or approval for that toxic chemical substance for two

725. Article 18(1) of the Toxic and Concerned Chemical Substances Control Act.
726. Article 21(1) of the Toxic and Concerned Chemical Substances Control Act.
727. Article 21(2) of the Toxic and Concerned Chemical Substances Control Act.
728. Article 13(1) of the Toxic and Concerned Chemical Substances Control Act.
729. Article 13(2) of the Toxic and Concerned Chemical Substances Control Act.
730. Article 13(3) of the Toxic and Concerned Chemical Substances Control Act.
731. Article 14 of the Toxic and Concerned Chemical Substances Control Act.
732. Article 15 of the Toxic and Concerned Chemical Substances Control Act.

years.[733] Those handlers that have partially or completely suspended work or business pursuant to the regulations of this act must submit explanations and verification documents concerning the completion of improvements before the resumption of work or business and may resume activities only after verification and approval by the special municipality, county or city competent authority. This also applies to those that have been ordered to make improvements within a limited period by the competent authority and that voluntarily report the suspension of work or business.[734]

383. For those circumstances in which the handling of Class 1, 2, or 3 toxic chemical substances is to be *suspended*[735] for a period that exceeds one month, the statutory responsible person shall, within thirty days from when the handling is suspended, submit a list of the remaining toxic chemical substances to the special municipality, county, or city competent authority for approval and handle the remaining toxic chemical substances in compliance with the following methods:[736]

(i) Return to the original manufacturer or vendor.
(ii) Sale or transfer to others.
(iii) Return to overseas exporter.
(iv) Disposal pursuant to relevant waste disposal regulations.
(v) Other methods officially announced or approved by the central competent authority.

V. Pollution Improvement

384. Each industry competent authority shall provide guidance for pollution abatement work for toxic chemical substances.[737]

---

733. Article 16(1) of the Toxic and Concerned Chemical Substances Control Act.
734. Article 16(2) of the Toxic and Concerned Chemical Substances Control Act.
735. Article 20 of the Toxic and Concerned Chemical Substances Control Act: 'The following circumstances in which Class 1, Class 2, and Class 3 toxic chemical substances are handled shall be deemed as the suspension of handling:

I. Those circumstances in which handling is suspended for one year or more without the approval of the special municipality, county or city competent authority.
II. Those circumstances in which handling is suspended for six months or more and the special municipality, county or city competent authority determines there is concern of pollution of the environment or the endangerment of human health.
III. Those handlers of a toxic chemical substance whose permit, registration, or approval has been revoked or cancelled, or that have been ordered to terminate business, pursuant to the regulations of this Act.'

736. Article 20 of the Toxic and Concerned Chemical Substances Control Act.
737. Article 22 of the Toxic and Concerned Chemical Substances Control Act.

VI. The Handling of Toxic Chemical Substances by Government Agencies and Academic Organisations

385. The handling of toxic chemical substances by government agencies and academic organisations should be managed in compliance with the following regulations:[738]

(i) The central competent authority, in consultation with the central industry competent authority, shall determine implementation procedures governing management authority over and use of the handled toxic chemical substances; the employment of professional technical management personnel; transport; record production, reporting, and length of preservation; marking, storage, checking, prevention, joint prevention, emergency response and other binding matters.
(ii) The central industry competent authority shall submit management methods for individual handling circumstances to the central competent authority for approval.

§3. Assessment, Prevention and Management of Concerned Chemical Substances

386. 'Concerned chemical substances' refers to chemical substances other than toxic chemical substances that have been officially announced by the central competent authority as environmental pollutants or are a suspected threat to human health based on substance characteristics or public consumer issues of domestic or foreign concern, and are controlled by the central competent authority.[739]

387. The central competent authority must, based on management requirements, *officially announce* as a chemical substance of concern any chemical substance with characteristics that meet the chemical substances of concern, as in the above definition.[740] Unless other regulations apply, the handling of chemical substances of concern shall be conducted in compliance with *methods* officially announced or approved by the central competent authority.[741] The central competent authority must, based on management requirements, *officially announce control concentration standards and graded handling quantity* for such substances.[742]

388. Enterprises handling chemical substances announced as concerning must apply to the special municipality, county, or city competent authority *for approval*

738. Article 23 of the Toxic and Concerned Chemical Substances Control Act.
739. Article 3 of the Toxic and Concerned Chemical Substances Control Act.
740. Article 24(1) of the Toxic and Concerned Chemical Substances Control Act.
741. Article 24(2) of the Toxic and Concerned Chemical Substances Control Act.
742. Article 24(3) of the Toxic and Concerned Chemical Substances Control Act.

and shall implement handling in compliance with the approval document content.[743] In addition, the handler shall *produce regular reports* concerning the specified handling of the chemical substances of concern, and such records must be properly preserved for future reference.[744] Moreover, in compliance with regulations, the handler shall *mark* toxicity and pollution control items on the containers of chemical substances of concern as well as handling premises and facilities and shall *keep safety data sheets* for the substances in question on hand.[745]

389. Finally, there is a limitation on the transfer of these substances. Those who handle chemical substances of concern *may not sell or transfer* these chemicals to those who have not obtained approval. However, the case shall not be subject to this restriction if it has been reported to and received the approval of the special municipality, county, or city competent authority in advance. The sale or transfer may not be conducted through mail order, online shopping, or any other transaction platform that prevents the identification of the given parties.[746]

§4. Registration and Reporting of Chemical Substances

390. Those that manufacture or import certain quantities of existing chemical substances each year are required to *apply to register* chemical substance data from the competent authority before the specified deadline. Enterprises that manufacture or import new chemical substances must apply to register chemical substance data from the competent authority ninety days prior to their manufacture or import. Both existing and new chemical substances (registered chemical substances thereafter) shall be allowed to manufacture or import *after approval of their registration.*[747] The manufacturer or importer must proactively *maintain and update the data* of approved and registered chemical substances.[748] Chemical substances subject to registration must be *regularly declared* in compliance with the central competent authority's regulations.[749] The registered content of chemical substance data includes the status of manufacture or import, physical, chemical, toxicological, and exposure characteristics, as well as hazard assessment and other data items designated as required for the registration by the central competent authority. Based on the annual quantities of manufacture and import along with the substance type, registration may be divided into *standard registration, simplified registration, and small quantity registration.*[750]

743. Article 25(1) of the Toxic and Concerned Chemical Substances Control Act.
744. Article 26 of the Toxic and Concerned Chemical Substances Control Act.
745. Article 27(1) of the Toxic and Concerned Chemical Substances Control Act.
746. Article 28 of the Toxic and Concerned Chemical Substances Control Act.
747. Article 30(1) of the Toxic and Concerned Chemical Substances Control Act.
748. Article 30(2) of the Toxic and Concerned Chemical Substances Control Act.
749. Article 30(3) of the Toxic and Concerned Chemical Substances Control Act.
750. Article 30(4) of the Toxic and Concerned Chemical Substances Control Act.

391. If the central competent authority judges that the characteristics of a new chemical substance can be defined as a toxic chemical substance or chemical substance of high concern, an *additional clause* shall be appended at the time of registration *requiring the submission of chemical substance hazard information, updated registered report data, or regular reporting of handling conditions and, when necessary, prohibition or restriction of handling of the chemical substance.* When discovered after approval and registration, the central competent authority may also modify or add required or prohibited or restricted items.[751] If the central competent authority confirms that the toxicity of a new chemical substance is compliant with the aforementioned definition of toxic chemical substance classes, the substance shall be announced. If the characteristics of said chemical substance meet the definition of a chemical substance of high concern, an announcement of its prescription will also occur.[752]

392. Registration and declaration may be *performed individually or through joint consultation.*[753] When different parties apply to register the same chemical substance jointly or sequentially, they may use common data needed for registration through consultation and do not need to repeat testing.[754]

393. The *approved chemical substance data* for registration should be used to manage chemical substances that are utilised by the industry competent authority. Moreover, the data should be provided as the basis for assessment, screening, and announcement of toxic chemical substances and chemical substances of high concern. The same applies in the case of data reported for future reference.[755]

394. Finally, regarding the handling and management of chemical substances whose registration has been approved, apart from their announcement as toxic chemical substances or chemical substances of high concern and handling in compliance with this act, the chemical substances must be handled in compliance with the *laws and regulations of other central industry competent authorities.*[756]

§5. Accident Prevention and Emergency Response

I. General Measures

395. The handlers of Class 1, 2, and 3 toxic chemical substances and concerned chemical substances that central competent authorities have specified and announced as hazardous must submit *risk prevention and response plans* to the special municipal, county, or city competent authority to be filed for future reference, and must *implement measures* in compliance with the content of the risk prevention

751. Article 31(1) of the Toxic and Concerned Chemical Substances Control Act.
752. Article 31(2) of the Toxic and Concerned Chemical Substances Control Act.
753. Article 32(1) of the Toxic and Concerned Chemical Substances Control Act.
754. Article 32(2) of the Toxic and Concerned Chemical Substances Control Act.
755. Article 33 of the Toxic and Concerned Chemical Substances Control Act.
756. Article 34 of the Toxic and Concerned Chemical Substances Control Act.

and response plans.[757] The competent authority will make the complete risk prevention and response plans publicly available via a specified website and in other appropriate places for public review.[758]

396. Handlers of Class 1, 2, and 3 toxic chemical substances and concerned chemical substances that have been specified and announced as hazardous by the central competent authority must *adopt measures necessary to protect third parties* and will, according to regulations, purchase *liability insurance to cover handling risks*.[759]

II. Prevention

397. Handlers of toxic chemical substances and concerned chemical substances that have been specified and announced as being hazardous by the central competent authority must take active steps to *prevent accidents from occurring* and must assign or commission *emergency responders or emergency response organisations* certified by the central competent authority to bear responsibility for the adoption of necessary protective, emergency response, and clean-up operations in the event of an accident.[760] A handler shall order the emergency responders to participate in training and retraining operated by the central competent authority itself or a designated agency and preserve training records.[761] An enterprise that manufactures, uses, stores, or transports Class 1, 2, or 3 toxic chemical substances and concerned chemical substances that have been specified and announced as hazardous by the central competent authority is required to *establish a mutual aid group* and must submit its establishment plan to the competent authority for future reference. Such mutual aid groups have to assist with protective, emergency response, and clean-up operations in the event of an accident.[762]

398. The normal operation of *discharge and leakage prevention facilities* will be maintained, and emergency response, *detection and alarm equipment* must be kept available while Class 1, 2, or 3 toxic chemical substances and concerned chemical substances that have been specified and announced as hazardous by the central competent authority are being handled.[763]

III. Transportation

399. Owners of Class 1, 2, and 3 toxic chemical substances and concerned chemical substances that have been specified and announced as hazardous by the

757. Article 35(1) of the Toxic and Concerned Chemical Substances Control Act.
758. Article 35(2) of the Toxic and Concerned Chemical Substances Control Act.
759. Article 36 of the Toxic and Concerned Chemical Substances Control Act.
760. Article 37(1) of the Toxic and Concerned Chemical Substances Control Act.
761. Article 37(2) of the Toxic and Concerned Chemical Substances Control Act.
762. Article 38(1) of the Toxic and Concerned Chemical Substances Control Act.
763. Article 39(1) of the Toxic and Concerned Chemical Substances Control Act.

central competent authority must, before transport, submit a transport manifest to the special municipality, county, or city competent authority at the place of dispatch, and are required to send a copy of the *authorised transport manifest* to the special municipality, county, or city competent authority at the destination.[764] Vehicles transporting chemical substances must have regularly maintained *real-time tracking systems* installed.[765]

IV. Emergency Measures

400. When one of the following circumstances applies in relation to handlers of toxic chemical substances and concerned chemical substances that have been specified and announced as hazardous by the central competent authority, the handler shall promptly *adopt emergency control measures* and, within thirty minutes, notify the competent authority for the area where the accident occurred:[766]

(i) Where the environment surrounding the handling site is polluted by leakage, chemical reaction, or other unexpected accident.
(ii) When an unexpected accident occurs during transport, and there is concern that environmental pollution will endanger human health, the operator or owner must dispatch professional emergency response personnel within two hours or commission a professional emergency response organisation to the site of the accident to take charge of accident emergency response and other follow-up tasks.[767]

401. In addition to taking immediate measures, the competent authority *must order a stop to operations* where the accident occurred or to the entire operation.[768] The handler will be required to bear responsibility for *clearance and disposal* as shown in relevant regulations and must also *submit a report* to the competent authority for reference.[769]

402. Emergency response vehicles dispatched by a competent authority or the handler to an accident *are not subject to vehicle speed limit regulations, traffic signs, or other signals* when they have illuminated their warning lights and turned on their sirens.[770]

---

764. Article 40(1) of the Toxic and Concerned Chemical Substances Control Act.
765. Article 40(2) of the Toxic and Concerned Chemical Substances Control Act.
766. Article 41(1) of the Toxic and Concerned Chemical Substances Control Act.
767. Article 41(4) of the Toxic and Concerned Chemical Substances Control Act.
768. Article 41(3) of the Toxic and Concerned Chemical Substances Control Act.
769. Article 41(5) of the Toxic and Concerned Chemical Substances Control Act.
770. Article 43 of the Toxic and Concerned Chemical Substances Control Act.

V. Cost Bearing

403. All costs incurred by the competent authority in the course of handling accidents shall be borne by the operator or owner. Fees may be paid from the appropriate fund and then claimed from the handler or owner.[771]

§6. Audit, Inspection

404. The competent authority may send personnel bearing identifying documents to enter public or private premises and examine the handling of toxic chemical substances, chemical substances of high concern, and other chemical substances that must be registered, relevant goods or premises; they may also request relevant information. They may demand the provision of stocking, production, sales, and inventory documents, account books, relevant statements, and other production/marketing or import/export data as needed to audit substance flows. When necessary, such personnel may request the presentation of receipts, take samples of relevant chemical substances or goods, implement inspection, and provisionally seal the premises, which shall be left under the safekeeping of the statutory responsible person.[772]

405. When an audit is performed, the audit results shall be handled as follows:[773]

(i) If the regulations of this act have been violated, the violator shall be punished pursuant to the regulations of this act, and the handler must dispose of the substance or goods within a specified period of time in compliance with waste clearance and disposal laws and regulations.
(ii) When a sealed substance or article has been determined to be waste, the handler may be ordered to dispose of the substance or article within a specified period of time in compliance with waste clearance and disposal laws and regulations. If it is determined that improvement may be made or the substance may be converted to another substance, the seal shall be removed, the items handed back, and the handler will be asked to make the improvements under supervision within a specified time or perform conversion. If the handler fails to make improvements or perform the conversion in the time provided, the handler may be ordered to dispose of the substance or article within a limited period in compliance with waste clearance and disposal laws and regulations.
(iii) The seal shall be removed and the items handed back if there was no violation of this act.

771. Article 42 of the Toxic and Concerned Chemical Substances Control Act.
772. Article 44(1) of the Toxic and Concerned Chemical Substances Control Act.
773. Article 45 of the Toxic and Concerned Chemical Substances Control Act.

§7. FUND

406. The central competent authority shall establish a fund to collect *handling fees from handlers* on the basis of the handling, release quantities, state of dispersion, accident hazard or risk of substances for the purpose of management, screening, assessment, and control of announced chemical substances.[774]

407. The sources for the fund are as follows:[775]

(i) Income from chemical substance handling fees.
(ii) Fund yield income.
(iii) Allocations from relevant environmental protection funds.
(iv) Appropriations from the central competent authority following budgetary procedures.
(v) Chemical substance registration and reporting fees and other fees that must be collected pursuant to this Act.
(vi) Fees from emergency responders training and retraining.
(vii) Reimbursements for expense claims in accordance with this act.
(viii) Allocation of some fines for violating this act and income from the recovery of outstanding debts by competent authorities pursuant to Article 66.
(ix) Fines levied and paid pursuant to this act and cash or income from the sale of confiscated or recovered proceeds due to violations of this act.
(x) Other income connected with chemical substance management.

408. The fund shall have the following uses:[776]

(i) Expenses for chemical substance management, coordination, consulting, hazard assessment, prevention, incentives, subsidies and assistance.
(ii) Expenses for personnel, equipment and materials as required for environmental accident monitoring and handling measures.
(iii) Expenses connected with chemical substance checking, verifying, and auditing and the commissioning or subsidising of testing organisations to carry out testing of chemical substances.
(iv) Expenses connected with chemical substance release quantities, dispersion surveys, health risk assessments and management.
(v) Expenses for chemical substance technology research, promotion, development, science and technology exchanges, personnel training and international work.
(vi) Expenses connected with the collection of chemical substance handling fees, fund claims, litigation and related administrative and personnel maintenance.
(vii) Other expenses related to chemical substance management and hazard assessment and prevention approved by the central competent authority.

---

774. Article 47(1) of the Toxic and Concerned Chemical Substances Control Act.
775. Article 47(3) of the Toxic and Concerned Chemical Substances Control Act.
776. Article 48 of the Toxic and Concerned Chemical Substances Control Act.

Article 49

409. The *Toxic Substances and Chemical Substances Management Fund* shall establish a *fund management committee* to bear responsibility for management and use; the management committee may establish a working technology team when necessary.[777] This management committee shall designate members who will be appointed for two years. Experts and scholars must constitute at least two-thirds of the total number of committee members, and neither gender should occupy less than one-third of the seats of the committee.[778]

§8. Information Disclosure and Confidentiality

410. Handlers shall publicly disclose the permits, registration documents, or approval documents approved by the competent authority, the materials declared in accordance with this Act, and the certificate numbers of professional technical management personnel and environmental analysis and testing organisation to a website designated by the central competent authority.[779] Competent authorities at all levels may publicly disclose individual and statistical information related to the auditing and punishment of handlers, professional technology management personnel, environmental analysis and testing organisations on a website designated by the central competent authority.[780]

411. Chemical substance registration information pursuant to this Act will be disseminated to the public. However, the central competent authority possesses the authority to maintain confidentiality of information involving national defence as well as industrial or commercial confidentialities subject to the application submitted by the manufacturer or importer that has received approval from the central competent authority.[781]

412. When one of the following circumstances occurs, information confidentiality shall not be subjected to this restriction pursuant to the authority of the central competent authority:[782]

(i) It is necessary for benefitting the public.
(ii) It is necessary for protecting people's lives, bodies and health.
(iii) Consent has been obtained from the manufacturer or importer.

413. Confidentiality shall be maintained concerning reviews, checking, and the collection of samples and testing performed pursuant to this act that involves

777. Article 49(1) of the Toxic and Concerned Chemical Substances Control Act.
778. Article 49(2) of the Toxic and Concerned Chemical Substances Control Act.
779. Article 70(1) of the Toxic and Concerned Chemical Substances Control Act.
780. Article 70(2) of the Toxic and Concerned Chemical Substances Control Act.
781. Article 69(1) of the Toxic and Concerned Chemical Substances Control Act.
782. Article 69(2) of the Toxic and Concerned Chemical Substances Control Act.

national defence, industrial, or commercial secrets. However, the identity, physical properties, chemical, toxicity, classification, labelling, and relevant safety information about chemical substances shall not be subject to this restriction.[783]

§9. Rewards

414. The competent authority may grant incentives to those that comply with one of the following conditions:

(i) The handler has not violated the regulations of this act for ten consecutive years.[784]
(ii) The handler has achieved outstanding results in its toxic chemical substance and chemical substances of very concern risk prevention and equipment improvement efforts.
(iii) Those that have invented or improved methods for the reduction of dangers or pollution created through the manufacture, transport, storage or use of toxic chemical substances and chemical substances of very concern that are appropriate for promotion.

§10. Public Interest Litigation

415. If the competent authority is negligent in enforcement when a handler, person responsible for registration and reporting, or other person with relevant responsibilities violates the regulations of this act or orders determined under its authorisation, victims or public interest groups may notify the competent authority in writing and state the specific content of the negligent enforcement. If the competent authority still has not made appropriate enforcement within sixty days, the victim or public interest group may initiate a lawsuit in administrative court addressing the negligence in implementation of duties taking the competent authority as the defendant and with the goal of ordering the competent authority to perform implementation.[785]

416. Regarding the administrative court's decision and in accordance with its authority, the court may order the defendant agency to pay appropriate legal expenses, detection and appraisal fees, and other lawsuit-related expenses to a plaintiff who has made a substantive contribution to the control of environmental pollution by chemical substances.[786]

783. Article 69(3) of the Toxic and Concerned Chemical Substances Control Act.
784. Article 72(1) of the Toxic and Concerned Chemical Substances Control Act.
785. Article 73(1) of the Toxic and Concerned Chemical Substances Control Act.
786. Article 73(2) of the Toxic and Concerned Chemical Substances Control Act.

Part II. Nature Conservation and Management

Chapter 1. Heritage Preservation

§1. Introduction

417. In Taiwan, there are two laws governing the preservation of cultural and natural heritages. The Cultural Heritage Preservation Act, passed in 1982 and revised in July 2016, deals with the preservation, conservation, promotion, and transfer of heritage.[787] The Underwater Cultural Heritage Preservation Act, passed in 2015, preserves, protects, and manages the underwater cultural heritage, establishes a link between the nation and its history, promotes the characteristics of this ocean Nation, and values the spirit of the Convention on the Protection of the Underwater Cultural Heritage of the United Nations and related international agreements.[788] Therefore, in this chapter, we discuss these two laws with a focus on the natural heritage of Taiwan.

§2. Cultural Heritage Preservation Act

418. This act is applied to 'cultural heritage', which means 'designated or registered, tangible or intangible, cultural heritages, which are of cultural value from the point of view of history, art or science,[789,790] including tangible cultural heritage[791] and intangible cultural heritage'.[792] Measures to preserve tangible cultural

787. Article 2 of the Cultural Heritage Preservation Act.
788. Article 1 of the Underwater Cultural Heritage Preservation Act.
789. Article 3 of the Cultural Heritage Preservation Act.
790. *Ibid.*
791. (1)Monuments: Architectural works and their ancillary facilities built for the needs of human life, which are of universal historical, artistic or scientific value.

(2) Historic Buildings and Sites: Buildings and sites and their ancillary facilities where historical events occurred or which are of historical, artistic or scientific value and need to be preserved.
(3) Commemorative Buildings: Buildings and their ancillary facilities that have a connection with people who have made important historical, cultural or artistic contributions and should be preserved.

heritage, such as natural landscapes and monuments, historic buildings, and commemorative buildings, are relevant to environmental law. Therefore, this chapter will elaborate on their legal regime.

I. Competent Authority

419. This act is unique, with multiple ministries acting as the competent authority. In general, the Ministry of Culture (central government level), the municipal government (municipality level) and the county/city government (county/city level) are the cultural authority in charge of this act. In addition, the jurisdiction for natural landscapes and natural monuments likes with the Council of Agriculture of the Executive Yuan (the COA) as the central competent authority.[793] Other ministries, i.e., 'related authorities', may have jurisdiction over two or more cultural heritage subjects.[794]

420. In addition, there is a coordination process for multiple local government jurisdictions. For cultural heritage under two or more jurisdictions of specific municipalities or counties/cities, the local competent authority shall be jointly

---

(4) Groups of Buildings: Groups of separated or connected buildings, which, because of their architecture, homogeneity or place in the landscape, are of universal historical, artistic or scientific value.
(5) Archaeological Sites: Sites that contain the remains or vestiges of human life, which are of historical, aesthetical, ethnological or anthropological value(6) Historic Sites: Spaces and its ancillary facilities where historical events occurred and are of value from the point of view of history, art or science need to be preserved.
(6) Cultural Landscapes: Locations or environments formed through long-time interactions between human beings and the natural environment, which are of historical, aesthetical, ethnological or anthropological value.
(7) Antiquities: Any art, utensils of life or civility, books or documents and audio-visual materials of cultural significance, belonging to different eras and ethnic groups.
(8) Natural Landscapes and Monuments: Natural zones, land formations, geological phenomena, plants or minerals, which are important for preserving natural environment.

792. (1) Traditional Performing Arts: A traditional art that is created in front of or presented to an audience by an artist and is passed down through generations of ethnic groups or geographic regions.

(2) Traditional Craftsmanship: Traditional skills and crafts, mainly handmade, that are passed down through generations of ethnic groups or geographic regions.
(3) Oral Traditions and Expressions: Traditions passed down through generations via language, recitation or singing.
(4) Folklore: Traditional customs, ceremonies, religious rites, festivals and ceremonies related to citizens' life that are of special cultural significance.
(5) Traditional Knowledge and Practices: Knowledge, skills and related practices addressed to nature and environment that are accumulated or developed by ethnic or social groups over a long period to survive in, adapt to and handle nature.

793. Article 4(1) of the Cultural Heritage Preservation Act.
794. Article 4(2) of the Cultural Heritage Preservation Act: 'The Ministry of Culture or the COA shall cooperate with related authorities in charge to decide the preservation plan for and management of concurrent affairs of such cultural heritage.'

decided by the municipality and county/city governments at the location of the cultural heritage. The central competent authority shall coordinate and designate the competent authority, if necessary.[795]

421. Finally, to review the designation, registration or revocation of various types of cultural heritage and other important matters stipulated in this Act, the competent authorities shall organize 'review committees'.[796]

II. Monuments, Historic Buildings, Commemorative Buildings, and Groups of Buildings

A. *Identifying Heritage*

1. Identifying Heritage

422. The competent authorities shall 'periodically conduct general surveys' of, or 'accept reports from individuals or organisations' on, any sites and scopes deserving of the designation of monuments, historic buildings, commemorative buildings or groups of buildings and shall review, record, and trace.[797] In addition, the competent authority shall establish complete files of the investigation, research, preservation, conservation, restoration, and reuse of individual monuments, historic buildings, commemorative buildings, and groups of buildings.[798]

423. If it has been more than fifty years since the construction of a public building or its affiliated facilities, whether or not on public land, the owning or managing agency/institution shall evaluate its cultural heritage value before eradicating it.[799]

424. Upon the 'discovery' of a building or groups of buildings deserving of the designation of a monument, a historic building or a commemorative building, the monument, building or complex shall be forthwith reported to the competent authority.[800] If any constructed structure or a building complex of human settlements deserving of the designation of a monument, a historic building, or a commemorative building is discovered during construction work or other land development activities, the construction work or land development activities shall be immediately stopped and a report, thereon, shall be made to the competent authority.[801]

795. Article 5 of the Cultural Heritage Preservation Act.
796. Article 6 of the Cultural Heritage Preservation Act.
797. Article 14 of the Cultural Heritage Preservation Act.
798. Article 16 of the Cultural Heritage Preservation Act.
799. Article 15 of the Cultural Heritage Preservation Act.
800. Article 33(1) of the Cultural Heritage Preservation Act.
801. Article 33(2) of the Cultural Heritage Preservation Act.

2. Designation and Announcement

425. In general, monuments shall be classified as national, municipal or county (city) monuments and shall be reviewed, designated and publicised by the responsible authority. If a monument is designated by the municipal or county (city) government, the competent authority shall report to the central competent authority for recordation.[802] Owners of buildings may apply to the competent authority for the designation of the buildings as monuments. The competent authority shall review such applications.[803] The central authority may review the designated municipal, county or city monuments based on the reports from competent authorities at various levels, individuals or organisations or applications from building owners and 'designate and announce them as national designated monuments'.[804]

426. Historic or commemorative buildings shall be 'reviewed, registered, and publicly declared' by the municipal or county (city) authority and shall be reported to the central authority for recordation.[805] The owner of a building may 'apply' to a municipal, county, or city authority for registration of the building as a historic or commemorative building.[806] The authority shall review such applications according to the statutory procedures. The central authority may assist registered historic and commemorative buildings.[807] Once a registration application for groups of buildings passes the municipal, county, or city authority's review, the authority shall 'register and announce the designation' and file the same with the central authority for recordation.[808] Residents or groups may 'apply' to the municipal, county, or city authority for registration of groups of buildings. After accepting the application, the authority shall review the same according to the statutory procedures.[809] The central authority may review the groups of buildings registered in accordance with the procedure or in response to the reports by competent authorities of various levels, individuals or organisations or applications by residents or groups and register and announce the same as 'significant groups of buildings'.[810]

427. To protect the actual heritage designation, the status of 'interim monuments' is provided. Monuments, historic buildings, commemorative buildings, and groups of buildings undergoing review are deemed interim monuments.[811] Before the review procedure commencement, the competent authority may, in the event of an emergency, declare a building as an interim monument and notify the owners, users or managers of the same.[812] During the review period, the interim monument

802. Article 17(1) of the Cultural Heritage Preservation Act.
803. Article 17(2) of the Cultural Heritage Preservation Act.
804. Article 17(3) of the Cultural Heritage Preservation Act.
805. Article 18(1) of the Cultural Heritage Preservation Act.
806. Article 18(2)) of the Cultural Heritage Preservation Act.
807. Article 18(3) of the Cultural Heritage Preservation Act.
808. Article 19(1) of the Cultural Heritage Preservation Act.
809. Article 19(2) of the Cultural Heritage Preservation Act.
810. Article 19(3) of the Cultural Heritage Preservation Act.
811. Article 20(1) of the Cultural Heritage Preservation Act.
812. Article 20(2) of the Cultural Heritage Preservation Act.

shall be 'deemed as a monument' and shall be managed and conserved accordingly. The review period shall not exceed six months and may be extended once, if necessary. In case the competent authority does not complete the review within the stipulated time, the interim historic monument will lose its status upon the expiry of the review period.[813] When a building is registered as an interim monument, the competent authority shall compensate the owner of the building for any loss resulting from the new status. The compensation amount shall be negotiated at par with the loss.[814]

B. Maintenance Duty

1. Maintenance Duty

428. Monuments, historic buildings, commemorative buildings, and groups of buildings shall be managed and conserved by their owners, users, or managers.[815] The competent authority at the location of a monument, a historic building, a commemorative building or a group of buildings shall provide professional consultation on the management and conservation thereof and may provide assistance thereto, if necessary.[816]

429. The management and conservation of monuments shall include the following:[817]

(1) Routine conservation and periodic restoration.
(2) The current and later operation and management of the monuments.
(3) Anti-burglary, anti-disaster, and insurance measures.
(4) Establishment of a contingency plan.

430. The owner, user, or manager of the designated monument shall draft the management and 'conservation plan' and report to the competent authority for recordation.[818] The competent authority shall 'provide assistance' if the owner, user, or manager of the designated monument encounters difficulty in drafting the management and conservation plan.[819]

---

813. Article 20(3) of the Cultural Heritage Preservation Act.
814. Article 20(4) of the Cultural Heritage Preservation Act.
815. Article 21(1) of the Cultural Heritage Preservation Act.
816. Article 21(2) of the Cultural Heritage Preservation Act.
817. Article 23(1) of the Cultural Heritage Preservation Act.
818. Article 23(2) of the Cultural Heritage Preservation Act.
819. Article 23(3) of the Cultural Heritage Preservation Act.

2. Reparation

431. Monuments shall be preserved in their original appearance and construction method. In the event of destruction or damage, where the main structure and building materials survive, restoration shall be made to the original appearance, with priority given to the preservation of the value of the cultural heritage. Depending upon its characteristics, the owner, user, or manager of the said site may submit a proposal to adopt appropriate restoration methods or reuse the said site to the competent authority. On approval, if necessary, the competent authority at the municipality, county or city location of the monument may assist in such restoration or reuse.[820] The restoration plan may include, if necessary, modern technologies and construction methods to enhance the monument's resistance to earthquakes, natural disasters, floods and termites and its durability,[821] while the reuse plan may, if necessary, include proposals to add other necessary facilities without affecting the original appearance of the monument.[822] Where monuments are designated due to significant historical events or figures, the reasons for designation and the value of the monument shall be conserved or distinguished during the use or reuse of the monument.[823] During the overall restoration or reuse of monuments, presentations and public hearings shall be held in phases, the relevant information shall be made known to the public, and local residents shall be invited to the events.[824]

432. 'Groups of buildings' shall be preserved as per their original architectural styles or landscapes. In the event of destruction or damage, where the main texture and building construction survive, restoration shall be made to the original style with priority given to preserving the value of the cultural heritage. In case it suits the characteristics of the group of buildings, residents or groups may propose methods to restore or reuse the group of buildings. On approval, if necessary, the competent authority at the location of the group of buildings may provide assistance for such restoration or reuse.[825]

433. When the 'emergency restoration' of a monument becomes necessary due to a major disaster, the owner, user or manager shall, within thirty days of the disaster, submit an emergency restoration plan and, within six months of the disaster, submit a restoration plan. The plans shall be implemented after approval by the competent authority.[826] The competent authority shall provide assistance if the owner, user, or manager encounters difficulty in drafting the plans.[827]

434. If the competent authority determines, after review, that a monument, a historic building or a commemorative building is likely to be damaged or destroyed or

820. Article 24(1) of the Cultural Heritage Preservation Act.
821. Article 24(2) of the Cultural Heritage Preservation Act.
822. Article 24(3) of the Cultural Heritage Preservation Act.
823. Article 24(4) of the Cultural Heritage Preservation Act.
824. Article 24(5) of the Cultural Heritage Preservation Act.
825. Article 25(1) of the Cultural Heritage Preservation Act.
826. Article 27(1) of the Cultural Heritage Preservation Act.
827. Article 27(2) of the Cultural Heritage Preservation Act.

its value is likely to deteriorate due to mismanagement, they may notify the owner, user, or manager to rectify the problems within a stipulated time. Failure of a timely rectification may lead to the competent authority managing, conserving, and restoring such site directly, levying the fees on the owner, user, or manager, or expropriating the monument or building and the corresponding land.[828]

435. If necessary, the competent authority may provide appropriate subsidies for the management and conservation, restoration and reuse of private monuments, historic buildings, commemorative buildings, and groups of buildings.[829]

3. Planning and Zoning

436. To conserve monuments and preserve their environments and landscapes, the competent authorities, together with the concerned authorities, shall draft 'monument preservation plans' and announce and implement the plans.[830] Upon the announcement and implementation of a monument preservation plan, the concerned authorities shall revise the regional, urban or national park plans in accordance with the monument preservation plan within a stipulated time.[831] When drafting a preservation plan, the competent authority shall hold presentations, public hearings and exhibitions in phases for local community residents.[832]

437. When drafting monument preservation plans, the competent authorities may classify, designate or reclassify sites as 'monument preservation land or zones, other functional land or sub-zones' in accordance with the Regional Planning Act, the Urban Planning Act or the National Park Act to preserve and conserve such land and zones.[833] The following regulations may be stipulated, and incentives may be offered, if necessary:[834]

(1) Monument land or zone preservation and other functional land or sub-zones.
(2) Land development activities.
(3) Land use.
(4) Lot size or the ratio of reserved open space on the sites.
(5) Floor area ratio.
(6) Depth and width of the front yards, backyards, and side yards of the site.
(7) Appearance, height, and colouration of buildings on the site.
(8) Related traffic and landscape in such zones.

---

828. Article 28 of the Cultural Heritage Preservation Act.
829. Article 30 of the Cultural Heritage Preservation Act.
830. Article 37(1) of the Cultural Heritage Preservation Act.
831. Article 37(2) of the Cultural Heritage Preservation Act.
832. Article 37(3) of the Cultural Heritage Preservation Act.
833. Article 39(1) of the Cultural Heritage Preservation Act.
834. Article 39(2) of the Cultural Heritage Preservation Act.

438. For instance, the classification of preservation land and zones, other functional land or sub-zones or special reserved zones for monuments, historic buildings or commemorative buildings shall be subject to the approval of the government agencies in charge of the relevant affairs in the following regards:[835]

(1) Construction, addition, alteration, restoration, relocation, demolition, or changes in the appearance and/or colours of the buildings and other construction work on the sites.
(2) Establishment of residential land, land developments, restoration and widening of roads, and other topographical alterations.
(3) Lumbering of bamboo and trees and the quarrying of sand and stones.
(4) Advertisement installation.

C. Historic Sites and Cultural Landscapes

1. Identification, Registration and Announcement

439. The municipal, county or city competent authorities shall 'periodically conduct general surveys' of, or accept reports from individuals or organisations about, any sites and scopes deserving of the designation of historic sites or cultural landscapes and shall 'review, record and trace'.[836]

440. The municipal, county or city authorities shall review and register historic sites and cultural landscapes and 'announce' and report them to the central authority for recordation.[837] The central authority may review the historic sites, and cultural landscapes registered following the protocols or in response to the reports by competent authorities of various levels, individuals or organizations and register and announce the same as significant historic sites or cultural landscapes.[838] In the event of destruction or a diminished value, the competent authority may revoke its registration or reclassify the historic site or cultural landscape and announce the new status.[839]

2. Planning and Zoning

441. The principles governing the preservation and conservation of historic sites and cultural landscapes shall be decided on a case-by-case basis by a review committee organised by the municipal, county or city competent authority and may be adjusted following the characteristics and development of historic sites and cultural

835. Article 42 of the Cultural Heritage Preservation Act.
836. Article 60 of the Cultural Heritage Preservation Act.
837. Article 61(1) of the Cultural Heritage Preservation Act.
838. Article 61(2) of the Cultural Heritage Preservation Act.
839. Article 61(3) of the Cultural Heritage Preservation Act.

landscapes.[840] The competent authorities shall, according to the above-decided principles, draft 'historic site and cultural landscape preservation and conservation plans' to supervise and protect historic sites and cultural landscapes and help the owners, users or managers cooperate with such preservation and conservation plans.[841] To conserve historic sites and cultural landscapes and preserve their environments, the competent authorities of such sites, together with other concerned authorities, may draft preservation plans and classify, designate or reclassify the sites as 'historic site and cultural landscape preservation land or zones, other functional land or sub-zones' in accordance with the Regional Planning Act, the Urban Planning Act or the National Park Act to preserve and conserve such land and zones.[842]

3. Exemption

442. To facilitate the preservation and protection of buildings and facilities inside historic sites and cultural landscapes, the construction management, land use and fire safety measures for such sites and landscapes shall be exempt, in whole or in part, from the Regional Planning, Urban Planning, National Park, Building, and Fire Services Act restrictions and other applicable laws and regulations.[843]

D. Natural Landscapes and Natural Monuments

1. Classification

443. Natural landscapes shall be categorised as natural reserves or geoparks, depending on their characteristics. Natural monuments include valuable and rare plants, minerals, and special topographic and ecological phenomena.[844]

444. Natural landscapes and monuments shall be graded as national, municipal, county, or city natural landscapes or natural monuments, depending on the level of their competent authority and shall be reviewed, designated, and announced as such by their authority. Where a natural landscape or monument is designated by the municipal, county, or city government, it shall be reported to the central authority for recordation.[845]

840. Article 62(1) of the Cultural Heritage Preservation Act.
841. Article 62(2) of the Cultural Heritage Preservation Act.
842. Article 63(1) of the Cultural Heritage Preservation Act.
843. Article 64 of the Cultural Heritage Preservation Act.
844. Article 78 of the Cultural Heritage Preservation Act.
845. Article 81 of the Cultural Heritage Preservation Act.

2. Identification

445. The competent authorities shall periodically 'conduct general surveys' of, or 'accept reports' from individuals or organisations about, any sites and scopes deserving of the designations of natural landscapes or natural monuments and shall review, record, and trace.[846]

446. The authorities shall set up complete files of the investigation, research, preservation, and conservation of natural landscapes and monuments.[847] The competent authorities shall implement commemorative plans for education about and preservation of natural monuments.[848]

447. Any discovery of a site deserving of the designation shall forthwith be reported to the competent authority.[849] If a site deserving of the designation is discovered during a construction project or land development activity, such construction or development work shall be immediately suspended, and the discovery shall be reported to the competent authority.[850]

3. Maintenance

448. Natural landscapes and monuments shall be managed and conserved by their owners, users, or managers, and the competent authority may provide necessary assistance to manage and conserve private natural landscapes.[851]

449. Anyone who manages and conserves natural landscapes and monuments shall draft management and conservation plans for the same and file the plans with the competent authority for recordation.[852]

4. Interim Natural Landscapes or Natural Monuments

450. Places undergoing the designation review procedure shall be deemed interim natural landscapes or natural monuments.[853] In the event of an emergency, the competent authority may announce a place as an interim natural landscape or natural monument before the review process and notify its owner, user, and manager of such announcement.[854]

---

846. Article 79(1) of the Cultural Heritage Preservation Act.
847. Article 80(1) of the Cultural Heritage Preservation Act.
848. Article 80(2) of the Cultural Heritage Preservation Act.
849. Article 88(1) of the Cultural Heritage Preservation Act.
850. Article 88(2) of the Cultural Heritage Preservation Act.
851. Article 82(1) of the Cultural Heritage Preservation Act.
852. Article 82(3) of the Cultural Heritage Preservation Act.
853. Article 84(1) of the Cultural Heritage Preservation Act.
854. Article 84(2) of the Cultural Heritage Preservation Act.

5. Prohibition

451. Natural monuments shall not be destroyed by picking, plucking, chopping, felling, excavating or any other means, and their ecological environments shall be conserved. Nevertheless, this Article shall not apply if any of the foregoing acts is necessary for indigenous peoples' traditional ceremonies or religious rites or for research, display, and international exchange by research institutions with approval from the competent authority.[855] Moreover, any alteration of or damage to the natural status of a reserve is prohibited. To conserve the natural status of a reserve, no one is allowed to enter the designated zone without the permission of the competent authority unless otherwise provided in other laws.[856]

§3. Underwater Cultural Heritage Preservation Act

452. Underwater cultural heritage includes all traces of human existence with a historical, cultural, archaeological, artistic, or scientific character, which have been partially or totally under water, periodically or continuously, such as:[857]

(1) sites, structures, buildings, artefacts, and human remains, together with their archaeological and natural context;
(2) vessels, aircraft, other vehicles, or any part thereof, their cargo or other contents, together with their archaeological and natural context;
(3) objects of prehistoric character.

I. Competent Authority

453. The main competent authority of this Act is the Ministry of Culture,[858] yet, other ministries in the central government may be involved when required.[859]

454. The competent authority shall convene a 'review committee' of underwater cultural heritage to review the following subjects:[860]

(1) applications for activities directed at underwater cultural heritage;
(2) coordination with other authorities with respect to activities affecting underwater cultural heritage;
(3) the recordation and management of underwater cultural heritage;

855. Article 85 of the Cultural Heritage Preservation Act.
856. Article 86 of the Cultural Heritage Preservation Act.
857. Article 3 of the Underwater Cultural Heritage Preservation Act.
858. Article 2(1) of the Underwater Cultural Heritage Preservation Act.
859. Article 2(2) of the Underwater Cultural Heritage Preservation Act: 'Whenever the matters prescribed in this Act involve with the competence of other authorities in charge of other matters, it is for the competent authority to consult with such other authorities for the undertaking of such matters.'
860. Article 8 of the Underwater Cultural Heritage Preservation Act.

(4) the zoning of underwater cultural heritage protection areas.

II. General Principle

455. Any activities related to underwater cultural heritage shall avoid the unnecessary disturbance of human remains or venerated sites.[861] Underwater cultural heritage shall not be the object of commercial exploitation except for the purposes of public access and educational promotion, as approved by the competent authority.[862]

III. Identification and Research

456. The competent authority shall undertake a general survey of underwater cultural heritage and record and manage the files after investigation, research, and review, in accordance with the procedures prescribed by this Act, based on the reports from individuals or organisations that indicate the presence of a suspected underwater cultural heritage.[863]

457. The competent authority shall set up a comprehensive case data for the investigation, research, excavation, preservation and restoration of underwater cultural heritage. The data shall be permanently preserved in accordance with the Archives Act and its relevant regulations.[864] The competent authority shall disclose the data in an appropriate manner unless the disclosure might endanger or otherwise put at risk the preservation, protection, and management of such underwater cultural heritage.[865]

458. Individuals or organisations who discover suspected underwater cultural heritage shall terminate any activity that may influence such heritage, maintain the completeness of the site and promptly report the discovery to the competent authority. However, ongoing activity may not be terminated, assuming that there is a need to prevent an urgent and severe danger or there is a substantial public interest at stake. Nevertheless, the discovery shall be reported to the competent authority.[866]

IV. Duty of the Private Person, Government, and Public Companies

459. If an EIA is required for an exploitation activity or a governmental agency and state-owned enterprise makes or ratifies a plan with respect to the exploitation

861. Article 4(1) of the Underwater Cultural Heritage Preservation Act.
862. Article 4(2) of the Underwater Cultural Heritage Preservation Act.
863. Article 5 of the Underwater Cultural Heritage Preservation Act.
864. Article 6(1) of the Underwater Cultural Heritage Preservation Act.
865. Article 6(2) of the Underwater Cultural Heritage Preservation Act.
866. Article 13 of the Underwater Cultural Heritage Preservation Act.

and utilisation of a water area, a prior investigation must be conducted related to the existence of or suspected underwater cultural heritage A notification of discovery shall be submitted to the competent authority, if any.[867]

460. The authorities in charge of other affairs shall notify the competent authority before issuing an approval or permit for activities involving the seabed or sea subsoil.[868]

V. Education

461. The competent authority shall educate and train the relevant professionals with respect to underwater cultural heritage to undertake its preservation.[869] The competent authority shall promote underwater cultural heritage education at each school level. The competent authority shall stipulate regulations for the implementation and encouragement of the aforesaid education in consultation with the Ministry of Education.[870]

VI. Regulation for Activities Directed at Underwater Cultural Heritage

462. In general, the competent authority shall supervise all activities directed at underwater cultural heritage.[871] Such activities shall not be undertaken unless an application with an 'activity plan' is filed by a scholar, expert or academic/ professional scientific research institution to the authority and approved thereby.[872] The applicant shall follow the approved plan, produce a periodic activity report within a stipulated time and send it to the authority for memorandum.[873]

463. In case of need for emergency protection of underwater cultural heritage during activities, it should be immediately reported to the authority, and the following measures must be taken:[874]

(1) Stop the relevant activity immediately.
(2) Take temporary protection measures and produce a report for the authority's memorandum.
(3) Request the authority's assistance.

867. Article 9(1) of the Underwater Cultural Heritage Preservation Act.
868. Article 10(1) of the Underwater Cultural Heritage Preservation Act.
869. Article 11 of the Underwater Cultural Heritage Preservation Act.
870. Article 12 of the Underwater Cultural Heritage Preservation Act.
871. Article 23(1) of the Underwater Cultural Heritage Preservation Act.
872. Article 22(1) of the Underwater Cultural Heritage Preservation Act.
873. Article 22(3) of the Underwater Cultural Heritage Preservation Act.
874. Article 24 of the Underwater Cultural Heritage Preservation Act.

A. *Enforcement*

464. To supervise the activities, the authority may send personnel or authorise professional institutions to conduct an inspection. The person subject to the inspection must not evade, interfere with or refuse such inspection. If the person is likely to evade, interfere with or refuse the inspection, the authority may request assistance from the coast guard or police agency within its jurisdiction.[875]

VII. Preservation of Underwater Cultural Heritage in Situ

465. The preservation in situ of underwater cultural heritage shall be the priority before allowing or engaging in any activities directed at the heritage, including 'recordation management, protection zone or other proper preservation measures'.[876]

A. *Zone Regulations*

466. Detailed rules have been provided for zonal regulations. When the review committees decide to 'designate a specific underwater cultural heritage protection zone status', the competent authority should consult with the relevant authorities to designate and publicise the protection zone to preserve the underwater heritage in situ.[877] The competent authority may request a relevant authority to utilize buoys, seaway, navigation facilities, marine charts, national maritime zone management plans or other methods to identify the location of a publicly 'declared underwater cultural heritage protection zone or other in situ preserved underwater cultural heritage'.[878] In addition, the competent authority shall consult with a relevant authority to provide a management and protection plan for such a protection zone.[879]

---

875. Article 25 of the Underwater Cultural Heritage Preservation Act.
876. Article 27 of the Underwater Cultural Heritage Preservation Act.
877. Article 28(1) of the Underwater Cultural Heritage Preservation Act.
878. Article 29 of the Underwater Cultural Heritage Preservation Act.
879. Article 30(1) of the Underwater Cultural Heritage Preservation Act.

Article 30(2) of the Underwater Cultural Heritage Preservation Act: 'The content of the management and protection plan set forth in the preceding paragraph should include the following subjects:

1. basic data: location, measure of area, significance of the underwater cultural heritage, description, and scope diagram of research
2. range classification
3. accountable authority distribution and reporting system
4. routine maintenance: preservation, maintenance, and recordation of the environmental landscape
5. emergency maintenance: prevention of natural or human damage and emergency disaster disposal
6. education and promotion: production and exhibition of promotional material as well as education activities
7. source of funding

467. A permit is required to enter an underwater cultural heritage protection zone.[880] The following activities are prohibited within an underwater cultural heritage protection zone, except otherwise stated in this Act:[881]

(1) Salvage from the underwater cultural heritage.
(2) Usage of explosives.
(3) Trawling or anchoring.
(4) Exploration for, or collection of, minerals.
(5) Installation of electric cables, pipelines, facilities, or construction.
(6) Discarding wastewater, oil, waste, or hazardous substances.
(7) Excavating, dredging seaway, and construction of ocean engineering.
(8) Diving.

B. Enforcement

468. To facilitate enforcement, the competent authority may request assistance from the coast guard agency for the management and protection of the underwater cultural heritage and for curbing illegal activities.[882]

C. Education and Public Visit

469. For social education, the competent authority may open, partially or entirely, an underwater cultural heritage protection zone for a public visit if the preservation, protection, and management remain undisturbed.[883]

VIII. Excavating Out of the Water

470. Any excavation required an underwater cultural heritage preservation and maintenance plan with the inclusion of non-destructive technology and survey method.[884] Underwater archaeologists, underwater operators and preservation scientists shall jointly participate in the excavation or emergency disposal measures.[885]

---

8. management plan of entrust
9. other matters related to management and protection'

880. Article 31(1) of the Underwater Cultural Heritage Preservation Act.
881. Article 31(2) of the Underwater Cultural Heritage Preservation Act.
882. Article 32 of the Underwater Cultural Heritage Preservation Act.
883. Article 33 of the Underwater Cultural Heritage Preservation Act.
884. Article 35(1) of the Underwater Cultural Heritage Preservation Act.
885. Article 35(2) of the Underwater Cultural Heritage Preservation Act.

471. The underwater cultural heritage shall not be excavated out of the water except in the following situations:[886]

(1) The underwater cultural heritage related to historical status or recognition of the nation.
(2) The absence of such underwater cultural heritage could be detrimental to a complete understanding of human history.
(3) The underwater cultural heritage is of substantial commercial value that cannot be protected without excavating it out of the water.
(4) Excavation is necessary for the investigation and research of underwater cultural heritage.
(5) The underwater cultural heritage cannot be sufficiently preserved, protected, or managed without excavating it out of the water due to an emergency or change in the existing environment.

472. An excavation report and the associated recordation shall be submitted to the competent authority before the designated date.[887] The underwater cultural heritage shall be preserved and maintained by the means designated by the competent authority. The competent authority may assign preservation or archive agencies (institutions) to preserve or maintain such underwater cultural heritage, if and when necessary.[888] The competent authority may assign related agencies (institutions) of its own, delegate power to local government or authorise other agencies (institutions), non-governmental bodies or individuals to undertake exhibitions and educational or promotional activities of the excavated underwater cultural heritage.[889]

IX. Reward or Subsidies

473. The competent authority may provide reward or subsidies to those who contribute to the preservation, restoration, protection, talent personnel cultivation and educational promotion of or has merit in approved underwater cultural heritage activities.[890]

886. Article 34 of the Underwater Cultural Heritage Preservation Act.
887. Article 36(1) of the Underwater Cultural Heritage Preservation Act.
888. Article 36(2) of the Underwater Cultural Heritage Preservation Act.
889. Article 36(3) of the Underwater Cultural Heritage Preservation Act.
890. Article 42 of the Underwater Cultural Heritage Preservation Act.

Chapter 2. National Park

§1. Competent Authority

474. The governance of national parks is stipulated under the National Park Act.[891] The 'Ministry of the Interior' is the competent authority for the country's national parks.[892] To assist the national park issues, the MOI establishes the 'National Park Planning Commission' to review the designation, alteration or abolishment of areas for national parks and review national park plans.[893] The 'National Park Headquarters' is established at each national park, and the general rules for their administration are enacted independently.[894]

475. However, the local government may play a certain role in regulating 'the national park enterprises'.[895]

§2. Designation and Planning

476. In general, there are two types of national parks defined in the National Park Act:[896]

(1) National Park: An area designated by the competent authority in accordance with this law for the sustainable conservation of unique national landscapes and ecosystems, the preservation of biodiversity and cultural diversity, and to provide for public recreation and research.
(2) National Nature Park: An area designated by the competent authority in accordance with this law that has a relatively limited resource abundance or a small surface area.

I. Designation

477. The criteria for the selection of 'national parks' are as follows:[897]

891. National Park Law, Amended Date: 2010-12-08, available at: https://law.moj.gov.tw/ENG/LawClass/LawAll.aspx?pcode=D0070105.
892. Article 3 of the National Park Act.
893. Article 4 of the National Park Act.
894. Article 5 of the National Park Act.
895. Article 11 of the National Park Act: 'Ministry of the Interior shall regulate '*the national park enterprises*' (National Park Enterprise: An enterprise set up in accordance with the National Park Plan to facilitate recreation, ecotourism, and conservation of park resources.) in accordance with the National Park Plan. The competent authority of each national park shall regulate the enterprises in their respective parks. If necessary, the competent authority of a national park may approve the request that an enterprise be invested in and operated by a local government, a public institution, or a joint public/private enterprise. Such an enterprise shall operate under the supervision of the National Park Headquarters.'
896. Article 8 of the National Park Act.
897. Article 6(1) of the National Park Act.

(1) Areas having unique landscapes, significant ecological systems or habitats with biodiversity that are representative of the country's natural heritage.
(2) Areas having an important cultural heritage or historical sites and natural and human environments that have a rich cultural or educational significance. Such areas are important for cultivating national identity and require long-term preservation efforts by the nation.
(3) Areas with natural recreational resources and unusual features that may serve as tourist destinations and leisure activity venues for the public.

478. An area that meets these criteria, however, has a relatively limited resource abundance, or a small surface area may be designated by the competent authority as a 'national nature park'.[898]

479. All decisions pertaining to the establishment and abolition of national parks, and the declaration and alteration of their boundaries, shall be submitted by the MOI to 'Executive Yuan for approval'.[899]

II. Plan

480. Separate comprehensive plans should be provided for the management, protection, utilisation and development of the entire area of each national park and national nature park.[900]

III. Measures to Assist the Management

481. Application may be made 'for appropriation of public land' required for the implementation of the national park plan in accordance with the law.

482. Private land within a park may continue its present use in accordance with the national park plan. However, when private land is required to implement the national park plan, it may be 'appropriated' in accordance with the law.[901]

483. The MOI or its designated agency, to investigate the national park area or alter the national park plan, may assign qualified individuals to enter private and public land to 'conduct studies and surveys'. Prior notification of this entry must be given to the landowners or tenants.[902] Any damage caused by this entry to crops,

898. Article 6(2) of the National Park Act.
899. Article 7 of the National Park Act.
900. Article 8 of the National Park Act.
901. Article 9 of the National Park Act.
902. Article 10(1) of the National Park Act.

trees, bamboo or other items that belong to the landowners or tenants shall be 'compensated'. The amount of compensation shall be based on an agreement between the parties. If such an agreement is not reached, it shall be arbitrated by a superior authority.[903]

484. The MOI shall regulate 'the national park enterprises' in accordance with the national park plan.[904] The competent authority of each national park shall regulate the enterprises in their respective parks. If necessary, the competent authority of a national park may approve the request that an enterprise be invested in and operated by a local government, a public institution, or a joint public/private enterprise. Such an enterprise shall operate under the supervision of the National Park Headquarters.[905]

§3. Zoning and Zonal Regulations

485. For management purposes, a national park may be divided into the following zones in accordance with existing land use patterns and resource characteristics (*see* Table 16):[906]

Table 16 Different Zones Within National Park

Zones	*Definitions*
General Area	The land and water areas in national parks which do not belong to other zoning areas and are allowed to maintain the original land and water use, including existing villages.
Recreation Area	An area suitable for outdoor recreational activities within which it is permissible to construct appropriate recreational facilities with a limited use of resources.
Historical Preservation Area	An area established to preserve important historic buildings, monuments, settlements, sites, ruins, cultural landscapes, and ancient objects, as well as recognised ancestral graves, places of worship, sites related to cultural origins, old tribal lands, culturally historic locations, and monuments of the indigenous peoples, which are to be preserved in accordance with indigenous cultures and customs.

903. Article 10(2) of the National Park Act.
904. Article 11(1) of the National Park Act.
905. Article 11(2) of the National Park Act.
906. Article 12 of the National Park Act.

Zones	*Definitions*
Special Landscape Area	An area with unique natural landscapes that cannot be recreated artificially and for which strict limits are placed on the area's development.
Ecological Protection Area	An area requiring strict protection of ecological communities and habitats to preserve biodiversity and facilitate ecological research.

(*Source*: Articles 8 and 12 of the National Park Act).

I. General Rules

486. In general, the following prohibitions are applied to all areas:[907]

(1) Burning of vegetation or setting fire to clear land.
(2) Hunting animals or catching fish.
(3) Polluting water or air.
(4) Picking or removing flowers or other vegetation.
(5) Carving into or writing on trees, bark, stones, or signs.
(6) Discarding fruit skins, paper, or any other materials.
(7) Driving outside of designated areas.

II. General Regulations

487. Academic institutions may engage in scientific research in national parks. However, they must first send a research proposal to the National Park Headquarters for approval.[908]

488. To promote the educational value of the national parks, the National Park Headquarters shall employ professionals to explain natural scenery and historic sites to visitors and provide other appropriate need-based interpretive services.[909]

489. The operating budget of the national parks shall be borne by the National Treasury upon the direction of the government. The cost of park concessions shall be borne by the operator for public institutions and other private or public entities.[910] The national park operating budget shall be reviewed by the National Park Planning Commission and submitted by the MOI to the Executive Yuan for

907. Article 13 of the National Park Act.
908. Article 21 of the National Park Act.
909. Article 22 of the National Park Act.
910. Article 23(1) of the National Park Act.

approval.[911] The MOI may accept donations of funds or lands from individuals or groups for the purpose of developing national parks.[912]

III. Permit

490. A permit scheme is provided for different zones:

Zones	*Actions*	*Authorities*
General area or a recreation area	1. Building or demolishing public or private structures, roads, or bridges 2. Filling in, diverting, or expanding water areas or waterways 3. Prospecting or exploring for minerals, earth, or gravel 4. Land reclamation or change of use 5. Fishing or livestock grazing 6. Constructing cable car systems or other mechanised transport systems 7. Utilisation of water from hot springs 8. Posting advertisements or erecting signboards or similar items 9. Adding or altering equipment or their use in existing factories	National Park Headquarters
Historical preservation areas	1. Repairing antiquities or monuments 2. Repairing or reconstructing existing buildings 3. Altering original landscapes or landforms	Ministry of the Interior
Historical preservation, special landscape and ecological protection areas	1. Building or demolishing public or private structures, roads or bridges 2. Constructing cable car systems or other mechanised transport systems	National Park Headquarters

911. Article 23(2) of the National Park Act.
912. Article 23(3) of the National Park Act.

Zones	*Actions*	*Authorities*
Special landscape and ecological protection area	1. Introducing exotic animals or plants 2. Collecting specimens 3. Using pesticides or herbicides	National Park Headquarters
Ecological protection area	1. Ecological protection areas take precedence over publicly owned lands. Within these areas, the collection of specimens, use of pesticides or herbicides, and construction of man-made facilities are prohibited. However, exceptions may be granted with the permission of the MOI for scientific research or special needs related to public safety and park management. 2. Any decisions related to the development of water resources or mineral sites within special landscape and ecological protection areas shall be subject to review by the National Park Planning Commission, and the review shall be submitted by the MOI to the Executive Yuan for approval.	Ministry of the Interior
Ecological protection areas	1. Entrance to ecological protection areas shall be allowed only after obtaining a permit from the relevant National Park Headquarters	National Park Headquarters

Source: Compiled by the author from Articles 14 to 20 of the National Park Act.

Chapter 3. Wild Life Conservation and Protection

491. To conserve wildlife, protect species diversity and maintain the balance of natural ecosystems, the Wildlife Conservation Act was promulgated on 23 June 1989 and amended on 23 January 2013.[913]

492. Wildlife, under this Act, is classified into two categories:[914]

(1) Protected Species: Endangered species, rare and valuable Species, and other conservation-deserving wildlife.
(2) General Wildlife: All other wildlife not included in the previous category.

493. Several special species of Taiwan have been published on the list, stone tiger (*Prionailurus bengalensis euptilurus* or *Prionailurus bengalensis chinensis*), Taiwanese clouded leopard (*Neofelis nebulosa brachyura*) and Taiwanese black bear (*Ursus thibetanus formosanus*).[915]

§1. Competent Authority

494. The AC and the Executive Yuan (at the central level), municipal governments (at the municipal level) and the county and city governments (at the county/city level) are the responsible government authorities for this act.[916]

495. To assist with wildlife conservation, the AC is authorised to establish a 'Wildlife Conservation Advisory Committee'. The members of the advisory committee are not paid for this role. The regulations for establishing the committee are determined by the AC. Academic experts, private conservation organisation members, aborigines, and other non-governmental representatives must comprise at least two-thirds of the total committee membership.[917]

496. To strengthen wildlife conservation, the AC should establish a Wildlife Research Institute. In addition, the AC may invite academic institutions or private organisations to conduct wildlife surveys, studies, conservation, utilisation, education, or promotion.[918]

---

913. Wildlife Conservation Act, Amended Date: 2013-01-23, available at: https://law.moj.gov.tw/ENG/LawClass/LawAll.aspx?pcode=M0120001.
914. Article 4(1) of the Wildlife Conservation Act.
915. The list of protected land species, available at: https://law.coa.gov.tw/GLRSnewsout/LawContent.aspx?id=GL000556.
916. Article 2 of the Wildlife Conservation Act.
917. Article 5 of the Wildlife Conservation Act.
918. Article 6 of the Wildlife Conservation Act.

§2. CONSERVATION OF WILDLIFE

I. Development Activities

497. Any construction or land use in major wildlife habitats 'should be conducted in ways and areas, which least affect the habitat, and do not harm the original ecological functions of the habitat'. If necessary, the authorities may ask the owners, users or occupants of a land use project to 'conduct an Environmental Impact Assessment'.[919] If land use proceeds before or without the EIA, the authorities may inform and consult other responsible government agencies to halt the project. If wildlife habitat destruction is recorded, the authorities and other appropriate government agencies shall request the responsible parties for a 'rehabilitation plan' within a certain period and monitor this process. If the responsible parties do not present a rehabilitation plan, or in case of emergency, the authorities may require the responsible parties to bear the resultant costs of necessary rehabilitation procedures.[920]

498. Any farming, forestry, fishery or animal husbandry development; mine exploration, earth or rock removal or related works; repair or construction of railroads, public roads or other roads; construction or establishment of parks or cemeteries; land utilisation for recreation, sporting or forest recreation areas; waste disposal or any other utilisation of major wildlife habitats may begin only after application to and approval from the proper local authorities and the AC. Following this approval, an application for development may be made to the relevant business authorities.[921] Areas with utilisation approval, yet experiencing damage to wildlife habitats, may be required to present a rehabilitation plan to the authorities within a certain period. In case damage occurs in areas without utilisation approval, in addition to the rehabilitation plan, the Authorities would require the responsible parties to pay for any emergency methods used to curb the damage.[922]

II. Protection Zone

499. Local authorities may establish wildlife refuges for major wildlife habitats with special conservation needs and formulate and conduct conservation plans in those areas. If necessary, they may commission other agencies or organisations to conduct the plans.[923] Establishment of a wildlife refuge, its modification or elimination shall be authorised and announced by the AC after an on-site public hearing of the plan where the opinions of the local residents are heard, and approval is received from the Wildlife Conservation Advisory Committee.[924] In emergency or necessary situations, the AC may, with the approval of the Wildlife Conservation

919. Article 8(1) of the Wildlife Conservation Act.
920. Article 9 of the Wildlife Conservation Act.
921. Article 8(2) of the Wildlife Conservation Act.
922. Article 13 of the Wildlife Conservation Act.
923. Article 10(1) of the Wildlife Conservation Act.
924. Article 10(2) of the Wildlife Conservation Act.

Advisory Committee, designate or modify the wildlife refuges.[925] For the wildlife refuge conservation plan, the authorities may announce further restrictive measures regarding the following:[926]

(1) Disturbance, abuse, hunting or killing of wildlife.
(2) Collection or cutting of plants.
(3) Pollution or destruction of the environment.
(4) Other prohibited or approved actions.

500. Upon announcement of the establishment of a wildlife refuge, the land within its boundaries may be purchased or expropriated by the authorities according to the law and, subsequently, managed by them.[927] For land not purchased or expropriated by the authorities, the owner, user or occupant shall provide a suitable wildlife habitat according to the stipulations announced by the authorities. Before the authorities announce the stipulations, if the land were used or profited from in a way that would be harmful to wildlife conservation, they may order the modification or elimination of such behaviour. Construction works of national importance are exempt from the stipulations if they do not negatively affect the wildlife and have the approval of the Wildlife Conservation Advisory Committee and the AC.[928] The Authorities shall compensate the owner or user of the land for any losses resulting from the above.[929]

III. Enforcement

501. To carry out wildlife resource inventories and conservation planning, the authorities or commissioned organisations may send authorised people into public and private areas for investigation and application of conservation measures. The owners, users or managers of the public or private land shall not avoid or hinder the investigation except when involving possible military secrets, in which case the investigation shall be carried out in the presence of military authorities.[930] If the investigation runs into obstructions or conservation measures are to be applied, the authorities shall inform the public or private owner, user or manager of the land. In case there is no way of communicating the information, the authorities may use a public announcement.[931] On completion of the investigation, the conservation authorities or personnel shall keep any industrial or military secrets, that they may have come across in the course of the investigation, confidential.[932] The owners or users of the public or private land shall be compensated for any losses incurred due to the investigation or conservation measures. The amount of compensation shall be

925. Article 10(3) of the Wildlife Conservation Act.
926. Article 10(4) of the Wildlife Conservation Act.
927. Article 11(1) of the Wildlife Conservation Act.
928. Article 11(2) of the Wildlife Conservation Act.
929. Article 11(3) of the Wildlife Conservation Act.
930. Article 12(1) of the Wildlife Conservation Act.
931. Article 12(2) of the Wildlife Conservation Act.
932. Article 12(3) of the Wildlife Conservation Act.

decided by negotiation. If the negotiations fail, authorities shall set the amount.[933] The above-mentioned regulation for investigations or conservation measures shall be determined by the AC.[934]

IV. Measures Relating to Protecting Wildlife

A. *Protected Wildlife*

502. Protected wildlife, that has no owner or is vagrant, or ownerless protected wildlife products shall be dealt with by the authorities. The authorities may commission a related agency or organisation to shelter, temporarily care for, administer first-aid to and protect or terminate the animals or products.[935]

503. Protected wildlife shall not be disturbed, abused, hunted, killed, traded, exhibited, displayed, owned, imported, exported, raised, or bred unless under special circumstances recognised in this or related legislation. Similarly, protected wildlife products shall not be traded, exhibited, displayed, owned, imported, exported, or processed unless under special circumstances recognised in this or related legislation.[936]

504. Protected wildlife should be conserved and not be disturbed, abused, hunted, killed, or otherwise utilised, except in the following cases:[937]

(1) When population size exceeds the carrying capacity of the area.
(2) For academic research or educational purposes, with proper approval from the AC.

B. *General Wildlife*

505. Except for academic research or educational purposes, hunting of general wildlife, including mammals, birds, reptiles, and amphibians, shall be conducted in areas designated by the local authorities after obtaining the proper permit issued by the local authorities or contracted organisations or groups.[938]

506. Parties who wish to hunt general wildlife or fish within the designate areas shall register with the commissioned management organisation or group when

933. Article 12(4) of the Wildlife Conservation Act.
934. Article 12(5) of the Wildlife Conservation Act.
935. Article 15 of the Wildlife Conservation Act.
936. Article 16 of the Wildlife Conservation Act.
937. Article 18 of the Wildlife Conservation Act.
938. Article 17 of the Wildlife Conservation Act.

entering the area and shall carry their permit at all times. Upon exiting, the parties shall report the species and the number hunted and pay a corresponding fee.[939]

V. Hunting

507. Hunting shall not be undertaken by the following methods:[940]

(1) Use of dynamite or explosives.
(2) Use of poisons.
(3) Use of electricity, narcotics, or other immobility methods.
(4) Use of nets set up on land.
(5) Use of firearms other than an authorised hunting rifle.
(6) Use of traps, snares, or other hunting equipment.
(7) Use of other prohibited items or methods as declared by the authorities.

508. The authorities may tear down or destroy any unapproved nets, snares, traps, or other hunting devices. The owners, users or managers of the land on which such devices are located shall not avoid, refuse or hinder such actions.[941]

509. Wildlife may be hunted or killed under one of the following circumstances and with the necessary approvals; however, in accordance with the prohibition guidelines (disturbed, abused, hunted, killed or otherwise utilized) and without the use of prohibitive methods (e.g., use of dynamite, explosives or poisons.). Any prohibited action against protected wildlife shall be reported to the authorities, except in case of emergencies:[942]

(1) Danger to public safety or human life.
(2) Damage to crops, poultry, livestock, or aquaculture.
(3) Being a disease vector of zoonoses or other pathogens.
(4) Danger to the safety of air transportation.
(5) Other reasons approved by the authorities.

510. When protected wildlife causes damage to crops, poultry, livestock, or aquaculture and it has not been reported to the Authorities, such protected wildlife, in case of emergency, may be hunted or killed using humane methods approved by the authorities to prevent further damage.[943]

511. Wildlife may be hunted or killed for traditional, cultural or ritual hunting, killing or utilisation needs of Taiwanese aborigines with the required approval; however, in accordance with the prohibition guidelines (disturbed, abused, hunted,

939. Article 20 of the Wildlife Conservation Act.
940. Article 19(1) of the Wildlife Conservation Act.
941. Article 19(2) of the Wildlife Conservation Act.
942. Article 21(1) of the Wildlife Conservation Act.
943. Article 21(2) of the Wildlife Conservation Act.

killed, or otherwise utilized) and without the use of prohibitive methods (e.g., use of dynamite, explosives or poisons.)[944] Any hunting, killing or utilisation of wildlife shall be approved by the authorities. The application process, hunting method, hunted species, bag limit, hunting season, location, and other regulations shall be announced by the AC and the National Aborigine Authority.[945]

VI. Personnel

512. A Conservation Police Force shall be established to help conserve wildlife.[946] Authorities or commissioned organisations or groups may use wildlife conservation or investigation personnel to conduct investigations, crackdowns, or other conservation work in wildlife refuges. If necessary, local police may be called in to cooperate with the conservation work.[947]

VII. Rewards

513. Authorities may give awards to law enforcement officials, common people or organisations that actively participate or assist authorities to crack down illegal activities or report offences to the authorities. The awards-related regulation shall be announced by the authorities.[948] The authorities may assist or encourage any non-government organisation or individual to join or attend international wildlife conservation meetings or other related activities.[949]

VIII. Donation

514. To bring together society's resources for wildlife conservation, the AC may establish a conservation donation account and accept private or anonymous donations. In addition, the AC may issue wildlife conservation stamps.[950]

§3. Import and Export of Wildlife

I. Import and Export

515. Import or export of live wildlife or protected wildlife products is not allowed without prior approval from the AC.[951] The import or export of live

944. Article 21-1(1) of the Wildlife Conservation Act.
945. Article 21-1(2) of the Wildlife Conservation Act.
946. Article 22(1) of the Wildlife Conservation Act.
947. Article 22(2) of the Wildlife Conservation Act.
948. Article 22(3) of the Wildlife Conservation Act.
949. Article 23 of the Wildlife Conservation Act.
950. Article 7 of the Wildlife Conservation Act.
951. Article 24(1) of the Wildlife Conservation Act.

specimens of protected wildlife is limited to academic research institutes, colleges, or universities and public or licensed private zoos for education or academic research.[952] Similarly, the import or export of live marine mammalian wildlife or products thereof is not allowed without prior approval from the AC.[953] The import or export of live marine mammalian wildlife or products thereof is limited to those hunted by indigenous people for their subsistence within their traditional territories.[954] The management and penal provisions of this Act apply to the import, export, trade, display or exhibition of live general marine mammalian wildlife or products thereof unless authorized by the AC. In case of violation, the live specimens or products may be confiscated.[955]

516. Academic research institutes, colleges, and universities, public or licensed private zoos, museums, and other wildlife exhibits shall receive the approval of the AC for the import or export of protected wildlife or their products.[956]

517. Any academic research institute, which cooperates with a foreign research institute and uses protected wildlife or their products for research, exchange, donation, or display shall issue a report to the AC within one year of import or export of the wildlife or product.[957]

518. The import or export of wildlife or wildlife products shall be inspected by customs, and the products must match their customs declaration. In addition, these shall be inspected and quarantined according to the inspection and quarantine regulations set by the authorities or their commissioned organisations.[958]

519. Wildlife epidemic disease prevention and follow-up examinations shall be conducted by the Plant and Animal Epidemic Disease Authorities according to relevant legislation.[959]

II. Export

520. The AC may, for cultural, hygiene, ecological protection, or policy reasons, ask trade authorities to announce a list of forbidden wildlife or wildlife products under the Foreign Trade Act.[960]

952. Article 24(2) of the Wildlife Conservation Act.
953. Article 24(3) of the Wildlife Conservation Act.
954. Article 24(4) of the Wildlife Conservation Act.
955. Article 24(6) of the Wildlife Conservation Act.
956. Article 25 of the Wildlife Conservation Act.
957. Article 28 of the Wildlife Conservation Act.
958. Article 29 of the Wildlife Conservation Act.
959. Article 30 of the Wildlife Conservation Act.
960. Article 26 of the Wildlife Conservation Act.

III. Import

521. In case of exotic wildlife, which is not endemic to Taiwan, imported for the first time, the applicant shall provide the AC with all the relevant information concerning the species and an Impact Assessment Report to address its effect on the native fauna and flora. Such wildlife may be imported only after the AC's approval.[961]

522. The municipal, city, or county authorities of the areas where the above-mentioned wildlife may be located shall investigate and monitor this wildlife regularly. If it is found that their importation has had a negative impact on the habitat of the native fauna or flora, the authorities shall order the owners or users to present a prevention or rehabilitation plan within a stipulated time and monitor this process. In addition, the situation shall be referred to the AC.[962]

§4. Wildlife Management

I. Notification/Consent

523. All persons raising or breeding protected wildlife or exotic wildlife dangerous to the environment, people or animals or those possessing protected wildlife products, as listed by the AC's Schedule of Protected Wildlife, shall fill out a data card and maintain records with their municipal or county (city) authorities. They must update these records regularly, especially in case of any change in status.[963] Those who may have legally imported, received through transfer or other legal means any protected wildlife or wildlife products shall submit documents to the municipal or county (city) authorities within a stipulated time. In addition, any change in status shall be registered in a similar manner.[964] If necessary, the authorities or a commissioned organisation or group may mark the wildlife or wildlife products. In addition, they may conduct regular or random investigations. The owner or keeper shall not avoid, refuse or hinder such investigations.[965] Registered owners or keepers may be allowed to continue to raise or hold their wildlife or wildlife products; however, no breeding shall be allowed except for academic research or educational purposes and with the prior approval of the authorities.[966]

524. Those who may have been engaged in raising or breeding any of the listed wildlife before the promulgation of the amendments shall be assisted by the authorities to cease all activities and change occupations within three years of the date of promulgation. If necessary, the animals may be purchased by the authorities.[967]

---

961. Article 27(1) of the Wildlife Conservation Act.
962. Article 27(2) of the Wildlife Conservation Act.
963. Article 31(1) of the Wildlife Conservation Act.
964. Article 31(2) of the Wildlife Conservation Act.
965. Article 31(6) of the Wildlife Conservation Act.
966. Article 31(3) of the Wildlife Conservation Act.
967. Article 31(4) of the Wildlife Conservation Act.

525. The purchase of wildlife shall be done in an appropriate and safe manner, and any wildlife may be sent to domestic or foreign educational or academic institutes and zoos or taken in and cared for by an appropriate organisation commissioned by the authorities.[968]

II. Management Measures

A. Set Free

526. Wildlife raisers shall not set their animals free without the permission of the authorities.[969]

B. Raising or Breeding

527. The authorities may send a representative to investigate raised or bred protected or dangerous wildlife. The owner or keeper of the wildlife shall not avoid, refuse or hinder the investigation.[970] The raising or breeding of protected or dangerous wildlife shall be accompanied by appropriate husbandry and attention to safety, sanitation, and proper facilities.[971]

C. Business Operation

528. Protected wildlife and its products shall not be traded, displayed, or exhibited in public areas without the permission of the authorities.[972]

529. The AC shall release a list of protected wildlife and products as per regulations.[973]

530. The for-profit raising, breeding, trading, processing, import, and export of wildlife shall be approved by the municipal or county (city) authorities and would require a business license.[974]

531. The AC shall set regulations regarding the conditions, application process, permit contents, and other measures governing the for-profit raising, breeding, trading, and processing of wildlife.[975]

968. Article 31(5) of the Wildlife Conservation Act.
969. Article 32 of the Wildlife Conservation Act.
970. Article 33 of the Wildlife Conservation Act.
971. Article 34 of the Wildlife Conservation Act.
972. Article 35(1) of the Wildlife Conservation Act.
973. Article 35(2) of the Wildlife Conservation Act.
974. Article 36(1) of the Wildlife Conservation Act.
975. Article 36(2) of the Wildlife Conservation Act.

D. Escape and Lost

532. Lost or wild animals, which are not endemic to Taiwan, may be dealt with by the authorities if found to be damaging Taiwan's plant or animal habitats.[976]

533. Endangered, rare, and valuable species shall be well managed during raising or breeding and must not escape. If an escape occurs, the owner or keeper shall, either themselves or with the assistance of local authorities, recover the animal.[977]

E. Death

534. If an endangered, rare or valuable species dies of illness or for an unknown reason, the owner or keeper shall have a veterinarian prepare an autopsy report determining the cause of death, which shall be sent to the municipal or county (city) authorities within thirty days for reference. If the reason for death is not a contagious disease, an academic research institute, public or licensed private zoo, museum, wildlife owner or keeper who wishes to use the carcass to make a specimen may get a veterinarian to sign a death certificate instead of an autopsy report, after approval by the authorities.[978]

535. If the carcass of a protected wildlife species is valuable for academic research or exhibition, academic or scientific research institutions, public or licensed private zoos or museums may purchase it from the owner or keeper.[979]

976. Article 14 of the Wildlife Conservation Act.
977. Article 37 of the Wildlife Conservation Act.
978. Article 38 of the Wildlife Conservation Act.
979. Article 39 of the Wildlife Conservation Act.

Chapter 4. Forest

536. The Forest Act was the early generation of environmental law. This Act is comprised of seventy-seven articles and was first proposed and duly passed by the government of the ROC, effective 15 September 1932. There have been eleven amendments to date, with the latest one implemented on 5 May 2021.

537. The Act originally covered only the general meaning of 'forest', i.e., 'the land(s) and its collateral trees and bamboo, collectively'.[980] In the ninth amendment, the protection was expanded to cover trees in non-forest areas under Chapter V-I Protection of Trees in July 2015.[981] Therefore, this Act applies to trees in urban areas as well.

§1. Competent Authority

538. The main competent authorities for this Act are the Council of Agriculture and the Executive Yuan (at the central government), the municipal government (at the municipal level) and the county (city) government (at the county (city) level).[982]

539. However, the following authorities may play a role in certain related affairs:

(1) Central Land Administrative Authority: The central government shall request them to classify and promulgate undeveloped mountains and lands suitable for forestry as forestland.[983]
(2) Central Government Authority of the Aboriginal People: If a forest is in the traditional territory of aboriginal people, the aboriginal people may utilise forest products for their living needs. The harvesting area, variety, time, payment, and other rules are decided by the central government agency along with the Central Government Authority of the Aboriginal People.[984]
(3) Relevant Fire Prevention Institution: Fires shall not be started in forest and forest protection areas. However, parties with a fire permit from a relevant fire prevention institution are not bound by this limitation. The permitted party must notify the owner or manager of adjacent forests prior to conducting a sanctioned fire.[985]
(4) Central Water Conservation Government Agency: The water-right fee in section 1 and the proportion of the allocation from the engineering budget for water resource development projects in section 4 are regulated by the Central Water Conservation Government Agency in conjunction with the central government. In addition, at the time of permit issuance for hill development, the

980. Article 3(1) of the Forestry Act.
981. Article 3-1 of the Forestry Act.
982. Article 2 of the Forestry Act.
983. Article 6(1) of the Forestry Act.
984. Article 15(4) of the Forestry Act.
985. Article 34(1) of the Forestry Act.

reciprocation fund fee in section 2 is paid. The obligated party, calculation format, payment schedule, time, procedures, and regulations are decided by the central government and submitted to the Executive Yuan for approval.[986]

§2. FORESTRY ADMINISTRATION

I. Principles

540. Forests, principally, belong to the nation.[987] 'Preserving the long-term integrity of the national lands' is the primary goal of the administrative management of the forestry industry.[988]

II. Classification of Forestland

541. The AC shall request the Central Land Administrative Authority to classify and promulgate undeveloped mountains and lands suitable for forestry as forestland.[989] A land designated as forestland 'cannot be changed to any other designation'. However, a forestland can be redesignated with approval from the municipal and county (city) governments, which must be reported to the central government and the Central Land Management Agency.[990] If a land belongs to the aboriginal people, approval from the Central Government Authority of the Aboriginal People is mandatory.[991]

III. Nationalization

542. Should a public or private forest have any of the following characteristics, the AC may 'appropriate' it to national ownership and 'compensate' the owner accordingly:[992]

(1) It is needed for reasons of national security or operation of the national forest.
(2) It includes a river, lake or other water source that provides important resources to the public.

986. Article 48-1(2) of the Forestry Act.
987. Article 3(2) of the Forestry Act.
988. Article 5 of the Forestry Act.
989. Article 6(1) of the Forestry Act.
990. Article 6(2) of the Forestry Act.
991. Article 6(3) of the Forestry Act.
992. Article 7(1) of the Forestry Act.

IV. Regulations

543. Should a national or public forest meet any of the following requirements, it may be 'leased, transferred or appropriated':[993]

(1) Appropriate for establishing a school, hospital, park, or other public facilities.
(2) Appropriate for national defence, transportation, or water conservation.
(3) Appropriate for establishing public works.
(4) Appropriate for establishing a duly-approved national park, designated scenic area or forest recreation park.

544. Should the applications stipulated above be violated, or the land is not used for the said purposes during the assigned period, the leased, sublet, or appropriated forestland shall be 'seized'.[994]

545. To carry out any of the following actions in a forest, an application shall be filed with the government agency, which shall, together with the relevant local agency, examine the specified area for its suitability for the proposed action. After approval, the action may be undertaken within the designated boundaries:[995]

(1) To build or repair a reservoir, roadway, or power transmission system or to develop a source of electricity.
(2) To mine or quarry.
(3) To build or repair other engineering works.

546. However, none of the undertakings should impair geological stability, national security, and forestry.[996] If there are concerns about forest damage, the government agency shall oversee that the party 'perform due water conservation measures or other necessary measures. The party may not refuse such supervision.[997]

547. The government agency can bar logging under any of the following circumstances:[998]

(1) The land is too steep or the soil too shallow for reforestation.
(2) The soil is likely to be eroded or affect public benefits after logging.
(3) The land is in a water reservoir collection area, headwaters of a river, on an eroded riverbank, windward coastal area, or sand dune area.
(4) The forest is in an area where logging prohibition is essential.

---

993. Article 8(1) of the Forestry Act.
994. Article 8(2) of the Forestry Act.
995. Article 9(1) of the Forestry Act.
996. Article 9(2) of the Forestry Act.
997. Article 9(3) of the Forestry Act.
998. Article 10 of the Forestry Act.

548. In addition, the government agency may, according to the forest location, 'limit or prohibit the harvest or excavation' of grass cover, tree roots, and grass roots for a specific period.[999]

§3. Forestry Management and Utilisation

I. Main Responsible Entity

549. Whereas national forests are classified and managed by the central government, public forests are managed by the owner or other assigned other legal entities and private forests are managed by private individuals.[1000] The central government may, according to the state of the forestry industry, regulate and implement the forest management plan.[1001]

550. To reinforce the water-retaining ability of the forest, forest management shall comply with the protection and management regulations of the water collection areas.[1002]

II. Management of National Forests

551. The 'national forest management plans' shall be regulated by the relevant administrative agency and submitted to the central government for approval.[1003] The annual plan for the national forest yields shall be based on the management plan for the relevant business area.[1004] In addition, the harvesting of the national forest yields must be carried out according to the annual logging plan and the national forest yields management code.[1005] Nevertheless, if a forest is in the traditional territory of the aboriginal people, they may take forest products for their living needs.[1006]

552. After a natural disaster, the local government has one month to 'clean-up' and tally the bamboo or trees carried outside the national forest boundaries by natural forces. After a month, local people may freely collect the displaced wood and bamboo.[1007]

---

999. Article 11 of the Forestry Act.
1000. Article 12(1) of the Forestry Act.
1001. Article 12(2) of the Forestry Act.
1002. Article 13 of the Forestry Act.
1003. Article 14 of the Forestry Act.
1004. Article 15(1) of the Forestry Act.
1005. Article 15(2) of the Forestry Act.
1006. Article 15(3) of the Forestry Act.
1007. Article 15(4) of the Forestry Act.

III. Related Areas

553. Should a national park or scenic area be designated in a forest area, the responsible party shall meet the government agency to conduct a field survey. The forest area within the demarcated boundaries shall be managed by the government agency in conjunction with the relevant national park or scenic area development plan.[1008]

554. A forest region, subject to approval after an environment impact assessment, may be designated as a forest recreation area.[1009] To maintain forest ecology and preserve biodiversity, a nature reserve may be designated within a forest area. The number of people and the amount of traffic allowed inside a nature reserve shall be regulated in accordance with the unique characteristics of the resources within the reserve.[1010]

IV. Personnel

555. Public and private forests with a commercial forest area of more than 500 hectares shall have a licensed forestry technician.[1011] Forest planters and loggers shall be assisted by forestry technicians or technical staff.[1012]

V. Other Regulations

556. Should business collaboration among forestry practitioners become necessary, the said practitioners may organise a 'forestry cooperative association' in accordance with the Cooperative Association Act. This association shall be counselled by the local government agency.[1013]

557. Should a forest owner need to use another's land to transport forest equipment and products or use, alter or remove implements in a water course without endangering the water supply or peoples' lives, the forest owner shall negotiate with the landowner or other interest-holders. Where negotiation is discordant or impossible, the parties shall file a request with the relevant local government agency for mediation. If the mediation fails, the central government shall resolve the issue.[1014]

1008. Article 16 of the Forestry Act.
1009. Article 17 of the Forestry Act.
1010. Article 17-1 of the Forestry Act.
1011. Article 18(1) of the Forestry Act.
1012. Article 18(2) of the Forestry Act.
1013. Article 19 of the Forestry Act.
1014. Article 20 of the Forestry Act.

558. On the following forestlands, the government agency may order the forest owner or stakeholder to undertake and complete reforestation and necessary water and soil conservation measures within an assigned period:[1015]

(1) Eroded gorge, steep exposed land, collapsed land, landslide area, fragmented belt, severely eroded land, and scattered sand dune.
(2) Water source area, reservoir collection area, coastal area, and riverbanks.
(3) Old fire site and flood eroded land.
(4) Logged site.
(5) Other areas where conservation is essential.

§4. CONSERVATION FORESTRY

I. Designation

559. Forests held by the state or a public or private entity, which meet any of the following requirements, can be classified as 'conservation forest' by the central government:[1016]

(1) Essential for preventing damage from floods, wind, tides, salt, and smoke.
(2) Essential for the conservation of a water source or protection of a reservoir.
(3) Essential for preventing damage from sand, soil erosion and blowing sand, falling rock, ice, or avalanche.
(4) Essential for national defence.
(5) Essential for public health.
(6) Essential for navigation.
(7) Essential for the fishing industry.
(8) Essential for the preservation of landmarks, historic relics, and scenery.
(9) Essential for nature conservation.

560. Hills or other lands, conforming to any of the following criteria, could be classified as 'conservation forest' by the central government and augment its conservation:[1017]

(1) Essential for preventing damage from floods, wind, tides, salt, and smoke.
(2) Essential for the conservation of a water source or protection of a reservoir.
(3) Essential for preventing damage from sand, soil erosion and blowing sand, falling rock, ice, or avalanche.
(4) Essential for national defence.
(5) Essential for public health.

1015. Article 21 of the Forestry Act.
1016. Article 22 of the Forestry Act.
1017. Article 23 of the Forestry Act.

II. Operation and Management

561. The management of conservation forests must prioritise, regardless of ownership, the public interest. All conservation forests shall be reasonably managed, cultivated, renewed, and logged according to their individual characteristics.[1018]

562. Logging, damage to wood or bamboo, development or livestock grazing, harvesting or excavating earth, rocks, grass cover or tree roots are prohibited in a conservation forest except with the prior approval of the government agency.[1019] In addition, the government agency may limit or prohibit the use of revenues generated through any prohibited activity by the conservation forest owner or dictate the method of operation and protection.[1020] The government agency may order reforestation or other essential restoration procedures if the prohibitions are violated.[1021]

563. Since conservation forests are protected against logging, landowners or crop owners may file for compensation equal to the amount of direct damage.[1022] For the owner of a conservation forest undertaking reforestation, the expenditure shall be considered as damages and can be claimed from the government.[1023] For the damages mentioned, the landowner shall be compensated by the central government, which may order the legal entity, organisation or private individual, that benefits from the conservation forest classification to bear part or all of the compensation.[1024]

III. Application for Designation and Declassification

564. The classification or declassification of a conservation forest requires an application to the municipality or county (city) government through a legal entity or organisation located in the vicinity of the forest or other parties with direct interests. The application must be presented to the central government for approval. If the forest falls under the jurisdiction of the central government, the application must be sent directly to them.[1025]

565. On accepting the application, the government agency must notify the relevant forest owner, landowner, and parties holding land rights and promulgate accordingly.[1026] Starting from the day of the promulgation to the day of final

1018. Article 24 of the Forestry Act.
1019. Article 30(1) of the Forestry Act.
1020. Article 30(2) of the Forestry Act.
1021. Article 30(3) of the Forestry Act.
1022. Article 31(1) of the Forestry Act.
1023. Article 31(2) of the Forestry Act.
1024. Article 31(3) of the Forestry Act.
1025. Article 26 of the Forestry Act.
1026. Article 27(1) of the Forestry Act.

classification or declassification, the concerned forest may not be developed or logged except with the approval of the government agency.[1027]

566. Should any party with direct interests object to the classification or declassification, the party may present a statement of opinion to the local government within thirty days of the promulgation.[1028]

567. The municipality or county (city) government shall present all documents related to the classification or declassification of a conservation forest to the central government for approval. In case there are objections filed, the statement of opinion shall be enclosed.[1029] The classification or declassification of a conservation forest, after approval by the central government, shall be promulgated by the relevant municipal or county (city) government and the forest owner shall be duly notified.[1030]

568. Should the subsistence of a conservation forest become unnecessary, subject to approval from the central government, it may be partially or completely declassified.[1031]

§5. Forest Protection

I. General

569. To protect the forest, forest police may be instituted. In the absence of the forest police, the local police shall assume the duties.[1032] The administration and district heads of villages (towns and cities) are responsible for assisting in forest protection.[1033]

570. The forest periphery may be designated a forest protection area. The area shall be delineated by a government-authorised agency, presented to the central government for approval and promulgated by the local government.[1034]

II. Fire Protection

571. Fires shall not be started in forest and forest protection areas. However, parties with a fire permit from a relevant fire prevention institution are not bound by this limitation. The permitted party must notify the owner or manager of adjacent

1027. Article 27(2) of the Forestry Act.
1028. Article 28 of the Forestry Act.
1029. Article 29(1) of the Forestry Act.
1030. Article 29(2) of the Forestry Act.
1031. Article 25 of the Forestry Act.
1032. Article 32(1) of the Forestry Act.
1033. Article 32(2) of the Forestry Act.
1034. Article 33 of the Forestry Act.

forests prior to conducting a sanctioned fire.[1035] In carrying out a sanctioned fire, the permitted party must have fire-extinguishing equipment on hand.[1036]

572. The government agency shall institute a forest fire squad based on forest conditions and organise a volunteer forest fire squad as needed.[1037] If a railway passes through a forest or forest protection area, fire and smoke prevention equipment must be available. The same applies to a factory situated near a forest protection area.[1038] If electrical wires pass through a forest or forest protection area, equipment that prevent electrical shorts must be available.[1039]

III. Biological Hazards or Disturbances

573. The forest owner is responsible for the elimination or prevention of biological hazards or disturbances in the forest. In such scenarios, the forest owner, subject to permission from the government and the necessity of the situation, may enter another's land to eliminate or prevent hazards to forest biology. In the event of damages, the forest owner shall be liable for compensation.[1040]

574. Should a forest be threatened or afflicted by biological organisms, the government may order the forest owner and other parties with interests to eliminate the organisms.[1041] The cost of said elimination or prevention shall be borne by the forest owner. However, if a prior agreement has been made regarding sharing of such costs, the terms of the agreement shall preside.[1042]

IV. Forest in Aboriginal People's Area

575. For national forests located within the traditional territory of the aboriginal people, the central government advises the aboriginal peoples' community development associations, legal entities, or individuals about reforestation and forest protection.[1043]

§6. Forestry Protection Outside the Forests

576. The local government shall inspect the trees located in its jurisdiction. Trees, bamboo groves, street trees, and individual trees important for ecology,

1035. Article 34(1) of the Forestry Act.
1036. Article 34(2) of the Forestry Act.
1037. Article 35 of the Forestry Act.
1038. Article 36(1) of the Forestry Act.
1039. Article 36(2) of the Forestry Act.
1040. Article 37 of the Forestry Act.
1041. Article 38(1) of the Forestry Act.
1042. Article 38(2) of the Forestry Act.
1043. Article 38-1(2) of the Forestry Act.

biology, geography, landscape, culture, history, education, research and community, recognised by a local government as trees subject to protection measures, must be recorded and announced.[1044]

577. The local government shall prioritise increased protection measures, maintaining the natural growth of the tree's crown and quality, providing regular care and health examinations, and protecting the growth habitat of the protected trees. The status of the trees shall be regularly announced on the local government website.[1045]

578. As a principle, trees that are located within the scope of lands marked for development, yet are subject to protection, shall remain in an 'as-is' condition. These trees may not be logged, transplanted, trimmed or sabotaged in any manner unless permitted by the local government. Furthermore, the growth habitat of the trees shall be well-maintained.[1046] To transplant protected trees, the developer must submit a transplantation and restoration plan for review and approval by the local government.[1047]

579. On approval for transplantation of protected trees from the local government, the developer shall hold a public explanation meeting to gather public opinion. Relevant organisations, agencies, and local residents may, within fifteen days of the public explanation meeting, submit their opinion in writing to the developer and a copy to the local government.[1048] The local government shall convene a public hearing and publish the date and venue of the said hearing in newspaper(s) and website(s) or publicise the information in any appropriate manner. Any member of the public may submit an opinion to the local government for reference. At the time of transplantation, the local government shall docket the trees for future tracking and regularly publish their status on the website.[1049]

580. For the transplantation of protected trees, the local government shall require the developer to provide land and funds for the replacement as compensation to the ecological environment.[1050]

581. For the management and protection of trees beyond the scale designated by the central government, planning, designing, and supervision shall be completed by legally registered technicians who are professionals in forestry and horticulture and have relevant skills or technical consulting institutes who hire such technicians. If the work is handled by the government at all levels, public corporations, and public

1044. Article 38-2(1) of the Forestry Act.
1045. Article 38-2(2) of the Forestry Act.
1046. Article 38-3(1) of the Forestry Act.
1047. Article 38-3(2) of the Forestry Act.
1048. Article 38-4(1) of the Forestry Act.
1049. Article 38-4(2) of the Forestry Act.
1050. Article 38-5 of the Forestry Act.

institutions, the work may be completed by people accredited as technicians in agencies, corporations, and institutions.[1051]

§7. SUPERVISION

582. A forest owner must provide the geographic name, area, tree, and bamboo species, its volume, a map of the forest location and a forest plan to the government for registration.[1052]

583. In case of forest neglect, over development for agriculture or over logging, the local government may assign specific management practices for the owner. If these practices are breached, the government may order the termination of logging and order reforestation.[1053] Should reforestation be ordered, however, not undertaken, the government may execute the order whose cost would be borne by the obligated party.[1054]

584. If publicly and privately held undeveloped mountains and lands are classified as forestry land, the government may order the owner to reforest within an assigned time. If reforestation is not completed within the specified time, the government may execute the order, the cost of which shall be borne by the obligated party.[1055]

585. In forest areas, unauthorised disposal of wastes or pollutants is prohibited.[1056] A harvester of state or public forests must maintain a record of the yield of each species, the volume, origins, and distribution channels. The harvester must choose a mark or seal to identify his forest products and file it with the local government. It must be used on all forest products before moving them out of the forest.[1057]

586. All forest products are subject to permit and inspection by the government before transport for distribution.[1058] The government shall set up checkpoints at crucial locations along the roadways to inspect the harvest. The government or public official engaged in such criminal investigation may, at their discretion, inspect the harvester's permit, account books, equipment, and materials.[1059]

1051. Article 38-6 of the Forestry Act.
1052. Article 39 of the Forestry Act.
1053. Article 40 of the Forestry Act.
1054. Article 41 of the Forestry Act.
1055. Article 42 of the Forestry Act.
1056. Article 43 of the Forestry Act.
1057. Article 44 of the Forestry Act.
1058. Article 45(1) of the Forestry Act.
1059. Article 45(2) of the Forestry Act.

§8. INCENTIVE

587. The taxation of forestry land and forest products is discounted or exempted.[1060] A forestry business that meets one of the following criteria may receive an award:[1061]

(1) Special achievement in reforestation or forestry management.
(2) A special forestry business whose products have significance to national defence or the nation's economic development.
(3) Large-scale cultivation of forests for supply to industries, national defence, ship building, road engineering and other important applications.
(4) Nurseries that propagate seedlings in large numbers for local reforestation.
(5) Those who invent or improve tree species or bamboo and wood applications and crafts.
(6) Significant contributions to extinguishing forest fires or mitigating damage caused by pests or pathogens and man-made disasters.
(7) Significant contributions to the research of forestry science.
(8) Significant contributions to the security of the nation's territory and conservation of water sources.

588. The award may be a cash prize, plaque, trophy, or commendation certificate. The qualifications, procedures and complete incentive measures for such issuance shall be decreed by the central government.[1062] In case of special achievements in protection or adoption of trees, rewards provisions shall apply *mutatis mutandis*.[1063]

I. Reforestation

589. To encourage reforestation by private individuals, aboriginal people and/or organisations, the government may, depending on actual needs, provide free seedlings, rewards, long-term low-interest loans or other assistance and rewards. The methods are decided by the central government and the Central Government Authority of the Aboriginal People.[1064] To encourage long-term reforestation by private individuals and/or organisations, the government shall establish a reforestation fund. The sources of funding would include:[1065]

(1) Allocation from water-rights fees.
(2) A reciprocation fund provided by those who undertake development of hillsides.

1060. Article 46 of the Forestry Act.
1061. Article 47(1) of the Forestry Act.
1062. Article 47(2) of the Forestry Act.
1063. Article 47-1 of the Forestry Act.
1064. Article 48 of the Forestry Act.
1065. Article 48-1(1) of the Forestry Act.

(3) Penalty fines for violation of this Act.
(4) Allocations from the engineering budget for water resource development projects.
(5) Allocations from government budgeting procedures.
(6) Donations.
(7) Other sources of income.

590. The water-right fee and the proportion of the allocation from the engineering budget for water resource development projects shall be regulated by the central water conservation agency in conjunction with the central government. At the time of permit issuance for hill development, the reciprocation fund fee shall be paid. The obligated party, calculation format, payment schedule, time, procedures, and regulations shall be decreed by the central government and submitted to the Executive Yuan for approval.[1066]

591. Undeveloped mountains and lands owned by the state shall be classified for forestry. Lands not reserved for state forestry operation may be designated and classified by the central government for reforestation and leased to the nationals of the ROC.[1067]

1066. Article 48-1(2) of the Forestry Act.
1067. Article 49 of the Forestry Act.

Chapter 5. Fishery Resources

592. There are two laws governing the allocation of fishery resources. The Fisheries Act, adopted on 11 November 1929, governs the fishery sector along with the Act for Distant Water Fisheries that came into effect in 2016. In general, the Act for Distant Water Fisheries regulates the 'use of any fishing vessel to conduct fishing in the high seas or in internal waters, territorial seas, and the exclusive economic zones of other countries'.[1068] However, the Fisheries Act deals with local fishery activities. Thus, both Acts complement each other to protect global fishery resources.

§1. Fisheries Act

I. Competent Authority

593. The main competent authorities for this Act are the Council of Agriculture and the Executive Yuan (at the central level), the municipal government (at the municipal level), and the county (city) government (at the county (city) level).[1069] The authorities are responsible for the fishery industries, including catching/harvesting and cultivating aquatic organisms, and the associated industries of processing, transportation and marketing.[1070]

594. For adjusting the fisheries structure, the competent authority may establish 'a fisheries advisory committee', which would consist of experts, scholars, fisheries associations and officials from relevant government agencies. The fisheries advisory committee shall be organised and operated in accordance with the regulations prescribed by the central authority.[1071]

II. Licensing

A. Persons

595. Any person who intends to operate a fishery in public or non-public waters must obtain an approval and a fishing licence from the competent authority.[1072] However, the authority may impose restrictions on these approvals for conserving aquatic resources or in public interest.[1073] The authority may collect fees from the applicants for the issuance of the fishing license.[1074]

1068. Article 4 of Act for Distant Water Fisheries.
1069. Article 2 of the Fishery Act.
1070. Article 3 of the Fishery Act.
1071. Article 13 of the Fishery Act.
1072. Article 6 of the Fishery Act.
1073. Article 9 of the Fishery Act.
1074. Article 7 of the Fishery Act.

596. However, the licence would not be issued to the following:[1075]

(1) Any fishery operator whose fishing licence has been revoked or abolished by the authority in accordance with this Act or the Act for Distant Water Fisheries.
(2) Any vessel that is forfeited or confiscated.
(3) Any vessel that is imported without permission from the authority.
(4) Any fishery operator who is presently restrained or suspended from the right to operate a fishery in accordance with Article 10 of this Act.
(5) Any fishery operator whose fishing licence is under administrative disposition of suspension in accordance with this Act or the Act for Distant Water Fisheries.
(6) Any fishery operator who has not paid the fine in accordance with this Act or the Act for Distant Water Fisheries.
(7) Any fishing vessel whose previous fishery operator violated this Act or the Act for Distant Water Fisheries but is yet to face punishment.

B. Boat

597. The building, modification or chartering of any fishing vessel used by a fishery operator for commercial operations must be permitted by the competent authority.[1076] The exportation or importation of any fishing vessel must be permitted by the competent authority in accordance with the regulations provided by the competent trade authorities.[1077]

C. Revoking of Licences

598. A licence may be revoked for violation of laws or other reasons:

(1) Any fishery operator who violates the provisions of this Act or any other regulations promulgated pursuant to this Act may be restrained or suspended from operating a fishery or rendering administrative services by the central government for not more than one year.
(2) If the violation is considered gross, the central government may withdraw the approval for fishery operation or revoke the fishing licence.
(3) The central government may suspend the Certificate of Fishing Vessel Officer or Fishing Vessel Crew Identification for not more than one year for any fishery employee who violates this Act or any other regulations promulgated pursuant to this Act.

1075. Article 7-1 of the Fishery Act.
1076. Article 8(1) of the Fishery Act.
1077. Article 8(2) of the Fishery Act.

(4) If the violation is considered gross, the central government may revoke the Certificate of Fishing Vessel Officer or Fishing Vessel Crew Identification.[1078]

599. Where any of the following circumstances occurs, the competent authority shall revoke the approval for fishery operation:[1079]

(1) A fishery operator who has no justification for being unable to undertake the fishery operation for more than one year from the date of approval or who suspends his/her fishery operation for more than two years without approval from the date of operation commencement.
(2) A fishery operator who applies and is approved to operate a fishery as a national of the ROC loses his nationality.
(3) Any applicant who obtains the approval of the fishery operation by fraud or illicit means.

1. Legal Implications of Licence Revoking

600. Any fishery operator's fishing vessel whose fishing licence or approval of fishery operation has been revoked shall not leave port, except those who have re-applied and been granted fishing licence by the competent authorities.[1080] Any fishery operator's fishing vessel whose fishing licence has been suspended or the right to operate fishery has been restrained or suspended shall not leave port during the period of administrative disposition.[1081] If a fishing vessel leaves the port in spite of the restriction imposed by the central government, the authority shall command the vessel to return to port within a designated period.[1082] Any fishing vessel leaving a port in violation of rules may be restricted by the central government, with the assistance of the Coast Guard, from leaving port or commanded to immediately return. In case of any resistance, the authority may take compulsory measures.[1083]

III. Crews

601. The central government shall prescribe regulations on the management of crew members of fishing vessels for the purposes of maintaining the orderly operation of fishing vessels and navigation and operation safety.[1084]

1078. Article 10 of the Fishery Act.
1079. Article 11 of the Fishery Act.
1080. Article 11-1(1) of the Fishery Act.
1081. Article 11-1(2) of the Fishery Act.
1082. Article 11-1(3) of the Fishery Act.
1083. Article 11-1(4) of the Fishery Act.
1084. Article 12 of the Fishery Act.

IV. Conservation and Management

A. Restrains or Prohibitions

602. For the purposes of resources management and fisheries structure adjustment, the competent authority may promulgate regulations on the following matters:[1085]

(1) Restriction or prohibition of catching, harvesting or processing aquatic organisms.
(2) Restriction or prohibition of the sale or possession of aquatic organisms or the products made therefrom.
(3) Restriction or prohibition of the use of fishing gear and fishing methods.
(4) Restriction or prohibition of fishing area and fishing period.
(5) Restriction or removal of objects obstructing the migratory routes of aquatic animals.
(6) Restriction or prohibition of placing or dumping objects harmful to aquatic organisms.
(7) Restriction or prohibition of placing or removal of protective objects necessary for the propagation of aquatic organisms.
(8) Restriction or prohibition of transplantation of aquatic organisms.

603. Aquatic organisms shall not be caught or harvested using:[1086]

(1) Toxic substances.
(2) Explosives or other dynamites.
(3) Electricity or other narcotics.

604. However, these restrictions do not apply to experimental and research purposes done with permission from the central/municipal government.

B. Zone and Planning

605. For the purposes of conserving aquatic resources, the competent authority may designate and establish an 'aquatic organisms propagation and conservation zone'.[1087]

606. However, the establishment of these zones shall be subject to the approval of the municipal government. In the case of the county(city), the competent authority shall submit a 'management plan of the conservation zones' to the central government for approval and promulgate the establishment on approval. In case of the

1085. Article 44 of the Fishery Act.
1086. Article 48 of the Fishery Act.
1087. Article 45(1) of the Fishery Act.

establishment of conservation zone involving two or more provinces (municipalities), approval must be received from the central government.[1088]

C. Survey

607. For the purposes of conserving aquatic resources, the competent authority may undertake a 'survey of respective fisheries regarding their catch volume, operation conditions, and sea conditions'.[1089] In undertaking the investigation, the competent authority may request the fishery operator or employee to submit a report on catch volume, operation period, fishing gears, fishing methods, and other relevant information. The fishery operator or employee shall not refuse.[1090]

D. Enforcement

608. The competent authority may designate officer(s) to a fishing vessel, fishing grounds, fish farms of inland aquaculture or other relevant sites to inspect the operator's catch, fishing gears, account books, and other objects and to question any relevant party. The Coast Guard Administration may, pursuant to its mandate, designate officer(s) to the fishing vessel for inspection and questioning of any relevant party. The relevant party shall not evade, obstruct, or deny any inspections.[1091]

609. If the officer finds discrepancies or offences during inspection, he is, however, not in the position to request the judicial authority to proceed with the search in time; the officer may provisionally seize the fishing vessel, the catch, and any other object that may serve as evidence. In case of violation of the provisions of this Act, the catch, the fishing gears, and other objects may be sealed.[1092] The provisional seizure or seal shall be witnessed by any person in charge of the fishing vessel or the site or any civil servant. An inventory must be made of the objects provisionally seized or sealed.[1093]

V. Fishery Development

A. Loan and Insurance

610. For the purposes of facilitating accommodation of fisheries fund, the competent authority may, in consultation with the concerned authorities, consult with

1088. Article 45(2) of the Fishery Act.
1089. Article 46(1) of the Fishery Act.
1090. Article 46(2) of the Fishery Act.
1091. Article 49(1) of the Fishery Act.
1092. Article 49(2) of the Fishery Act.
1093. Article 49(3) of the Fishery Act.

financial institutions for providing fishery loans. If necessary, the financial and fisheries authorities may approve the establishment of fisheries financial institutions.[1094]

611. For promoting fisheries investment and assuring fisheries security, the competent authority shall coordinate with the concerned authorities to conduct fisheries insurance programmes or designate fishermen's associations or consult with public or private insurance institutions to undertake the programmes.[1095]

612. For the safety of fishermen's lives and property, the competent authorities may prescribe regulations regarding salvage operations for fishing vessels in maritime distress, assistance for fishermen and fishing vessels in distress, awards to motor-powered vessel owners and insurance for fishermen and their sea operations.[1096]

B. Government Measures

613. For assuring fishery security and maintaining an orderly operation, the competent authority shall undertake the following:[1097]

(1) Construction and maintenance of fishing ports and fisheries infrastructures.
(2) Disposition of patrol fleets for salvage, patrol, and fishery protection.
(3) Establishment of fisheries radio broadcasting stations.
(4) Establishment of safety facilities such as beacons, sign poles, and weather forecasting systems.
(5) Prescription of regulations governing the operation of fishing grounds and fishing vessels.
(6) Requisition to the Ministry of Defence and other authorities for necessary assistance and protection.

C. Rewards and Funds

614. The competent authority may provide awards or incentives to those who have performed any of the following:[1098]

(1) Improving facilities conducive to fisheries safety and salvage.
(2) Improving fishing vessels, fishing gears, fishing methods or processing methods for fisheries products with remarkable results.

1094. Article 52 of the Fishery Act.
1095. Article 53 of the Fishery Act.
1096. Article 53-1 of the Fishery Act.
1097. Article 54 of the Fishery Act.
1098. Article 55 of the Fishery Act.

(3) Promoting fisheries education or conducting fisheries research with remarkable results.
(4) Exploiting fisheries resources conducive to fisheries development.
(5) Any other performance with a significant contribution to fisheries development.

615. To promote fisheries development, the government shall establish fisheries development fund. The competent authority shall propose the amount of the said fund to the Executive Yuan for approval and duly appropriate its budget.[1099]

616. To encourage fishermen to voluntarily cease fishing and reward them for complying with the prohibited fishing period, which lasts every year for two months or above, the central government shall annually budget a reward.[1100]

D. Price Stabilisation Scheme

617. For coping with price fluctuation of fisheries products and stabilising the market of fisheries products, the competent authority may take guiding measures to maintain stable prices and SD of industries.[1101]

E. Tax Incentives

618. Fishing vessels, fishing gears and materials imported for fisheries production are exempted from or receive discounts in import duties. Items imported by fisheries research institutes for experimental and research purposes are exempted from import duties.[1102] Fuel for powered equipment used in fisheries is exempted from commodity tax. The Executive Yuan shall decide the standard of preferential price for the fuel.[1103]

§2. Distant Water Fisheries Act

619. The motivation to promulgate additional laws to govern distant water fisheries is related to the EU's fishing ban. Taiwanese fish products may face an import ban in Europe after the European Commission issued a yellow card on 1 October 2015 over illegal, unreported, and unregulated (IUU) fishing. Taiwan and Comoros have six months 'to propose measures to be incorporated into an action plan with clear benchmarks and criteria'. If they fail to show enough commitment, they will face a red card, i.e., a ban on export to the EU. Red cards have already been handed

1099. Article 56 of the Fishery Act.
1100. Article 59-1 of the Fishery Act.
1101. Article 57 of the Fishery Act.
1102. Article 58 of the Fishery Act.
1103. Article 59 of the Fishery Act.

to Cambodia, Guinea, and Sri Lanka.[1104] Therefore, this Act was promulgated on 20 July 2016 to ensure the conservation of marine fisheries resources, strengthen distant water fisheries management, curb IUU fishing and improve traceability of catches and fisheries products to promote the sustainable operation of distant water fisheries.[1105]

I. Competent Authority

620. Like the Fishery Act, the main authority is the Council of Agriculture and the Executive Yuan in the central government. However, as the distant fishery matters are international in nature,[1106] selected other authorities may play a role. For instance, the coastal guard authority may dispatch personnel to inspect fishing vessel(s), catches and fisheries products, fishing gear(s), account books, and other objects and question distant water fisheries operators, employees or data holders who shall not refuse, evade or obstruct such request.[1107] The police may inspect the catches or fisheries products, account books, and other objects and question any relevant party.[1108]

II. Planning

621. The competent authority shall, taking reference from international conventions, treaties, agreements, and conservation and management measures, draw up and promulgate 'national plans of action' on the following matters with a precautionary principle, ecosystem-based approach and the best available scientific advice:[1109]

(1) Conservation, management, utilisation, and maintenance of maximum sustainable yield of marine fisheries resources.
(2) Measures in response to the change of marine fisheries resources and marine ecosystem.
(3) Goals for sustainable operation, development strategies, and implementing steps for distant water fisheries.
(4) Measures to balance the fishing capacity and the marine fisheries resources.

1104. Taiwan could face EU fish ban, 2 Oct. 2015, available at: https://euobserver.com/green-economy/130528.
1105. Article 1 of the Distant Water Fisheries Act.
1106. Article 3 of the Distant Water Fisheries Act.
1107. Article 16 of the Distant Water Fisheries Act.
1108. Article 25(1) of the Distant Water Fisheries Act: 'The competent authority may dispatch personnel to the vessels, offices, storages, or other relevant sites of the industry related to distant water fisheries to inspect the catches or fisheries products, account books and other objects, as well as to question any relevant party who shall not refuse, evade, or obstruct. If necessary, such inspection may be conducted by the competent authority together with personnel from the coast guard authority or police authorities.'
1109. Article 5 of the Distant Water Fisheries Act.

(5) Measures to guide, assist, and subsidise the distant water fisheries operators, distant water fisheries employees, and the industry related to distant water fisheries in response to the structural adjustment of the distant water fisheries.
(6) Establishment of a supervision and management system for distant water fisheries and human resource training.
(7) Training of human resources for distant water fisheries and development of relevant technologies and equipment.
(8) Cooperation with other countries and international fishery organisations.
(9) Prevention, deterrence, and elimination of IUU fishing.

III. Licence

622. Any person with the nationality of the ROC who intends to engage in distant water fisheries must obtain a fishing licence pursuant to the Fisheries Act and apply to the competent authority for a distant water fisheries permit.[1110] The issuing guidance is stipulated in Articles 7[1111] and 8,[1112] and failing to meet any of

1110. Article 6 of the Distant Water Fisheries Act.

1111. Article 7 of the Distant Water Fisheries Act: 'In case that any applicant referred to in Article 6, paragraph 1 has any of the following circumstances, the issuance of the distant water fisheries permit shall be denied:

(1) A person is declared incompetent or limited capacity;
(2) A person is subject to the order of the commencement of guardianship or assistance, and such order is not yet revoked;
(3) A person is declared bankrupt and having not yet resume his/her rights;
(4) A person is sentenced imprisonment for violating this Act, the Fisheries Act or the Act to Govern Investment in the Operation of Foreign Flag Fishing Vessels and such sentence is not yet executed, not executed completely, or is on probation whose period is not yet expired, or 2 years have not passed since such sentence is executed completely, on probation which is expired, or pardoned;
(5) A person is sentenced to a short-term imprisonment or criminal fine for violating this Act, the Fisheries Act or the Act to Govern Investment in the Operation of Foreign Flag Fishing Vessels and such sentence is not yet executed, not executed completely or 2 years have not passed since such sentence is executed completely;
(6) A person whose fishing vessel is sentenced to revocation or withdrawal of fishing license pursuant to this Act or the Fisheries Act and 2 years have not passed since such sentence is executed completely;
(7) The fishing vessel that applies for the distant water fisheries permit is sentenced to a fine pursuant to this Act, the Fisheries Act or the Act to Govern Investment in the Operation of Foreign Flag Fishing Vessels and such fine is not paid completely;
(8) The fishing vessel that applies for the distant water fisheries permit is sentenced to suspension of its fishing license pursuant to this Act or the Fisheries Act, and such sentence is not executed completely.'

1112. Article 8 of the Distant Water Fisheries Act: 'In any of the following circumstances, the competent authority shall deny the issuance of the distant water fisheries permit. For the distant water fisheries permit that has been issued, the competent authority shall adjust, limit, or revoke:

(1) The restriction placed by conservation and management measures is changed;
(2) In responses to the conclusion as a result of consultation between the Republic of China and other countries or international fisheries organizations;

these may lead to a rejection of application, adjustment, limitation or revocation:[1113]

IV. Regulations

623. Any fishing vessel of distant water fisheries must be installed with a vessel monitoring system (hereinafter referred to as VMS) and electronic logbook system (hereinafter referred to as E-logbook) before leaving port. Regulations on the management and guidance of the VMS and E-logbook, the electronic navigational chart and the monitoring centre shall be prescribed by the competent authority.[1114]

624. All fishing vessels of distant water fisheries shall comply with conservation and management measures and international standards of fishing on the high seas.[1115]

V. Prohibition

625. No fishing vessel of distant water fisheries shall conduct transshipment in-port or at-sea or landing in-port without authorisation.[1116] Fishing vessels must not enter waters under national jurisdictions of other countries. Notwithstanding this provision, authorised fishing vessels from other countries can engage in fisheries activities and may fish in the exclusive economic zones of other countries.[1117]

626. Any person with the nationality of the ROC would also be prohibited under certain conditions,[1118] such as falsification or alteration of catch certificate documents, using catch certificate documents not issued for the concerned catch or intentionally using falsified or altered catch certificate documents to sell catches or

---

(3) The fishing vessel is subject to a voluntary or interim conservation and management measure adopted by an international fisheries organization under establishment;
(4) The country with which the fishing vessel engages in fisheries cooperation is incapable of controlling and managing foreign fishing vessels fishing in the waters under its national jurisdiction.
(5) The country with which the fishing vessel engages in fisheries cooperation is listed on the IUU fishing non-cooperating countries list or is subject to a letter of identification for more than 2 years by other countries, international fisheries organizations, or other economic integrated organizations;
(6) Where it's necessary for the management of marine fisheries resources.'

1113. Article 8 of the Distant Water Fisheries Act.
1114. Article 9 of the Distant Water Fisheries Act.
1115. Article 10 of the Distant Water Fisheries Act.
1116. Article 11 of the Distant Water Fisheries Act.
1117. Article 12 of the Distant Water Fisheries Act.
1118. Article 13 of the Distant Water Fisheries Act: 'Any person with the nationality of the Republic of China shall not conduct any of the following serious infringements:

fisheries products. If sufficient and concrete evidence indicates a fishing vessel being involved in serious infringement, the competent authority shall order the

---

(1) Conducting distant water fisheries without the fishing license or the distant water fisheries permit referred to in Article 6, paragraph 1, or conducting distant water fisheries during the period of the execution of suspension of the fishing license;
(2) Leaving ports without installing VMS or E-logbook system onboard fishing vessels, in violation of Article 9, paragraph 1;
(3) Conducting trans-shipment at-sea, in-port or landing in-port without the authorization of the competent authority, in violation of Article 11, paragraph 1;
(4) Engaging in fisheries cooperation without the approval of the competent authority in violation of Article 12, paragraph 1, and fishing in waters under national jurisdictions of other countries;
(5) Falsifying, altering or concealing Chinese/English vessel name, names of registry port, CT numbers, or international radio call sign;
(6) Intentionally causing the VMS to misreport vessels positions or rendering VMS non-functional when fishing;
(7) Continuing catching species with catch limit when the total catch of such species of the fishing vessel has exceeded 20 percent of the quota allowed by the competent authority pursuant to the regulations prescribed in accordance with subparagraph (4) of Article 10, paragraph 2;
(8) Fishing in prohibited fishing areas or periods;
(9) Using fishing gears prohibited by the competent authority;
(10) Engaging in fishing activities that are not authorized by the competent authority;
(11) Fishing for, retaining, trans-shipping, landing or selling prohibited species;
(12) Not submitting or filling in logbooks or catch reports, in violation of the regulations prescribed in accordance with Article 10, paragraph 2, or seriously misreporting logbooks or catch reports;
(13) Refusing, evading, or obstructing any observer dispatched by the competent authority, the international fisheries organization or the country that the fisheries cooperation in engaged with for carrying out his/her observing duties;
(14) Refusing, evading, or obstructing any inspection referred to in Article 11, paragraph 2; Article 12, paragraph 2; Article 16; Article 17, paragraph 1; or Article 25, paragraph 1; or any audit conducted pursuant to the regulations prescribed in accordance with Article 25, paragraph 4;
(15) Falsifying, altering, destroying or concealing evidence related to violation of this Act;
(16) Providing catch certificate documents of a fishing vessel for the use of catches of other fishing vessel(s), or using catch certificate documents of other fishing vessel(s) for selling catches caught by itself;
(17) Falsification or alteration of catch certificate documents, using catch certificate documents not issued to the catch concerned, or intentionally using catch certificate documents that are falsified or altered to sell catches or fisheries products;
(18) Participating in joint fishing with, trans-shipping with or supplying any fishing vessel listed on the IUU fishing vessel lists of the international fisheries organizations or stateless vessel;
(19) Trading (purchasing, selling, marketing, etc.) or processing catches or fisheries products with the knowledge that such catches or fisheries products originate from any of the following circumstances:
    i. Any circumstances as stipulated in subparagraph (1) to the preceding subparagraph of this Article; or
    ii. Catches are caught by any fishing vessel listed in the IUU fishing vessel lists of the international fisheries organizations.'

fishing vessel to stop fishing and navigate to a designated port within the required time for further inspection.[1119]

627. Any person with the nationality of the ROC shall not engage in or support IUU fishing. If a person of Chinese nationality is hired on board a foreign fishing vessel suspected of IUU, the competent authority shall, without prejudice to the sovereignty of the flag, take appropriate measures to prevent IUU fishing. The competent authority shall cooperate with international fishery organisations or other countries to prevent and deter Chinese nationals from engaging in or supporting IUU fishing.[1120]

VI. Facilitation of Law Enforcement

628. For fisheries management or for the submission of relevant data of individual fishing vessels to relevant international fishery organisations, the competent authority may request the distant water fishery operators, employees or data holders to provide information on catch quantities, fishing area(s), fishing period(s), fishing gear(s), fishing method(s), vessel positions, operational level data, transshipment, landing, selling and other relevant information. Distant water fishery operators, employees or data holders shall not refuse such request.[1121]

629. The competent authority or the Coast Guard Administration may, pursuant to their mandates, dispatch personnel to inspect fishing vessel(s), catches and fisheries products, fishing gear(s), account books, and other objects and question distant water fishery operators, employees or data holders who shall not refuse, evade or obstruct such request.[1122]

630. Any fishing vessel fishing on the high seas shall accept the boarding and inspection conducted by the designated inspectors of countries who conduct reciprocal high seas boarding and inspection of the ROC or inspectors from vessels designated by international fishery organisations. Distant water fishery operators and employees shall not evade, obstruct or refuse such inspection.[1123] The international fishery organisations or countries that conduct reciprocal high seas boarding and inspection with the ROC and the names and registration numbers of the designated vessels shall be promulgated by the competent authority.[1124]

1119. Article 18 of the Distant Water Fisheries Act.
1120. Article 14 of the Distant Water Fisheries Act.
1121. Article 15 of the Distant Water Fisheries Act.
1122. Article 16 of the Distant Water Fisheries Act.
1123. Article 17(1) of the Distant Water Fisheries Act.
1124. Article 17(2) of the Distant Water Fisheries Act.

VII. Port Regulations: Ban on Leaving or Entering the Port

631. In case of any of the following circumstances, the fishing vessel shall not leave the port.[1125] This ban is also imposed under other infringements of this Act:[1126]

(1) A fishing vessel whose fishing licence has been revoked.
(2) A fishing vessel whose fishing licence is suspended and is serving punishment.

632. Any foreign-flagged fishing vessel that intends to enter a Chinese port must obtain permission from the competent authority and comply with the regulations of the shipping administration, customs, sanitary, immigration, inspection, quarantine and coast guard. In case of force majeure or distress, the port entry may be granted after notification.[1127] In any of the following circumstances, fishing vessels shall be denied port entry:[1128]

(1) The fishing vessel is listed on the IUU vessel list of other countries, international fishery organisations or other regional economic integrated organisations.
(2) The flag state of the fishing vessel is identified as IUU fishing non-cooperating country or is subject to a letter of identification for more than two years by other countries, international fishery organisations or other regional economic integrated organisations.
(3) The fishing vessel is involved in IUU fishing.
(4) Where there is a written request from another flag state to prohibit such fishing vessel from entering the port.
(5) When a fishing vessel cannot be identified.

633. The competent authority may dispatch personnel to the fishing vessels, relevant offices, storages or other sites to inspect the catches or fisheries products, account books and other objects and question any relevant party who may not refuse, evade, or obstruct. If necessary, such inspection may be conducted by the competent authority together with personnel from the coast guard authorities or the police. The course of the inspection must be recorded and filed for reference.[1129]

1125. Article 20(1) of the Distant Water Fisheries Act.
1126. Article 21 of the Distant Water Fisheries Act: 'For any fishing vessel that leaves the port against the provisions stipulated in Article 9, paragraph 1; Article 19, paragraph 2; and Article 20, paragraph 1, the competent authority may commission the Coast Guard Administration to take appropriate measures to stop such fishing vessel from leaving the port. In case that such fishing vessel resists, the Coast Guard Administration may take compulsory measures. For such fishing vessel that has left the port, the competent authority shall order such fishing vessel to navigate to the designated port within required timeframe.'
1127. Article 22(1) of the Distant Water Fisheries Act.
1128. Article 22(2) of the Distant Water Fisheries Act.
1129. Article 23(1) of the Distant Water Fisheries Act.

VIII. Other Regulations

A. High-Risk Fishing Vessels

634. In case any distant water fisheries operator meets one of the following conditions, the competent authority shall categorise his/her fishing vessels as high risk and implement special management measures:[1130]

(1) A serious infringement stipulated in Article 13, paragraph 1 is conducted by the distant water fisheries operator.
(2) Accumulated fines of over 2 million New Taiwan Dollars have been imposed upon the distant water fisheries operator within three years for violating this Act.
(3) The accumulated period of fishing licence suspension is for more than three months, and three years have not passed since the completion of the punishment.

B. Export and Issuance of Catch Certificate Documents

635. Industries related to distant water fisheries who intend to conduct export trade of catches or products of distant water fisheries shall establish a code of conduct and operating procedures for purchase and sales and submit them to the competent authority for approval.[1131]

636. The application for catch certificate documents shall only be made by industries related to distant water fisheries with approval to conduct export trade of catches or products of distant water fisheries.[1132]

C. Hire Foreign Crew Member

637. Any distant water fisheries operator intending to hire foreign crew members must obtain permission from the competent authority. Such hiring shall be done by the distant water fisheries operator personally or through domestic intermediaries or agents (hereinafter referred to as the agents).[1133]

1130. Article 24(1) of the Distant Water Fisheries Act.
1131. Article 25(3) of the Distant Water Fisheries Act.
1132. Article 25(4) of the Distant Water Fisheries Act.
1133. Article 26 of the Distant Water Fisheries Act.

D. Dispatch Staff Stationed Abroad

638. To strengthen the management of distant water fisheries and promote cooperation with other countries and international fishery organizations, the competent authority shall assign and dispatch staff stationed abroad responsible for fisheries.[1134]

E. Comprehensive Information System

639. The competent authority shall establish an integrated, comprehensive information system on distant water fisheries to strengthen their management.[1135]

F. Commission Professional Institution(s)

640. The competent authority may commission professional institution(s) to conduct the following:[1136]

(1) Providing advice and guidance to distant water fisheries.
(2) Monitoring and management of vessel position.
(3) Development and management of E-logbook reporting software.
(4) Collection, statistics, analysis, and utilisation of catch data.
(5) Transshipment in-port or landing in-port inspection.
(6) Dispatching observers.
(7) Assisting fishery associations to implement management policy and measures prescribed by the competent authority.

IX. Industry Development of Distant Water Fisheries

A. Planning

641. The competent authority shall draw up and implement a 'distant water fisheries development plan'.[1137] This will take into account the fisheries' production, livelihood of fishermen, and marine ecology to develop a sustainable operation for Taiwanese distant water fisheries.[1138]

1134. Article 27 of the Distant Water Fisheries Act.
1135. Article 28 of the Distant Water Fisheries Act.
1136. Article 29 of the Distant Water Fisheries Act.
1137. Article 30(1) of the Distant Water Fisheries Act.
1138. Article 30(2) of the Distant Water Fisheries Act.

642. Any distant water fisheries operator who intends to conduct exploratory fishing to develop new fishing gear(s), fishing method(s) or fishing ground(s) must submit an exploratory fishing plan and apply to the competent authority for permission.[1139]

B. Assistance and Subsidy

643. The competent authority may assist private sectors to conduct the following matters:[1140]

(1) Negotiations related to distant water fisheries or conclusion of agreement(s) with other countries, international fishery organisations or foreign organisations or institutes related to fisheries.
(2) Exchange of international information, technology, and human resource related to distant water fisheries.
(3) Standardisation of international technology, joint research, and cooperation on technology related to distant water fisheries.
(4) Holding international academic meetings or exhibitions related to distant water fisheries.
(5) Research on overseas markets for fisheries products or the dissemination of information related to distant water fisheries.
(6) Training of native or foreign crew members, officers, or observers.

644. To encourage distant water fisheries operators to introduce and implement new technology for conserving marine ecosystem environment and sustainable operation, the competent authority may give appropriate financial aid depending on the financial situation of the government.[1141]

C. Research and Development

645. To promote scientific and technological research related to distant water fisheries, the competent authority may conduct the following:[1142]

(1) International cooperation for research and assessment of marine fisheries resources.
(2) Exploitation of new fishing grounds.
(3) Research on marine fisheries biodiversity.
(4) Research and evaluation on sustainable operation of distant water fisheries.

1139. Article 31 of the Distant Water Fisheries Act.
1140. Article 32 of the Distant Water Fisheries Act.
1141. Article 33 of the Distant Water Fisheries Act.
1142. Article 34 of the Distant Water Fisheries Act.

Part III. Spatial Planning

646. Taiwan's spatial planning legal regime has long featured multiple laws and fragmented legislation. The Urban Planning Act[1143] was promulgated in mainland China on 8 June 1939. However, the Regional Plan Act came about on 31 January 1974.[1144] Thus, urban land has long been governed by the Urban Planning Act, while non-urban land is governed by the Regional Plan Act. The Executive Yuan planned to provide a single planning Act on 11 May 1995.[1145] However, the bill failed to get approval in the parliament and was finally adopted in 2015 and published in 2016.[1146] This Act replaced the Regional Plan Act, which ceased to exist in the municipalities and counties (cities) authorities publicly revealed the functional zone maps.[1147] Nevertheless, environmental conservation zones may still be subject to both the National Spatial Plan Act and the National Park Act, while the urban-rural development zones may be subject to both the National Spatial Plan Act and the Urban Plan Act.

647. Thus, in this section, we will elaborate on the latest legal regime of national spatial planning.

1143. Urban Planning Law, Announced Date 1939-06-08, Amended Date: 2021-05-26, available at: https://law.moj.gov.tw/ENG/LawClass/LawHistory.aspx?pcode=D0070001.

1144. Regional Plan Act, Announced Date: 1974-01-31, Amended Date: 2000-01-26, available at: https://law.moj.gov.tw/ENG/LawClass/LawAll.aspx?pcode=D0070030.

1145. Ministry of Interior, Special website for National Spatial Planning Act, available at: https://www.cpami.gov.tw/%E6%9C%80%E6%96%B0%E6%B6%88%E6%81%AF/%E6%A5%AD%E5%8B%99%E6%96%B0%E8%A8%8A/10182-%E5%9C%8B%E5%9C%9F%E8%A8%88%E7%95%AB%E6%B3%95%E5%B0%88%E5%8D%80.html.

1146. 6 January 2016.

1147. Article 45(3) of the National Spatial Plan Act.

Chapter 1. National Spatial Planning

648. The National Spatial Planning Act was adopted on 6 January 2016. However, since this Act was adopted after the GHG Management Act of 2015, the consideration for climate change has been indicted in its legal purpose: 'This Act specifically establishes guidelines concerning measures to cope with climate change, assure land use safety, conserve the natural environment and cultural assets, promote the reasonable allocation of resources and industries, strengthen land consolidation and management mechanisms, and restore sensitive areas and damaged land in pursuit of sustainable development.'[1148]

§1. Competent Authority

649. The competent authorities for this Act are the MOI at the national level, the municipality government at the municipality level and the county (city) government at the county (city) level.[1149] The work is further distributed among the central[1150] and local authorities.[1151]

1148. Article 1 of the National Spatial Plan Act.
1149. Article 2 of the National Spatial Plan Act.
1150. Article 3 of the National Spatial Plan Act: 'The following terms, used in this Act, shall be defined as follows.

1. Spatial plan: establishment of spatial development plan to set guidelines for the conservation and utilization of resources on the land and in marine under the jurisdiction of the ROC government, to achieve the sustainable development goal.
2. National spatial plan: a plan established with specific objectives and consistent with relevant policies, concerning the land use throughout the country.
3. Municipality or county (city) spatial plan: a plan established for the development and control of land and marine under the jurisdiction of a municipality or county (city) government.
4. Metropolitan area: an area that consists of one or more central cities as the core and municipalities, counties (cities) and townships (towns, cities, and districts) that are socially and economically associated closely with the core.
5. Specific area: an area designated by the central competent authority as having natural, economic, cultural significance or other properties.
6. Sectoral spatial development strategy: a development strategy that has been established by the competent authority after consultation with the relevant authorities.
7. Functional zone: demarcation of environmental conservation zones, marine resource zones, agricultural development zones and urban-rural development zones consistent with the characteristics of land resources to facilitate conservation, utilization, and management of the land.
8. Growth management: management policies and measures established to promote land use effectively, ensure sustainable development, improve environmental quality and protect social justice, by taking into account the carrying capacity of the environment, public facility service standards and financial burden, user rights and obligations, and profit-loss balance, to regulate urban-rural development and to define the locations and timelines of future development of various areas.'

1151. Article 4 of the National Spatial Plan Act: 'The central competent authority shall be responsible for the following.

I. Main Authorities

650. The agencies that are responsible for the establishment, review, and approval of the National spatial plan are as follows:[1152]

(1) National Spatial Plan: to be established and reviewed by the MOI and presented to the Executive Yuan for approval.
(2) Municipality or county (city) Spatial Plans: to be established and reviewed by the competent authority of *each municipality or county (city) government* and presented to the MOI for approval.

651. For specific areas in the National Spatial Plan, including land and sea, that belong to indigenous people, these areas shall be jointly established by the central government and the Central Competent Authority for Indigenous Peoples in accordance with Article 21 of the Indigenous Peoples' Basic Law.[1153]

§2. General Principles and White Paper

652. The basic spatial planning principles are as follows:[1154]

(1) Spatial planning shall comply with international conventions and regulations and promote SD.

---

1. Establishment, announcement, revision, and enforcement of the National spatial plan.
2. Review, approval, and supervision of the spatial plan that are established by municipality or county (city) governments.
3. Establishment of functional zone demarcated priorities and principles.
4. Establishment of land use permit systems and regulatory measures for land use control.
5. Issuance of land use permits for environmental conservation zones and marine resource zones, review and approval of permit changes and revocation of permits.
6. Other relevant issues.

The competent authorities of municipalities or counties (cities) shall be responsible for the following.

1. Establishment, announcement, revision and enforcement of municipality, county (city) spatial plans.
2. Demarcation of functional zones.
3. Enforcement of land use control measures and establishment and enforcement of municipality and county (city) land use control measures.
4. Issuance of land use permits for agricultural development zones and urban-rural development zones, review and approval of permit changes, and revocation of permits.'

1152. Article 11(1) of the National Spatial Plan Act.
1153. Article 11(2) of the National Spatial Plan Act.
1154. Article 6 of the National Spatial Plan Act.

(2) Natural conditions, water resources and climate change shall be taken into consideration in spatial planning to prevent disasters on land and facilitate emergency responses.
(3) Environmental conservation zones shall be used for conservation purposes, and other uses may be prohibited or restricted.
(4) Marine resource zones shall be used with consideration for resource sustainability, diverse needs shall be consolidated, and priorities of uses shall be established.
(5) Agricultural development zones shall be used to ensure food security. Important agricultural production environments and facilities shall be safeguarded, and fragmented development shall be avoided.
(6) Urban-rural development zones shall be guided toward compact development and placed under growth management to create suitable and harmonious living environments and efficient production environments and provide sufficient public facilities.
(7) Metropolitan areas shall be developed in sympathy with regional characteristics and overall development, whereas cross-region consolidation shall be reinforced to achieve the complementation of resources and strengthen regional functions to improve competitiveness.
(8) Specific areas shall be developed in accordance with topography, geomorphology, geographic features, and cultural characteristics of the region and the requirements set forth in other regulations.
(9) If spatial planning involves indigenous people's land, traditional cultures, territories, and knowledge shall be respected and preserved, and mechanisms to achieve mutual benefits and prosperity shall be established.
(10) Spatial planning shall be conducted with extensive public participation and informational transparency.
(11) Environmental conservation shall be considered for land use, and fair and efficient regulatory mechanisms shall be established.

653. The central competent authority shall release a spatial planning white paper periodically through regular channels on the Internet and other appropriate channels.[1155]

§3. National and Local Spatial Plan

I. Types of Spatial Plan

654. The types of spatial plans are as follows:[1156]

(1) National Spatial Plan.
(2) Municipality or county (city) Spatial Plans.

1155. Article 5 of the National Spatial Plan Act.
1156. Article 8(1) of the National Spatial Plan Act.

655. However, the Municipality or county (city) Spatial Plans must not conflict with the National Spatial Plan.[1157] In addition, national park plans, urban plans and departmental plans established by specific competent authorities must not conflict with the National Spatial Plan.[1158]

II. Preparation

656. To improve the drafting process and transparency, opinions of scholars, specialists and related NGOs shall be extensively solicited through seminars or other means to support the establishment of the National Spatial Plan. Each spatial plan must be publicly exhibited for thirty days, and public hearings shall be held before it is presented for review and approval. The dates of the exhibition and hearings shall be posted in government gazettes, newspapers and the Internet and publicised through other appropriate channels. Within the public exhibition period, private individuals and groups may present in writing their opinions to the competent authority, indicating their names or titles and addressees. The competent authority shall review such opinions and present them, the results of its review, and the plan, to the Executive Yuan or the central competent authority for decisions. The process, outcomes, the decisions concerning the opinions of private individuals and groups and related information of the review shall all be posted on the Internet, in government gazettes or publicized through other appropriate channels for public viewing.[1159]

III. Reviewing

657. Before approval, a proper reviewing process is established. The Executive Yuan shall recruit and appoint scholars, specialists, representatives from NGOs and relevant authorities to form a spatial planning committee to meet and conduct:[1160]

(1) Review and approval of the National Spatial Plan.
(2) Coordination of sectoral plans with the National Spatial Plan.

658. The central competent authority shall recruit and appoint scholars, specialists, representatives from NGOs and relevant authorities to form a spatial planning committee to conduct:[1161]

(1) Review and approval of the National spatial plan drafts and changes.
(2) Review and approval of the municipality or county (city) spatial plans.
(3) Reconsideration of the municipality or county (city) spatial plans.

1157. Article 8(3) of the National Spatial Plan Act.
1158. Article 8(4) of the National Spatial Plan Act.
1159. Article 12 of the National Spatial Plan Act.
1160. Article 7(1) of the National Spatial Plan Act.
1161. Article 7(2) of the National Spatial Plan Act.

(4) Review and approval of applications for permits to use environmental conservation zones and marine resource zones and review and approval of permit changes and revocation of permits.

659. The competent authority of each municipality or county (city) shall recruit and appoint scholars, specialists, representatives from NGOs and relevant authorities to form a spatial planning committee to conduct:[1162]

(1) Review and approval of the municipality or county (city) spatial plan drafts and changes.
(2) Review and approval of applications for permits to use agricultural development zones and urban-rural development zones and review and approval of permit changes and revocation of permits.

IV. After Approval

660. Once a spatial plan has been approved, the agency that drew up the plan shall publicly announce the implementation thereof within thirty days of receiving the approval document, and it shall also send a copy of the plan to each concerned municipality or county (city) government and township (town, city, district) office, to be publicly exhibited for at least ninety days. At the same time, the outline of the plan shall be published in government gazettes, newspapers and on the Internet and publicised through other appropriate channels. If a municipality or county (city) government fails to make such an announcement, the central competent authority may do so on its behalf.[1163]

661. A municipality or county (city) government, having established a spatial plan, may apply for reconsideration of a decision made concerning the plan by filing such an application before the implementation of the plan is announced, following the regulations. This application may be filed once only. If the original decision is upheld after reconsideration, then the government shall comply with the aforementioned regulations and announce the implementation of the plan.[1164]

V. After Publication

662. After the National spatial plan has been announced, the competent authorities of the municipality or county (city) government shall draw up or revise their spatial plan within the period that has been specified by the central competent authority. However, municipalities or counties (cities) governments that had already

1162. Article 7(3) of the National Spatial Plan Act.
1163. Article 13 of the National Spatial Plan Act.
1164. Article 14 of the National Spatial Plan Act.

announced the implementation of urban plans or national park plans for all their administrative districts may be excluded.[1165]

663. After the implementation of the National spatial plan has been announced, the central competent authority shall revise it every ten years. After the implementation of the municipality or county (city) spatial plan has been announced, the municipality or county (city) competent authority shall revise it every five years. However, under any of the following conditions, the plan may be revised as soon as possible:[1166]

(1) Damage has occurred because of war, an earthquake, a flood, a storm, fire or any other critical incident.
(2) The conservation of resources or prevention of a major disaster is deemed necessary.
(3) National defence or important public facilities or a public utility project is deemed necessary.
(4) The National spatial plan and the establishment or revision of its contents concerning a metropolitan area or a specific area are deemed necessary.
(5) The plan is a municipality or county (city) spatial plan, and adjustments are deemed necessary to accommodate the National spatial plan.

664. After announcing the implementation of a municipality or county (city) spatial plan, the competent authority of a municipality or county (city) shall notify the local urban planning authority to establish or revise urban plans consistent with the guidelines outlined in the spatial plan.

VI. Power to Ensure Enforcement

665. When competent authorities of various levels need to enter public or private land or buildings to perform investigations or surveys in pursuit of the establishment or revision of spatial plans, the owners, occupants, managers, or users of such properties may not refuse. However, to enter land and facilities that are used for national defence purposes, the consent of authorities with jurisdiction over such land and facilities shall be required.[1167] Personnel who enter public or private property for investigation or survey, as stated in the preceding paragraph, shall present documentary proof or certificates and notify the owners, occupants, managers or users of the property seven days before entry.[1168] If certain obstacles must be removed or dismantled to conduct an investigation or survey and doing so causes damage to the property of the owners or users, appropriate compensation shall be provided, and the amount shall be decided by negotiation.[1169]

1165. Article 15(1) of the National Spatial Plan Act.
1166. Article 15(3) of the National Spatial Plan Act.
1167. Article 18(1) of the National Spatial Plan Act.
1168. Article 18(2) of the National Spatial Plan Act.
1169. Article 18(3) of the National Spatial Plan Act.

666. When the competent authority needs to collect, coordinate, and consolidate spatial planning information and data concerning environmentally sensitive areas for the establishment of a spatial plan, all relevant authorities shall assist and provide such information and data. The central competent authority shall also survey land cover and monitor land use regularly.[1170]

§4. DEMARCATION OF FUNCTIONAL ZONE AND LAND USE CONTROL

I. Principles

667. One of the important items in the aforementioned Spatial Plan is the development of a Functional Zone to conduct further Land Use Control. The comprehensive functional zones and land use is provided in the table below:

Zones	*The Demarcation Principles*	*Land Use Principles*
1. Environmental conservation zones: To be demarcated by natural resources, ecology, landscape, disasters, and the deployment of corresponding disaster prevention facilities, shall be considered, and areas shall be classified by their degree of environmental sensitivity.	A. Type 1: areas with abundant resources, important habitats, an exceptional landscape, susceptibility to disaster and a highly sensitive environment. B. Type 2: areas with abundant resources, important habitats, an exceptional landscape or susceptibility to disaster and a weakly sensitive environment. C. Other necessary types.	A. Type 1: areas where the natural environment is to be protected and other uses are prohibited or restricted. B. Type 2: areas where the natural environment is to be protected as much as possible and conditional uses may be permitted. C. Other necessary types: areas where various degrees of use control are imposed as determined by the characteristics of the environmental resources.
2. Marine resource zones: to be demarcated by the current states of internal and territorial marine, future developmental requirements, current conservation and utilization of marine resources, traditional use of such resources by indigenous people, and special and other uses, and to be classified according to the needs of the use of marine.	A. Type 1: areas with exclusive use. B. Type 2: areas with compatible uses. C. Other necessary types.	A. Type 1: areas where public safety and welfare are to be protected or that meet the requirements for conditional exclusive uses, with other uses prohibited or restricted. B. Type 2: areas designated as public access or compatible uses. C. Other necessary types: areas not yet planned or used, where various degrees of use control are imposed as determined by the conditions of the marine resources.

1170. Article 19(1) of the National Spatial Plan Act.

Zones	*The Demarcation Principles*	*Land Use Principles*
3. Agricultural development zones: to be demarcated by the agricultural production environment, capacity to contribute to food security and quantities of existing agricultural improvement facilities, and to be classified according to the conditions of agricultural production resources therein.	A. Type 1: areas with excellent environments for agricultural production that can contribute to food security or have important agricultural facilities that have been improved. B. Type 2: areas with decent environments for agricultural production that can contribute to food security and support agricultural diversity. C. Other necessary types.	A. Type 1: areas to be used for agricultural production and that have production and marketing facilities, with other uses prohibited or restricted. B. Type 2: areas to be used for agricultural production and that have facilities for the development of a related industrial value chain with various degrees of use control imposed according to the characteristics of the industry and other uses prohibited or restricted. C. Other necessary types: areas where various degrees of use control are to be imposed according to the conditions of the agricultural resources.
4. Urban-rural development zones: to be demarcated by the degree of urbanization and developmental needs and to be classified according to the level of development.	A. Type 1: areas with higher levels of urbanization and higher concentrations of residential buildings or industrial activities. B. Type 2: areas with lower levels of urbanization but with a certain concentration of residential buildings or industrial activities. C. Other necessary types.	A. Type 1: areas to be used for a high intensity of residential activities, industrial activities, or other urban-rural development activities. B. Type 2: areas to be used for low intensity of residential activities, industrial activities, or other urban-rural development activities. C. Other necessary types: areas where various degrees of use control are to be imposed as determined by prevailing urban-rural development.

Source: Compiled by this author from Articles 20 and 21 of the National Spatial Plan Act.

II. Use Permit

668. The land use concerning functional zones and sub-zones that are special and of scale up to a certain threshold should apply for the permits.[1171] Applicants who have received land use permits may not change the functional zone and sub-zone; land reclamation shall be permissible only in urban-rural development zones

1171. Article 24(1) of the National Spatial Plan Act.

and must meet the requirements for coastal and marine spatial planning.[1172] After obtaining permits from the competent authority, applicants shall start using the land in the specified period. Once the specified period expires, the permit shall become invalid. Land use permits for applicants who do not use the land according to approved plans, violate relevant regulations, fail to make improvements within the specified period or have their plans annulled by the relevant authority of specific purpose, soil and water conservation or environmental protection shall be revoked.[1173]

669. To improve transparency, the application should be made public before reviewing. Having accepted a land use permit application and confirmed that the application meets the pertinent requirements, the competent authority of a municipality or county (city) shall publicly exhibit for thirty days the submitted documents and plans at the office of the township (town, city, district) that has jurisdiction over the location with which the application is concerned; this competent authority shall also hold public hearings before reviewing the application[1174] The time, location and procedure of each public hearing shall be posted on the Internet as well as in government gazettes, newspapers or through other appropriate channels for public access. The owners of the land referred to in the land use permit application shall also be notified in writing unless the public hearing has already been held under other regulations and relevant information has already been posted on the Internet for public access, with the landowners already notified in writing thereof.[1175] During the public exhibition period, private individuals and groups may present opinions to the competent authority, providing their names or titles and addresses. The competent authority shall compile such opinions within thirty days of the end of the public exhibition period and present them with the application and submitted documents and plans for review.[1176]

670. This Act provides guidelines to instruct the reviewing. When reviewing land use permit applications, the competent authority shall consider the suitability of the land use, the service level of transportation and public facilities, as well as the carrying capacity of the natural environment and man-made facilities. Applications that meet the following requirements shall be approved following the characteristics of functional zones:[1177]

(1) Environmental conservation zone and marine resource zone: Plans ensure environmental protection, natural conservation and disaster prevention and include effective measures to restore the ecological environment.
(2) Agricultural development zones: The integrity of the agricultural production environment and water resources are maintained and fragmental use or use

1172. Article 24(2) of the National Spatial Plan Act.
1173. Article 24(6) of the National Spatial Plan Act.
1174. Article 25(1) of the National Spatial Plan Act.
1175. Article 25(2) of the National Spatial Plan Act.
1176. Article 25(3) of the National Spatial Plan Act.
1177. Article 26(2) of the National Spatial Plan Act.

likely to affect other agricultural production environments is avoided. If agricultural facilities must be built, they must be related to local agricultural production and management.

(3) Urban-rural development zones: Urban growth management, the linkage impact of development trends, public construction timelines, and the completeness of water, power, and gas supply telecommunications systems.

671. Finally, once a land use permit application has been approved, the competent authority shall *issue the land use permit* and publicly exhibit the submitted documents and plans in the offices of the relevant municipality or county (city) governments and townships (towns, cities, districts) for no less than thirty days. At the same time, the competent authority may also publish the outline of the spatial plan in government gazettes, newspapers, on the Internet or through other appropriate channels for public access.[1178] The central competent authority shall collect environmental conservation fees from any applicant who receives land use permits to cover expenses related to environmental conservation. The competent authorities of municipalities and counties (cities) shall also collect impact fees from applicants, which shall be used to improve or construct public facilities. Impact fees may be paid in the form of constructible land inside the areas that are covered by land use permits.[1179] In addition, after receiving a land use permit from the competent authority, each applicant shall undertake the following before beginning to use the land according to the approved plan:[1180]

(1) Delineate areas to be registered as public facilities belonging to the municipality or county (city) or township (town, city, district) and transfer the ownership of such areas to the municipality or county (city) government or township (town, city).
(2) Pay the environmental conservation fee to the central competent authority and the impact fee to the competent authority of the municipality or county (city).
(3) Change the land for designated use according to the land use plan.

III. The Effect of Functional Zone Map

672. After announcing a functional zone map, the competent authority of each municipality or county (city) shall act according to the regulations outlined in the Act and impose land use control. Besides reparation of existing legal buildings and facilities or buildings and facilities that were built before the implementation of regional plans, or facilities that are not subject to the land use control provisions, no new construction or reconstruction may be conducted. If necessary, the competent authority of the municipality or county (city) may assess the situation and order a change of land use or require that the users of existing legal buildings and facilities relocate, providing appropriate compensation for costs incurred from relocation.

1178. Article 27(1) of the National Spatial Plan Act.
1179. Article 28(1) of the National Spatial Plan Act.
1180. Article 29(1) of the National Spatial Plan Act.

Before ordering a change of land use or relocation, the competent authority of the municipality or county (city) may allow uses that were permitted before the implementation of regional plans, original legal uses, or change the use of such buildings and facilities to that is less against to the purposes.[1181] When changing constructible land to non-constructible land in a spatial plan, the competent authorities of municipalities or counties (cities) shall provide compensation for damage thus incurred.[1182]

673. If the government deems necessary the acquisition of land, buildings, or facilities to enforce environmental protection and ecological conservation, then the relevant authorities shall act according to the other law and appropriate funds to purchase or expropriate such properties.[1183]

IV. Public Interest Litigation Clause

674. If an applicant for a land use permit violates this Act or orders that have been established following this Act, and the competent authority is negligent in supervision, then citizens or public interest groups whose rights and interests had been violated may present written statements that include detailed descriptions of such negligence to the competent authority. If the competent authority still fails to take necessary action under the law within sixty days of receiving such written statements, the said citizens or public interest groups may file with the Administrative Court lawsuits against the competent authority for negligence in the execution of its duty.[1184] The Administrative Court may order the defendant, the competent authority, to pay the lawyer's fees, appraisal costs and other litigation expenses of the plaintiffs.[1185]

§5. Environmental Restoration of National Land

675. The relevant authority may *demarcate the following areas as environmental restoration areas* to carry out restoration works.[1186] The central competent authority shall coordinate relevant authorities to identify the agency responsible for demarcating environmental restoration areas and shall request the Executive Yuan to identify that agency if the coordination among agencies fails:[1187]

(1) Areas with a high potential for mudslides.
(2) Areas with severe landslides.
(3) Areas with severe land subsidence.

1181. Article 32(1) of the National Spatial Plan Act.
1182. Article 32(2) of the National Spatial Plan Act.
1183. Article 33 of the National Spatial Plan Act.
1184. Article 34(1) of the National Spatial Plan Act.
1185. Article 34(2) of the National Spatial Plan Act.
1186. Article 35(1) of the National Spatial Plan Act.
1187. Article 35(3) of the National Spatial Plan Act.

(4) River basins with deteriorating ecological environments or safety hazards.
(5) Areas where the ecological environment has seriously deteriorated.
(6) Other areas that exhibit high geological sensitivity or are likely to have a severe impact on environmental conservation.

676. In principle, environmental restoration areas shall be used for conservation and development, and the installation of any facilities shall be prohibited. The demarcating agency shall establish restoration plans and execute them after they have been approved by the central relevant authority. If such areas include indigenous people's land, then the demarcating agency shall invite indigenous tribal settlements to send representatives to participate in plan establishment and execution and management.[1188] The restoration plans shall be comprehensively reviewed every five years. If changes are deemed necessary, the responsible agency shall request the Executive Yuan to approve such changes.[1189] When executing the restoration plans that are, each relevant authority may act under the law to purchase or expropriate private land and legal buildings in the area if necessary.[1190]

677. If existing settlements or buildings and facilities in environmental restoration areas are assessed by the central relevant competent authority or the municipality or county (city) government with jurisdiction over the area as having safety hazards, restriction of occupancy or forced relocation may not be imposed unless the immediate danger is expected.[1191] If areas are assessed as having safety hazards, then the central relevant competent authority, municipality or county (city) shall establish appropriate placement plans and complementary measures and obtain the consent of the residents to build homes that favour ecological sustainability on safe and suitable land to accommodate those residents and assist in their settling, finding employment, schools and retirement homes, and preserving their traditional culture. If necessary, the Executive Yuan shall coordinate and consolidate such undertakings.[1192]

§6. SD Fund for National Land

678. The central competent authority shall set up the SD Fund. The sources of the fund shall include the following:[1193]

(1) Environmental conservation fees that are collected from applicants for land use permits.
(2) Funds that have been appropriated by the government according to the budgeting procedure.

1188. Article 36(1) of the National Spatial Plan Act.
1189. Article 36(2) of the National Spatial Plan Act.
1190. Article 36(3) of the National Spatial Plan Act.
1191. Article 37(1) of the National Spatial Plan Act.
1192. Article 37(2) of the National Spatial Plan Act.
1193. Article 44(1) of the National Spatial Plan Act.

(3) A percentage of fees that are collected by the Taiwan Water Corporation.
(4) A percentage of fees that are collected by the Taiwan Power Company.
(5) A percentage of fines that are imposed for violations of this Act.
(6) Private donations.
(7) Accrued interest from the fund.
(8) Other income.

679. Starting on the day when this Act goes into effect, the central competent authority shall set up an annual budget to be appropriated from the government, based on the results of a review of, and changes to, the spatial plan review. The total amount to be appropriated in the ten years after this Act goes into effect shall not be less than *TWD 50 billion.*[1194]

680. The SD Fund shall be utilized for the following purposes:[1195]

(1) Payment of compensation under this Act.
(2) Spatial planning research and surveys and land use monitoring.
(3) Provision of subsidies from the source of funds for use by the competent authorities of municipalities and counties (cities) in investigating violations and encouraging the public to report unlawful land use.
(4) Expenses needed for other environmental conservation undertakings.

1194. Article 44(2) of the National Spatial Plan Act.
1195. Article 44(4) of the National Spatial Plan Act.

Part IV. Liability

681. According to the Basic Environment Act, Citizens, enterprises, and government entities at all levels jointly share the duties and responsibilities of protecting the environment,[1196] and those who pollute or destroy the environment are deemed responsible for the environmental harm or risk they create.[1197] Such 'responsibility' may be further divided into private law, administrative law, and criminal law liabilities.

682. In reality, the burden of proof and tracking the pollution sources are the major difficulties. Thus, for the former, Article 33 of the Environmental Basis Act stipulates that: 'The central government shall establish a mechanism for resolving environmental disputes, strengthen technology to assess reasons for dispute and *burden of proof education*, training, research and development, and provide an appropriate dispute resolution mechanism', while the central government is obliged to establish funds to bear responsibility for environmental cleaning, restoration, and *tracking and investigation of pollution sources* and the promotion of matters beneficial to environmental development under Article 31 of the Environmental Basis Act.

1196. Article 4(1) of the Environmental Basic Act.
1197. Article 4(2) of the Environmental Basic Act.

Chapter 1. Private Law Liability

§1. General Introduction

683. In general, private liability is provided in the Civil Code of Taiwan. Environmental harm could infringe on different obligations under the Civil Code, such as Contracts, Management Of Affairs Without Mandate, and Unjust Enrichment, yet the most frequent violation is torts.

684. According to Article 184 of the Civil Code, a person who, intentionally or negligently, has wrongfully damaged the rights of another is bound to compensate him for any injury arising as a result. The same rule shall be applied when the injury is done intentionally in a manner against the rules of morals. However, this provision has weaknesses when applying to environmental liability. For instance, such a clause places too high a burden of proof on victims to prove causation, leading to victims' failure when claiming compensation.[1198]

685. To correct such weakness, Article 191-3 was added to the Civil Code on 21 April 1999. A person who runs a particular business or does other work or activity shall be liable for the injury to another if the nature of the work or activity or an implement or manner used might damage another, except where the injury was not caused by the work or activity, or by the implement or manner used, or reasonable care was exercised to prevent the injury. This article is inherent in Article 2050 of the Italian Civil Code. The liability of this article is based on fault but not on strict liability. This article is a presumption of negligence and causation, whose scope of application is wider than that of strict liability. Second, the defendant upon whom the liability under this article may be imposed includes anyone who undertakes risky jobs or activities, regardless of whether they are a natural person or a legal person. The critical element in imposing liability under this article is whether a job or an activity is one with extraordinary risk. In order to make a decision as to extraordinarily dangerous activities, the court takes into account the following factors: (1) the defendant gains benefits from the risky enterprises; (2) the defendant is superior to the victim in taking precautions to prevent the loss; (3) it is unfair to impose upon the victim the burden of proving the defendant's fault; (4) the risky activity incurs a great personal injury on the victim, (5) the cost of preventing the losses incurred by the activity is small, compared to the large amount of losses incurred by that activity; (6) the activity shall be viewed as a risky resource in ordinary life; (7) the risk shall be special, extraordinary, high, and unreasonable; and (8) the defendant produces the risk and is able to control the risk and distribute the loss.[1199]

1198. Chen, H.H., Field Report: Professionals, Students, and Activists in Taiwan Mobilize for an Unprecedented Collective-Action Lawsuit Against a Former Top American Electronics Company, *East Asian Science, Technology and Society: An International Journal* 5(4), 555–565 (2011).

1199. Chen, T.F., The Strict Liability under European Continental Law and Comments on Article 191-3 of the Taiwanese Civil Code, *NTU Law Review* 40(2), 569–628 (2011).

686. In reality, the court is more willing to shift the burden of proof, as demonstrated in the following famous case of RCA.

§2. The RCA Case

687. RCA established subsidiaries in Taiwan between 1967 and 1970, running electronics production operations for twenty-two years. GE took over RCA in 1986 and sold it to Thomson Consumer Electronics (Thomson's US subsidiary) in 1987, whereupon it was renamed Technicolor in 2010. From 1988 to 1992, Thomson Consumer Electronics owned and operated the facility, which was shut down in 1992.[1200] RCA voluntarily poured organic solvents on the ground, leading to soil and groundwater pollution. It contaminated the workers' water supplies and potable water. 1,300 workers discovered they had cancer, of whom 221 died. The workers and their families constituted an employee association which filed a lawsuit in 2006 for damage compensation under Article 41 of the Code of Civil Procedure. Plaintiffs' claims amounted to TWD 2.7. This was one of the first class-action lawsuits in Taiwan's legal history.

688. In the beginning, the lower court denied damages to the 222 others, saying they either had not proved any illness from the factory's pollution or displayed no obvious exterior signs of being sick.[1201] Despite the legal basis of a general tort, that is, Article 184 of the Civil Code, the high court took a very active approach in reverting the burden of proof. As the defendant, RCA did not lawfully use organic solvents or save records regarding its measures to protect the health of its employees, the burden of proof should have been reversed from the plaintiffs to the defendants. If the defendant did not provide evidence, it would then benefit the plaintiffs. It is unnecessary to mention again that the plaintiffs were exposed to organic solvents during their work. Even though the high court had agreed that, in this case, the plaintiff's burden of proof should be relieved, its decision to deny the damages was based on the fact that they had failed to establish a causal relationship between their disease and the pollution[1202]

689. However, in a recent judgment of the Supreme Court of March 2020, the Supreme Court upheld a decision made by the high court in March 2020 to award TWD 54.7 million (USD 1.82 million) in compensation to twenty-four other plaintiffs in the class-action lawsuit brought by former RCA employees and relatives of deceased or injured workers against RCA, its parent company, and successor entities in 2004.[1203]

1200. Rebecca, RCA Case – 2015/04/17, available at: http://zoomlawcn.so-buy.com/files/15-1140-40536,c1712-1.php.

1201. Taipei Times, Former workers at RCA factory win Supreme Court case, 13 Mar. 2022, available at: https://www.taipeitimes.com/News/taiwan/archives/2022/03/13/2003774699.

1202. Focus Taiwan, Supreme Court reverses judgment denying damages to ex-RCA workers, 03/11/2022, available at: https://focustaiwan.tw/society/202203110029.

1203. Taipei Times, Former workers at RCA factory win Supreme Court case, 13 Mar. 2022, available at: https://www.taipeitimes.com/News/taiwan/archives/2022/03/13/2003774699 Jobin, P., The

Chapter 2. Administrative Law Liability

690. In general, administrative fines are the most frequently used administrative penalty for environmental law violations. Such a fine may be accompanied by 'improvement'. For instance, holding such folk activities as god altar worship, temple festivals, weddings, and funerals that impair the tranquillity of the lives of others within noise control zones is prohibited at times and in places or premises officially announced by the special municipality, county, or city competent authority under Article 8 of the Noise Control Act. The violators will be fined TWD 3,000–TWD 30,000 and will be required to promptly make improvements; those that fail to comply will be fined per violation.[1204]

691. The Administrative Penalty Act provides a general regime governing administrative penalties. In general, 'administrative penalties' refers to the following categories of adverse actions of a punitive nature:[1205]

(1) restrictive and prohibitive actions: Actions imposing restrictions on or suspension of business; suspension of certificates or licences; orders to stop work or to discontinue use; restricting passage of vehicles; prohibition of entry into or exit out of harbours, airports, or specific places; prohibitions on production, sales, export, or import; prohibitions against application or other restrictions on or prohibitions against doing certain acts;
(2) actions of deprivation or abolition of eligibility or rights: Orders to wind up business; orders of dissolution; revocation or annulment of permits or registration; revocation of certificates or licences; compulsory dismantlement; or other actions of deprivation or abolition of specific eligibility or rights;
(3) actions against reputation: Publicizing personal or trade names or photographs or other similar actions; and
(4) actions of disciplinary warnings: Disciplinary warnings; reprimands; recording of points for violation; recording of times of violation; reformatory courses, supplemental training classes, or other similar actions.

692. The above four types of penalties can be found in environmental legislation. To illustrate, certain examples are given as follows:

(1) Suspension of work or suspension of business: The Water Pollution Control Act provides that 'Sludge produced through wastewater or sewage treatment by enterprises, sewage systems, and building sewage treatment facilities shall be properly treated and may not be arbitrarily stored or dumped. Those enterprises, sewage systems, or building sewage treatment facilities that discharge wastewater or sewage into surface water bodies shall comply with effluent

---

Valuation of Contaminated Life: RCA in Taiwan and the Compensation of Toxic Exposure, *East Asian Science, Technology and Society: An International Journal* 1–26 (2021).

1204. Article 23 of the Noise Control Act.

1205. Article 2 of the Administrative Penalty Act.

standards.'[1206] In addition to administrative fines, in severe circumstances, livestock enterprises may be ordered to suspend work or business and, where necessary, may have their water pollution control permit (document) cancelled, or they may be ordered to terminate business.[1207]

(2) Annulment of authorisation: According to Article 43 of the Air Pollution Control Act, the central competent authority, in conjunction with the central competent authority in charge of transportation and communications, shall determine regulations for testing and treatment and commission regulations for air pollutant emission of transportation vehicles and other binding matters. In addition to fines of TWD 15,000–TWD 60,000, in severe circumstances, orders may be issued for the suspension of business and annulment of authorisation.[1208]

(3) Actions against reputation: According to Article 96(2) of the Air Pollution Control Act, Competent authorities at all levels shall *publish public or private premises that are determined to cause any of the severe circumstances.*[1209]

(4) Reformatory courses: According to Article 50-1 of the Waste Disposal Act, violators of provisions regarding the spitting of betel nut juice or fibre shall be required to attend a four-hour class to help them break their habit of chewing betel nuts.

1206. Articles 7 and 8 of the Water Pollution Control Act.
1207. Article 40(2) of the Water Pollution Control Act.
1208. Article 80 of the Air pollution control Act.
1209. Article 96(1) of the Air Pollution Act: '… 1. Those circumstances in which a pollution source that fails to legally register or obtain permission violates the Act;

2. Those circumstances in which a violator, after punishment, voluntarily reports the suspension of work and the implementation of improvements, and verification checks prove this to be untruthful;
3. Those circumstances in which a violator, having been notified twice within one year to make improvements within a limited period, still continues violating the Act;
4. Those circumstances in which a large quantity of air pollutants is emitted and seriously impacts the air quality of nearby areas;
5. Those circumstances in which there is concern of the endangerment of public health due to the emission of air pollutants that contain toxic substances;
6. Those circumstances in which air pollutants are emitted through exhaust pipes not authorized in operating permits granted to stationary pollution sources, or the flow direction of waste gases is adjusted so that air pollutants are emitted through the collection or treatment facilities that are not authorised in the permits; or
7. Other acts that seriously impact the air quality of nearby areas.'

Chapter 3. Criminal Law Liability

§1. Criminal Code

693. Several criminal offences provided in Chapter 11 of Offenses Against Public Safety are relevant to the criminal law liability relating to environmental damage.

694. The most relevant clause for environmental liability is Article 190-1 of the Criminal Code. A person who throws, abandons, drains, releases, or uses in any other manner a poisonous substance or any other substance that may harm health, allowing it to pollute the air, soil, rivers or other bodies of water and thereby causes harm shall be sentenced to imprisonment for no more than five years, detention, or a fine or combined with a fine of no more than TWD 10 million.[1210]A factory or business proprietor, supervisor, agent, employee, or other personnel who commits the offence in the performance of his occupation shall be sentenced to imprisonment for no more than seven years, which may be combined with a fine of no more than TWD 15 million. An enhanced penalty will be imposed if the act causes death or serious physical injury.[1211] Moreover, negligence or attempt to commit the offences are both punishable.[1212]

695. Yet other clauses may be relevant to environmental liability as well:

(1) A person who endangers public safety by causing to escape or *by obstructing the flow of steam, electricity, gas, or another gaseous substance* shall be sentenced to imprisonment for not more than three years, short-term imprisonment, or a fine of not more than TWD 9 thousand (Article 177(1) of the Criminal Code).
(2) A person who manufactures, sells, transports, or possesses nuclear raw material, nuclear fuel, nuclear reactor, a *radioactive substance*, or its raw material not according to law shall be sentenced to imprisonment of not more than five years (Article 187-1 of the Criminal Code).

1210. Article 191-1(1) of the Criminal Code.

1211. Article 191-1(3) and (4) of the Criminal Code: 'An offender who commits the offense set forth in paragraph 1 and causes death shall be sentenced to imprisonment for no less than three years but no more than ten years; if the offense results in serious physical injury, the offender shall be sentenced to imprisonment for no less than one year but no more than seven years.

An offender who commits the offense set forth in paragraph 2 and causes death shall be sentenced to life imprisonment or imprisonment for no less than seven years; if the offense results in serious physical injury, the offender shall be sentenced to imprisonment for no less than three years but no more than ten years.'

1212. Article 191-1 (5)–(7) of the Criminal Code: 'An offender who commits the offense set forth in paragraph 1 due to negligence shall be sentenced to imprisonment for no more than one year, detention, or a fine or combined with a fine no more than two million dollars.

An offender who commits the offense set forth in paragraph 2 due to negligence shall be sentenced to imprisonment for no more than three years, detention, or a fine or combined with a fine no more than six million dollars.

An attempt to commit the offenses set forth in paragraphs 1 and 2 is also punishable.'

(3) A person who endangers public safety by *releasing nuclear energy or radioactivity* that causes public danger shall be sentenced to imprisonment of not more than five years (Article 187-2 of the Criminal Code).
(4) A person who uses a radioactive substance without a justified season and causes damage to another's body or health shall be sentenced to imprisonment for not less than three years but not more than ten years (Article 187-3 of the Criminal Code).
(5) A person who places *poisonous or harmful substance sanitation in water sources, waterways, or reservoirs* intended to supply water to the public shall be sentenced to imprisonment for not less than one year but not more than seven years (Article 190 of the Criminal Code).

§2. Environmental Law

696. Criminal penalties have been adopted as a tool to ensure the enforcement of and compliance with environmental legislation. Imprisonment and criminal fines are frequently used. This book will use the obligation to adopt emergency measures as an example.

I. Non-compliance with Adopting Emergency Measures

697. According to Article 41 of the TCCSCA, for those toxic chemical substances and concerned chemical substances that have been specified and announced as being hazardous by the central competent authority for which one of the following circumstances applies, the handler must promptly adopt emergency control measures and, within no more than thirty minutes, notify the competent authority for the area where the accident occurred. When death results, the responsible party shall be subject to life imprisonment or at least seven years of imprisonment and may be fined from TWD 5 million to TWD 10 million; when serious injury results, the responsible party shall be subject to three years or up to ten years of imprisonment and may be fined from TWD 3 million to TWD 5 million; when health hazards causing disease result, the responsible party shall be subject to six months or up to five years of imprisonment and may be fined TWD 1 million to TWD 4 million.[1213]

698. Article 33 of the Air Pollution Control Act provides that when stationary pollution sources of public or private premises emit a large quantity of air pollutants due to a sudden accident, the statutorily responsible person shall promptly adopt emergency response measures and shall notify the special municipality, county or city competent authority within at most one hour. Those that fail to promptly adopt emergency response measures and thereby cause human death shall be punished by life imprisonment or a minimum of seven years imprisonment and may be fined a maximum of TWD 30 million, while those that cause severe injury shall be punished by three to ten years imprisonment and may be fined a maximum

1213. Article 50 of Toxic and Concerned Chemical Substances Control Act.

of TWD 25 million. Those that cause harm to human health such that it leads to illness shall be punished with six months to five years imprisonment and may be fined a maximum of TWD 20 million.[1214]

699. According to Article 51 of the Water Pollution Control Act, parties at fault that failed to adopt emergency response measures promptly shall be punished by a maximum of three years imprisonment, detention, and/or a fine of TWD 200,000–TWD 5 million.

700. A violation of the management regulations of Article 30 of the Environmental Agents Control Act governing environmental agent microbial preparation applications, physical and biological protective measures and emergency response measures at experiment sites, records and record preservation, and record reporting may entail a criminal penalty. The violator shall be fined TWD 60,000–TWD 300,000 and may be ordered to make improvements within a limited period; serious violators and those that fail to make improvements by the deadline shall have their permit or licence revoked or cancelled and may be ordered to suspend work, suspend business, or terminate business where necessary.[1215]

701. Under Article 34 of the Water Pollution Control Act, parties at fault that failed to adopt emergency response measures shall be punished by a maximum of three years imprisonment, detention and/or a fine of TWD 200,000–TWD 5 million.

702. However, in certain pieces of environmental legislation, such obligation to adopt emergency measures is imposed on the government. Thus, there is no criminal offence as such. For instance, under Article 40 of the Waste Disposal Act, when an enterprise endangers human health or agricultural or fishery operations while storing, clearing, or disposing of industrial waste, the competent authority shall promptly order it to make improvements and adopt emergency measures. A similar government responsibility clause can be found in Article 15 of the Soil and Groundwater Pollution Remediation Act.[1216]

703. Despite a lack of penalty clauses for violation of the obligation to adopt emergency measures, there are still certain criminal offences provided in these two Acts.[1217]

1214. Article 51 of the Air Pollution Control Act.

1215. Article 48 of Environmental Agents Control Act.

1216. Article 8 of Soil and Groundwater Pollution Remediation Act: 'The competent authorities with local jurisdiction shall, according to actual circumstances at control or remediation sites, adopt the following emergency response measures to mitigate pollution harm or prevent pollution expansion.'

1217. For example, Art. 46 of the Waste Disposal Act: 'In any of the following circumstances, one to five years imprisonment shall be imposed and may be combined with a fine of no more than fifteen million New Taiwan Dollars:

I. Arbitrary disposal of hazardous waste.

II. Other Criminal Offences in Environmental Law

704. In addition to the criminal penalties noted in the above environmental legislation, there are certain acts without such an emergency responsibility clause, which are part of the environmental legislation regulating issues of relatively light environmental pollution. For instance, compared to the large amount of imprisonment clauses in the acts mentioned above, there is only one imprisonment clause in the Resource Recycling Act.[1218] The *same holds true of the* Drinking Water Management Act.[1219]

705. However, in certain legislations, only administrative penalties without criminal offences have been stipulated:

– Noise Control Act.

II. The responsible person of the enterprise or relevant person fails to store, clear, dispose of or reuse waste pursuant to this Act, thereby causing environmental pollution.
III. Providing land refilling or waste piling without permission from the competent authority.
IV. Conducting waste storage, clearance, disposal without obtaining the waste clearance and disposal permission pursuant to Article 41, Paragraph 1; or storing, clearing and disposing of waste not in accordance with the content designated in the waste clearance and disposal permission.
V. Personnel of the enforcement authority authorize clearance and disposal of general waste to the enterprise without valid permission document; or authorize when knowing there is illegal conduct of clearance and disposal.
VI. Responsible person or relevant personnel of a public or private waste disposal organization, or personnel of the enforcement authority issue a false certificate for the waste not being disposed of.'

See also, Art. 33 of the Soil and Groundwater Pollution Remediation Act: 'Those that pollute the soil deliberately with the intention to change the classification of land use shall be punished by one to ten years imprisonment and may be fined a maximum of TWD 1 million.

Those who pollute the soil or groundwater deliberately, causing the land to become a pollution control site or remediation site, shall be punished by one to five years imprisonment.'

1218. Article 18 of the Resource Recycling Act: 'Enterprises officially announced and designated by the central competent authority shall report to the central competent authority their production, storage, collection, transport, reuse, recycling, import, export, transit, or transshipment of renewable resources via the Internet and in accordance with the format, items, content, and frequency required by the central competent authority. If authorized by the central competent authority, however, enterprises may report by some means other than the Internet.'

Article 25 of the Resource Recycling Act: 'Those having reporting obligations pursuant to Article 15 and Article 18 of this Act that knowingly report false information or keep false records of their operations shall be punished by a maximum of three years imprisonment, detention and/or a fine of a maximum of NT$1.5 million.'

1219. The imprisonment clause in this Act, *see*, e.g., Art. 13 of the Drinking Water Management Act: 'Those chemical agents used for drinking water quality treatment shall be limited to those officially announced by the central competent authority. Water supply units may apply to the central competent authority to officially announce an unlisted agent as chemical agent used for drinking water treatment. The central competent authority shall determine regulations governing application qualifications, documentation that shall be attached, procedures, approval conditions, rejection, corrections, and other binding matters.'; Art. 18 of the Drinking Water Management Act: 'Those that violate Article 13 shall be punished by a maximum of one year of imprisonment and detention, and/or may be fined a maximum of NT$60,000.'

- Greenhouse Gas Reduction and Management Act.
- Environmental Education Act.
- Indoor Air Quality Act.

Selected Bibliography

Anton Ming-Zhi Gao & Katherine Yuhh-chinn, *The Effect of the Basic Environmental Act on Environmental Governance in Taiwan: From the Aspect of Judicial Review*, in: Konrad-Adenauer-Stiftung Foundation (ed.), *Rule of Law for Good Environmental Governance* (2015), 140–153.

Anton Ming-Zhi Gao, *Transformation of the Principles of International Environmental Law in Taiwan*, in: Herausgegeben von Prof Dr Timo Hebeler (eds), *Protecting the Environment for International for Future Generations: Principles and Actors in International Environment Law* (23 January 2017), 231–278 (ISBN: 978-3-503-17174-3).

Juang Gao, *Genetic Technology and Food Safety in Taiwan*, in: Jörg Menzel & Rose-Liza Eisma-Osorio (eds), *Genetic Technology and Food Safety* (2015) (ISBN: 978-621-8017-10-8).

Gao, A.M.Z. & Juang, K.Y.C., The Effect of Basic Environmental Act on Environmental Governance in Taiwan: From the Aspect of Judicial Review. *Rule of Law for Good Environmental Governance*, 140, 2015.

Yang, W.T., et al. (2018). Road traffic noise, air pollutants, and the prevalence of cardiovascular disease in Taichung, Taiwan. *International Journal of Environmental Research and Public Health*, 15(8), 1707.

Wu, C.F., et al. (2020). A dynamic relationship between environmental degradation, healthcare expenditure and economic growth in wavelet analysis: Empirical evidence from Taiwan. *International Journal of Environmental Research and Public Health*, 17(4), 1386.

Yang, J.L. & Chen, L.H. (2018). Toxicity of antimony, gallium, and indium toward a teleost model and a native fish species of semiconductor manufacturing districts of Taiwan. *Journal of Elementology*, 23(1).

Chen, W.L. Chang, C.C. & Chao, F.L. (2020). Redesign of a traditional ritual furnace for reducing environmental impact. *International Journal of Environmental Science and Development*, 11(3).

M.S. Ho, *Environmental Movement in Democratizing Taiwan (1980–2004): A Political Opportunity Structure Perspective*. in: Jeffrey Broadbent & Vicky Brockman (eds), *East Asian Social Movements* 283–314, 292 (2011).

Tong, Y. (2005). Environmental Movements in Transitional Societies: A Comparative Study of Taiwan and China. *Comparative Politics*, 167–188.

Selected Bibliography

Index

The numbers here refer to paragraph numbers.

Air Pollution Control, 78, 132–156
- Air Pollution Control Plan, 134
- Air quality control Regions, 132–133
- Air quality monitoring stations, 139
- Cap and Trade, 135–138
- Emergency measures, 140–142
- Mobile pollution sources, 150–152
- VOC, 153

Air Pollution Control Act, 70, 76, 100, 692, 698
- emission trading scheme (ETS), 6
- Water Pollution Control Act, 5

Basic Environment Act, 20, 22, 99, 681
- Conservation, 58, 59

Civil code, 4–6, 97, 683–685, 688

Climate related authority, 90–92
- Committee on Energy Conservation and Emission Reduction (CECER), 86
- the Committee on the Promotion of New Energy, 86
- Office of Energy and Carbon Reduction, 88
- National Development Council, 89

Criminal code, 4, 5, 97, 693–695

Distant Water Fisheries Act, 619–645
- Competent Authority, 620
- Planning, 621
- License, 622
- Prohibition, 625–627
- Port Regulations: Ban on Leaving or Entering the Port, 631–633

Environmental authority, 9, 77
- Environmental Health Division, the Department of Health, Executive Yuan, 78
- Environmental Protection Administration (EPA), 78, 83, 84
- Ministry of Environment and Natural Resources, 83, 84

Environmental Education Act, 118–123

Environmental Impact Assessment Act, 124–131
- Policy EIA, 42, 129–131
- Project EIA, 124–128

Environmental legal principles:
- Common but Differentiated Responsibilities, 38–39
- Common Heritage and the Common Concerns of Humankind, 54–55
- Cooperation, 58–59, 62
- Duty to Adopt Effective National Law: The Duty to Enforce, 57
- Equitable Utilisation, 51–53
- Good Governance, 56
- Human Rights, 47–50
- Integration Principle, 23–25
- Intergenerational and/or Intragenerational Equity, 26–28
- Polluter Pays Principle, 33–37
- Precautionary Principle, 44–45
- Prevention Principle, 40–41
- Procedural Principles, 63
- Sovereignty over Natural Resources, 60–61
- State Responsibility and Liability, 29–32
- Sustainable Development, 19–22
- The Obligation Not to Cause Damage (No Harm Rule), 46
- Access to Information, 64–66

Access to Justice, 70–71
Public Participation, 67–69
Environmental legislations
Air Pollution Control Act, 80
Basic Environment Act, 80
Drinking Water Management Act, 80
Environmental Agents Control Act, 80
Environmental Impact Assessment Act, 80
Greenhouse Gas Reduction and Management Act, 80
Indoor Air Quality Act, 80
Noise Control Act, 80
Organic Act of the Environmental Professionals Training Institute, Environmental Protection Administration, Executive Yuan, 80
Organic Act of the Environmental Protection Administration, Executive Yuan, 80
Organic Act of the National Institute of Environmental Analysis, Environmental Protection Administration, Executive Yuan, 80
Organization Act of the Toxic and Chemical Substances Bureau, Environmental Protection Administration, Executive Yuan, 80
Public Nuisance Dispute Mediation Act, 80
Resource Recycling Act, 80
Soil and Groundwater Pollution Remediation Act, 80
The Environmental Education Act, 80
Toxic and Concerned Chemical Substances Control Act, 80
Waste Disposal Act, 80
Water Pollution Control Act, 80
Environmental movement, 74, 75
Environmental related authorities
Construction and Planning Office of the Ministry of the Interior (National Parks Division, Sewage Systems Office), 84
Ministry of Economic Affairs (Mines Department, Bureau of Mines, Central Geological Survey), the Ministry of Transportation and Communication (Central Weather Bureau), 84
Council of Agriculture (Forestry Bureau, Soil and Water Conservation Bureau, Taiwan Forestry Research Institute, Endemic Species Research Institute), 84
Veterans Affairs Council (Forest Conservation and Management Administration), 84
EPA, 6–9, 56, 78–84, 87, 93, 95, 100, 119, 121, 122, 126, 129, 131–135, 139, 141, 143, 144, 149, 151, 152, 163–165, 194–238, 240–242, 245, 247–252, 273, 318, 319, 333, 368, 370
Executive Yuan (the cabinet), 22

Fisheries Act, 592, 619–645
Boat, 597
Competent Authority, 593–594
Conservation and Management, 602–609
Crews, 601
Fishery Development, 610–618
Licensing, 595
Loan and Insurances, 610–612
Price Stabilisation Scheme, 617
Revoking of Licenses, 598–599
Rewards and Funds, 614–616
Tax, 618
Forest, 536, 537
Application for Designation and Declassification, 564–568
Biological Hazards or Disturbances, 573–574
Classification of Forestland, 541
Competent authority, 538–539
Conservation Forestry, 559–568
Fire Protection, 571–572
Forest in Aboriginal People's Area, 575
Forest Protection, 569–570
Forestry Administration, 540
Forestry Management And Utilisation, 549–550
Forestry Protection Outside The Forests, 576–581
Incentive, 587, 588
Management of National Forests, 551–552
Nationalization, 542
Personnel, 555
Reforestation, 589–591
Supervision, 582–586

Greenhouse Gas Reduction and Management Act, 6, 80, 91, 705

Heritage Preservation, 417
Competent authority, 419–421
Cultural Heritage Preservation Act, 418
Designation and Announcement, 425–427
Historic Sites and Cultural Landscapes, 439–442
Identifying Heritage, 422–424
maintenance duty, 428–430
Monuments, Historic Buildings, Commemorative Buildings, and Groups of Buildings, 422–438
Natural Landscapes and Natural Monuments, 443–450
Planning and Zoning, 436–438, 441

Indoor Air Quality, 157–160
Indoor Air Quality Act, 80, 705
International treaties:
Paris agreement, 95
Basel Convention, 95
Convention on Mercury, 95
The Stockholm Convention on Persistent Organic Pollutants, 95
Montreal Protocol, 95
Ionising Radiation Protection, 332
Competent authority, 333–335
The Duty of the Facility Operators, 341–345
Personnel and employers, 346–351
Regulation on Hospitals, 352
Product regulation, 353
Construction and Building Regulations, 354–357
Radiation protection service, 358
Management of Radioactive Material, Equipment Capable of Producing Ionising Radiation, 359–367

The Legislative Yuan (the Parliament), 8, 163, 371

Marine Pollution Control, 239
Competent authorities, 240–241
Emergency Plan, Financial Guarantee or Insurance, 248
Exemption from Sanction, 249
General measures, 242–244
Harbour pollution, 246
Liability for Damage Compensation, 265–267
Major Marine Pollution Accident, 245
Ocean as the Final Disposal Site, 247
public interest litigation clause, 268
The Prevention of Pollution from Marine Projects, 252–254
The Prevention of Pollution from Pollution Sources on Land, 250–251
The Prevention of Pollution from the Disposal of Waste at Sea, 255–260
The Prevention of Sea Pollution by Ships, 261–264

National Development Council (NDC), 9, 89
National Environmental Protection Plan, 107, 111
National Environmental Education Framework, 119
National Park, 84, 85, 132, 250, 436, 442, 543, 553, 655, 662
Competent authority, 474–475
Designation, 477–479
Measures to Assist the Management, 481–484
Plan, 480
Zoning and Zonal Regulations, 485–490
Net zero, 11, 89
Noise Pollution Control, 317
Competent authorities, 318–319
Noise Control Zone, 320–322
Motor vehicles and civil aircrafts, 323–325
Airport, 326–328
Administrative Inspection, 329–330
Nuclear-phase out, 10, 11, 27, 45, 88, 101, 333

Soil and Groundwater Pollution Remediation Act, 4, 70, 80, 194, 195, 198–201, 211, 212, 219, 227-229, 233, 702
Environmental Impact Assessment Act, 70
Soil and Underground Water Pollution Remediation, 194–198
Pollution Control Area, 198
Pollution Control Site, 198
Pollution Control Standards, 198
Pollution Monitoring Standards, 198
Pollution Remediation Goals, 198

Pollution Remediation Site, 198
Quality Indicators, 198
Spatial Planning
National Spatial Plan Act, 646
Regional Plan Act, 646
Urban Planning Act, 646
Spatial Planning Act, 10, 648
Sustainable development, 18–22, 26, 39, 62, 109, 648

Toxic Chemical Substances Control, 368–369
Competent authority, 370–372
Assessment, Prevention and Management of Toxic Chemical Substances, 373–375
Records and disclosure, 376
Permission and registration, 381–383
Pollution improvement, 384
Assessment, Prevention and Management of Concerned Chemical Substances, 386–389
Registration and Reporting of Chemical Substances, 390–394
Accident Prevention and Emergency Response, 395–403
Audit, Inspection, 404–405
Fund, 406–409
Information disclosure and confidentiality, 410–413
Rewards, 414
Public interest litigation, 415–416

Underwater Cultural Heritage Preservation Act, 452
Duty of the Private Person, Government, and Public Companies, 459–460
Education, 461
Enforcement, 464, 468
Excavating Out of The Water, 470–472
Identification and Research, 456–458
Preservation of Underwater Cultural Heritage In Situ, 465
Regulation for Activities Directed at Underwater Cultural Heritage, 462–463
Reward or Subsidies, 473
Zone Regulations, 466–467

Waste Disposal
Competent and Enforcement Authority, 273–275
Definition of Waste, 269–272
Designated clearance areas, 288–289
Disposal of General Waste, 276
Disposal of Industrial Waste, 290–307
Emergency measures, 307
Fee and fund, 284–285
Hazardous industrial waste, 302–304
Implementation of the clearance and disposal of general waste by special municipality, county, or city competent authority, 286–287
Import and export requirement and import ban, 300–301
Public interests litigation, 315–316
Recycle, 279–285
Reuse, 305–306
Reward, 310–311, 313–314
Tax credit, 312
Waste disposal hierarchy, 290
Water pollution
Administrative inspection, 187
Automatic monitoring system, 185
Control Measures, 168–171
Emergency measures, 183–184
Improvement assistance, 182
Permit, 175–178
Plan and permit, 168–170
Principle, 161–162
Professional personals, 179
Public authorities, 163–165
Public interest litigation clause, 192–193
Reporting, 180
Sewage systems that discharge wastewater or sewage, 172–174
Underground water and soil, 190–191
Water pollution control zones, 188–189
Water quality analysis, 181
Wild Life Conservation and Protection, 491–493
Competent authority, 494–496
Conservation of Wildlife, 497–498
Donation, 514
Enforcement, 501
General Wildlife, 505–506
Hunting, 507–511
Import And Export Of Wildlife, 515–522
Notification/Consent, 523–525
Personnel, 512
Protected Wildlife, 502–504
Protection Zone, 499–500
Rewards, 513

www.ingramcontent.com/pod-product-compliance
Ingram Content Group UK Ltd.
Pitfield, Milton Keynes, MK11 3LW, UK
UKHW020136290926
15471UKWH00003B/523

9 789403 528267